Franchising Hospitality Services

THE HOSPITALITY, LEISURE AND TOURISM SERIES

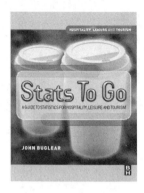

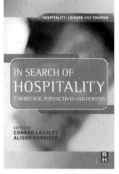

Franchising
Hospitality Services

Edited by
Conrad Lashley
and
Alison Morrison

BUTTERWORTH
HEINEMANN

OXFORD AUCKLAND BOSTON JOHANNESBURG MELBOURNE NEW DELHI

Butterworth-Heinemann
Linacre House, Jordan Hill, Oxford OX2 8DP
225 Wildwood Avenue, Woburn, MA 01801-2041
A division of Reed Educational and Professional Publishing Ltd

℞ A member of the Reed Elsevier plc group

First published 2000

British Library Cataloguing in Publication Data
Franchising hospitality services
　　1. Hospitality industry 2. Franchises (Retail trade)
　　I. Lashley, Conrad II. Morrison, Alison J.
　　338.4'7647'068

ISBN 0 7506 4772 8

Composition by Genesis Typesetting, Rochester, Kent
Printed and bound in Great Britain by
Biddles Ltd, www.biddles.co.uk

Contents

Editors and contributing authors

Conrad Lashley is British Institute of Innkeeping Professor of Licensed Retail Management, Leeds Metropolitan University.

Alison Morrison is Senior Lecturer and Director of Research at the Scottish Hotel School, University of Strathclyde.

Contributing authors

Stephen Ball is Principal Lecturer in Hospitality Management and the Leader of Hospitality Management Research in the Centre of International Hospitality Management at Sheffield Hallam University.

Christina Fulop is an Emeritus Professor, and from 1989 to 1996 was Deputy Director, Centre for Franchise Research at City University Business School.

Guy Lincoln is Senior Lecturer in Licensed Retail Management in the School of Tourism and Hospitality Management, Leeds Metropolitan University, with extensive experience as a practitioner in the licensed retail sector.

Angus Macmillan is Senior Franchise Manager, International with the Royal Bank of Scotland, where he has looked after the international franchise activities and clients since 1991.

Lesley Pender is Lecturer in Marketing at the University of Newcastle upon Tyne, specializing in Travel Trade and Transport, and Tourism Marketing.

Stuart Price is a brewing, pub and restaurant industry analyst at Credit Suisse First Boston. He has written a seminal piece of work in the form of the *Franchise Paradox*, published by Cassell.

Stephen Taylor is Lecturer at the Scottish Hotel School, University of Strathclyde, specializing in the areas of entrepreneurship and strategic management.

Foreword

A decade in the hotel and catering industry and a decade in the franchising sector has taught me one important lesson – generalizations are dangerous. Yet it is the business of professional study and the nature of a body of knowledge to be based on a history of generalized hypotheses propounded by 'researchers' and tested over time for their explanatory and predictive power. Such a history of investigation, hypothesis, testing and revision has to start somewhere. Franchising is a relatively young business method, which is only just beginning to attract the attention it deserves from the academic business community. This book represents a significant step along the road to the production of a body of knowledge on franchising. Undoubtedly, the book will stimulate debate, maybe even argument, which is all to the good, providing it is argument in pursuit of truth rather than fame or fortune.

Fulop makes the significant observation in Chapter 2 that franchising for franchisees 'is a distinct way of starting a new business'. Franchisors are not just in the business of distributing or marketing goods or services, they are in the business of starting legally independent businesses which are saleable by their owners with the benefit of the goodwill they have built in their business. This represents a defining characteristic of business format franchising and a characteristic that is evident even in conversion franchising. The introduction of saleability with a premium based on turnover and profitability was the major change made in the licensed trade first by Inns Partnership when it was part of Greenalls. In their excellent analysis of pub tenancies in the Licensed Retailing chapter Lincoln and Lashley touch on this change. I could similarly venture interpretations of the underlying factors principally at work in the changes in KFC, Wimpy, Pierre Victoire and Pizza Express. These may differ somewhat from the those offered by various authors in this work, but would focus in the end on the 'subjective factors'. The fact of the matter is that franchising is fundamentally a people business that makes investigation, explanation, interpretation and prediction an uncertain world where we are all at risk of claiming too much, or indeed too little.

Price, in Chapter 3, controversially challenges what is propounded as the franchise fraternity's rhetoric on the success rates of franchising. The challenge is made with a rhetorical fervour that outshines the franchise establishment's original claims, which in fact relate to its success in starting new businesses, that is to say in establishing successful franchisees. That claim is supported by the most extensive and consistent quantitative research on franchising in the world, the NatWest/BFA annual survey, which should nonetheless be open to criticism and debate if we are to secure continuous improvement.

There is in any case a real problem here that we must all address. Morrison and Macmillan powerfully describe the real cost of franchise entry for new franchisors. There are too many new franchisor withdrawals which are unnecessary and expensive and but for want of a better access to franchise know-how, could have been avoided. Fortunately, their impact on franchisee withdrawal rates overall is very small – though this is little comfort for those of their start up franchisees who are not bought back or otherwise survive in their business.

The strength of this book is particularly apparent where the considerations concentrate on a specific sector, for example Taylor's work on the international hotel business; or on a particular company, Lashley's work on McDonald's; or on a particular function, Morrison and Macmillan's work on franchise financing; the hypotheses put forward here seem to me to be more sustainable. But this does not mean that we should not venture to present generalized work on franchising, it means that we should do more of it until we do find interpretations and explanations of good franchising that will stand the test of time. Explanations that will offer a predictive power to prospective new franchisors to help them decide whether or not to adopt the franchising method.

This book makes a valuable contribution to the collection and presentation of such an organized body of knowledge on franchising that will I hope stimulate debate on franchising in business schools, by professional advisors and by the franchising community itself.

Brian Smart
Director General
British Franchise Association

Preface

The dimensions of franchising hospitality services

Franchising is growing in significance in Europe and internationally, as the traditional independent retailer structure falls away, the range of 'franchisable' services and products increases, and new social and economic trends create exciting novel commercial opportunities. In the UK this growth has been aided by the:

- general health of the UK economy;

- growth in consumer and commercial spending;

- general spread of the service sector in the wider economy;

- expansion of organizations into international markets as home markets reach saturation point;

- deregulation and easing of trading restrictions;

- advent of new retailing formats, including home shopping and the Internet;

- continuing number of new entrants to the UK franchising sector.

Consequently, franchising has become an established way of carrying out business. The most popular use of the term franchising is in relation to what is known as business format franchising, which is the subject of this book. It involves (DTI, 1998, p. 2):

> the granting of rights by a company (the franchisor) for a third party (the franchisee) to operate their business system using a common brand and common format for promoting, managing and administering the business.

Although by no means a new concept, business format franchising has become an established global enterprise trend within the service sector, in general, and specifically within the hospitality services sector. It represents a popular method of financing the expansion of multi-site chains that deliver a consistent service concept (Houston, 1984), and is a strategy adopted by franchisees to take advantage of a more entrepreneurial management system (Falbe and Dandridge, 1992). The number of separate businesses created by some 568 business format franchisors stands at 29,100 and more than 273,000 persons are directly employed in franchising (NatWest/BFA, 1998). Success stories are plentiful: for example, Holiday Inn, McDonald's, Burger King, Kentucky Fried Chicken, Benetton, Levi, Vision Express, Body Shop and Prontoprint, but franchising is not free from failure, as the demise of the Pierre Victoire restaurant company in 1998 illustrated.

From a European perspective, Stanworth (1995) predicts that service-oriented franchising is likely to experience growth rates notably faster than those that apply to franchising as a whole. Key Note (1998) forecasting that, by 2002, the UK franchising industry will be generating a turnover of £11.6 billion substantiates this. This represents a growth of 65.7 per cent over 1997, and catering, hotels, retail, domestic and personal services, and direct selling, are likely to be the fastest growth areas (Table 1).

In general, franchises represent a small percentage of the total market sector in which they operate. However, within catering and hotels it can be seen (Table 2) that the percentage is significant and growing. This is particularly the case within the fast food, themed pubs, budget hotel and travel sectors. Invariably the best franchises are based around strong brands or business concepts, such as Burger King, Tom Cobleigh's, Holiday Inn Express, and British Airways.

Given the seemingly unstoppable forward momentum of franchising, it is clear that its impact will be substantial on the structure and characteristics of the hospitality services sector over the coming decades. Increasingly, large franchise systems are replacing, absorbing or making redundant a vast array of atomistic, traditional small firms (Stanworth, 1995). Drawing on

	1998	1999	2000	2001	2002
Franchised systems	589	617	646	681	702
(% change year-on-year)	5.2	4.8	4.7	5.4	3.1
Franchised units	37,976	50,128	66,670	90,604	121,863
(% change year-on-year)	56.2	32.0	32.9	35.9	34.5
Total turnover (£bn)	5.6	6.4	7.3	10.3	9.6
(% change year-on-year)	6.6	10.5	10.7	10.8	10.6

Source: Key Note (1998, p. 53)

Table 1 Forecast for UK franchising (1998–2002)

Market share of business format franchising	9.1%
Growth in franchised units 1993–1997	3%
Number of franchised units in 1997	3,675
Growth in franchised systems 1993–1997	1%
Number of franchised systems in 1997	65

Source: Key Note (1998)

Table 2 Catering and hotel franchising summary information

the qualities of individual-operator franchisees, and blending proven business concept and local expertise, franchisors have the potential to benefit from the synergy of collective entrepreneurship (Falbe and Dandridge, 1992). Franchising is transforming the service sector previously characterized by small unit size, local orientation, resource poverty and absence of professional management skills (Lovelock, 1991).

The scope of this book

So it is that we present this book to you. Based on the foregoing discussion it is clear that, in the UK, Europe and internationally, franchising has taken strong roots that will support an ever-strengthening franchise sector. We as students, academics and practitioners associated with services in general, and hospitality services in particular, need to lift the lid off the seductive popularist understanding of what franchising is hyped up to be, and delve deep into its complexities, nuances and logic. In particular, it is important to look behind the associated dominant rhetoric of success. Only in this way can we all gain an understanding of this kaleidoscopic form of economic organization.

The objective of the book is to draw together a comprehensive and consolidated collection of streams of knowledge relative to franchising hospitality services into a package that rates high on 'readability'. We do this through structure, style, content and varied learning approaches.

The book is organized into two parts. Part One provides a rich exploration of theoretical frameworks and debates, and their application to hospitality services. It covers an array of themes, including: the theory of the firm; the historical development of franchising; the failure of literature adequately to test out the success rhetoric; franchisees as intrapreneurs; and empowering franchisees.

Part Two then moves to focus on some of the fundamental issues associated with the structuring and financing of franchising and the specifics of four sub-sectors of hospitality services – catering, hotels, licensed retail, and travel trade and transport. At this sub-sector level our understanding of franchising is progressed as various interpretations of franchising, similarities and disparities emerge. In particular, the concept of 'tight' and 'soft' brands, and 'hard' and 'soft' franchise systems has prominence throughout. Part Two culminates in a chapter dedicated to the McDonald's Restaurant Corporation, which serves to elucidate and consolidate the range of key issues that emerge from the previous chapters.

How to get the most out of the book

Each chapter ends with a summary. After the chapter summary, we have included debate topics and selected reading to further encourage readers to engage in, and reflect on, the content of the chapter. We have striven to help you get the most out of this book by enhancing its learning and expressive value in two major ways:

- theoretical debate has been supported with real world examples; and

- interactive learning features have been designed and integrated to increase understanding of franchising hospitality service concepts.

Put simply, this means that the content has been deliberately formulated to integrate learning and understanding through the use of multiple approaches. An overview of these approaches is now given, and together they form the structure of the content of the book.

Chapters

There are eleven chapters in all, written by leading experts on franchising and the hospitality services sector, and drawn from the worlds of both academia and commerce. These authors have reviewed the current state of knowledge, introduced real world examples and developed innovative perspectives on franchising hospitality services. The result is a content that is academically challenging, determined to stimulate, enable contextualization, and to facilitate the linkage of theory to practice.

Case studies

The content of the book is interspersed with short and more substantial case studies. In Chapter 1, Taylor draws heavily on the case of the McDonald's Restaurant Corporation as a means to illustration the theory of the firm as it relates to franchising. The same company is also used by Lashley in Chapter 11 to achieve an in-depth investigation of the company at a more operational level. The rationale for this singular focus is simply that McDonald's is arguably the most successful pioneer of business format franchising in hospitality services. Together, these two case studies are intrinsically fascinating and illuminate a substantial number of franchising issues. In Chapter 10, Pender brings in accounts of British Airways and the Advantage Travel Centres to provide strong linkages to the theoretical arguments presented.

Debate topics

A range of provocative debate topics can be found at the end of each chapter. It is anticipated that these may be used to form the basis of reflection on learning, and the stimulation of further intellectual debate. This may be carried out in class with debate groups, form the basis for group or individual assignments, or be addressed in private study mode.

Selected readings

For each chapter the author(s) have selected what, in their opinion, represent the most significant texts in the area, for those who wish to take the chapter theme to a higher level of understanding and analysis.

Finally, this book is intended for students in the latter stages of their management qualifications, whether at degree or post-graduate level. In addition, it is proposed that it will appeal to a wide range of audiences, including practitioners who may find the content challenging and containing ideas and concepts that could contribute to business success. We sincerely hope that you enjoy this book, as through enjoyment comes effective learning.

Conrad Lashley
Alison Morrison

References

DTI (Department of Trade and Industry) (1998) *Small Firms: Introduction to Franchising.* Department of Trade and Industry.

Falbe, C. and Dandridge, T. (1992) Franchising as a strategic partnership: issues of co-operation and conflict in a global market. *International Small Business Journal*, **3** (10), 40–52.

Houston, J. (1984) *Franchising and Other Business Relationships in Hotel and Catering Services.* Heinemann.

Key Note (1998) *Franchising Market Report.* Key Note Publications.

Lovelock, C. (1991) *Services Marketing.* Prentice Hall.

NatWest/BFA (1998) *Franchise Survey 1998.* Business Development Research Consultants.

Stanworth, J. (1995) A European Perspective on the Success of the Franchise Relationship. Presented at the Ninth Annual Conference of the Society of Franchising. San Juan, Puerto Rico, January.

PART 1

Franchising Organization and Debates

An introduction

Stephen Taylor

Key points

- Franchising represents a mode of organization that can be interpreted and understood from the perspective of the theory of the firm.

- In essence, a business format franchise is concerned with the transference of intellectual property rights that provides both parties to the transaction with access to valuable benefits.

- The existence of franchising as an organizational form can be explained through two main theories: resource scarcity and agency.

- The key to any successful franchise strategy is that franchisors recognize as an economic imperative the importance of having an ongoing interest in, and relationship with, franchisees.

Introduction

In the second half of this century a major revolution in business organization occurred. Originating in the USA during the post-war economic boom of the 1950s, franchising emerged as a powerful new way of facilitating the growth of service organizations. It was to prove to have a particularly strong efficacy within the hospitality services sector and became readily adopted by many hotel, fast food and restaurant organizations. Indeed, in the USA today, it is almost certainly the dominant organizational mode across these sub-sectors. It is estimated that franchising accounts for 41 per cent of all retail sales in the USA, which amounts to some $800 billion annually. Behind these figures are 550,000 franchised businesses and 8 million employees. In the UK it is estimated that there are 29,100 franchised businesses employing around 273,000 people. Around an eighth of these franchises operate in the UK hospitality services sector (NatWest/BFA, 1998).

While franchising has historically been less prevalent in a UK and, more generally, the wider European context, here too in the past twenty years it has emerged as an important element of the hospitality services sector. Further afield, in the newly emerged markets of Asia and the Far East, franchising is proving to represent a major instrument of growth in the modern hospitality services sector. In many instances this reflects the internationalization of the US-developed franchising organizations such as McDonald's (fast food), Holiday Inns (hotels) and Starbucks (coffee). However, there has also been a growing trend of indigenously developed concepts such a Wimpy (UK), Jollibee (Philippines) and Novotel (France). Accordingly, franchising is not simply an American phenomenon, but rather represents a more fundamental development in business organization that enjoys an increasingly global presence in the hospitality services sector. None the less, the questions remain as to what actually is franchising and why has it proved to be so successful in recent decades?

What is franchising?

While this is a seemingly innocuous question, franchising as a concept can be characterized as one that has been subject to a wide range of definitions resulting in a great deal of confusion. As Price (1997) highlights in his seminal contribution to the franchising literature, this confusion, in part, stems from the disparate types of business relationships to which this term has been applied. Indeed, 'franchising definition' can almost be viewed as a stream of literature in its own right. It is not intended to revisit this debate here (see Chapters 2 and 10), but rather to adopt a more pragmatic approach with a view to delimiting the focus of this chapter and those that follow. The franchising context with which this book is concerned is business format franchising (which is sometimes referred to as second generation franchising) as this represents the franchising mode most frequently deployed within the hospitality services sector. However, it is worth noting that franchising as a concept has its origins in the tied public house system in eighteenth-century Britain (Stern, 1998). These origins are discussed in full in Chapter 9. The business format franchise involves the owner of a brand name and business system (the franchisor) transferring the right via a contract (the franchise agreement) to use this name and format to another party (the franchisee), usually for a fixed time period in a prescribed geographic area. In return, the franchisee agrees to pay an initial up-front fee and thereafter a royalty based upon a percentage of actual revenues generated (see Chapter 6).

In essence, a business format franchise is concerned with the transference of intellectual property rights (in the form of trademarks and technical know-how) that provides both parties to the transaction with access to valuable benefits. In the case of the franchisor, these benefits are primarily in the form of access to a means of rapid growth at a minimum level of capital investment (the franchisee is responsible for capital expenditure on plant and equipment), and the 'recruitment' of highly motivated owner–managers to operate the business units. For the franchisor this provides the basis for establishing the critical mass (minimum efficient scale) required to gain access to the benefits inherent in operating a chain of hotels or restaurants. The franchisee benefits from acquiring the rights to own and operate a proven business format while gaining access to a level of support (managerial assistance, marketing support etc.) typically found only in large chain hospitality organizations. A critical advantage frequently cited for the franchisee is a considerably reduced level of risk of failure compared to other small business start-ups. That said, in Chapter 3 Price controversially challenges the empirical foundations of such propositions. Furthermore, the extent to which franchisees can be classified as entrepreneurs is debatable given the high level of conformity typically inherent in a business format franchise (see Chapters 4 and 5).

Franchising and the theory of the firm

Within economics, approaches to the theory of the firm seek to provide explanations for the existence of the firm, its scale and scope or, in other words, its existence as a mode of economic organization. For our purposes here, these can be broadly grouped into two distinct literature streams (Foss, 1996). As will be demonstrated below, the foci of these research paradigms closely mirrors that of the two main theories advanced to explain franchising (Carney and Gedajlovic, 1991):

- the **resource scarcity** thesis, which shares some of the concerns of the knowledge perspective of the firm; and

- the **agency thesis,** which shares some of the concerns of the efficient contracting literature on the theory of the firm.

However, before turning our attention to these explanations of franchising *per se*, it is useful as a means of providing a wider theoretical context, briefly to review these two broad groupings of research which attempt to explain the existence of the firm.

The first stream of literature in the theory of the firm are those explanations which are concerned with and share a **resource perspective** (e.g. the resource-based view: Conner, 1991; Conner and Prahalad, 1996; and the literature sharing a more evolutionary focus: for example, Kogut and Zander, 1992). Here the focus is upon investigating successful firm growth strategies, their technological development and the creation of competitive advantage. In this first group of explanations the main emphasis is upon the role of valuable resources (capital, managerial, know-how, reputation etc.) in the context of organizational growth and evolution. The resource-based category, is generally acknowledged to have its antecedents in the seminal contribution by Penrose (1959), *The Theory of the Growth of the Firm*, which was concerned with explaining firm evolution.

The second category of explanations are those which are concerned with the **efficient contracting perspective** (for example, Alchian and Demsetz, 1972; Williamson, 1975), where the focus is upon explaining firm existence, boundaries and internal organization. This efficient contracting approach has its origins in Coase's (1937) seminal contribution 'The Nature of the Firm', which posed the question: 'why do firms exist?'. Coase argued that 'the distinguishing mark of the firm was the suppression of the price mechanism' (1937/1952, p. 334). Instead of using the price mechanism to co-ordinate external transactions, the firm utilized the power of fiat (authority) for internal co-ordination. The resultant dichotomy of markets versus hierarchies (which is also referred to as the 'make or buy' decision – albeit with the order of the terms reversed), has been an enduring theme within this literature stream. Ultimately, a primary concern here is the issue of organizational control.

Why franchise?

A central question that occupies academic researchers is why firms choose to expand through franchising (equivalent to the market mode and the 'buy' decision) rather than through company-owned units (equivalent to the hierarchy mode and the 'make' decision). Two reviews of the franchising literature (Elango and Fried, 1997; Fulop and Forward, 1997) suggest that it is possible to identify two competing theories in relation to this question. These are, as indicated above, termed resource scarcity (or resource allocation theory) and agency theory. The former is concerned with resource constraints to firm growth, while the latter is concerned with the issue of incentives and organizational control (Lafontaine and Kaufmann, 1994). As such, these two theories closely parallel the two literature streams on the theory of the firm outlined above. That this is the case should not be surprising as each seeks to offer an explanation for the popularity of franchising as a mode of economic organization and, in addition, why firms frequently operate a mix of franchised and company-owned units.

Resource scarcity theory

This stream of research explains franchising as being a response to a shortage of the necessary resources required for firm expansion, such as financial capital, labour capital, managerial talent (Oxenfeldt and Kelly, 1969; Norton, 1988a) or local market knowledge (Minkler, 1990). This view has its origins in the seminal work of Oxenfeldt and Kelly (1969), who suggested a life-cycle model of franchising in which a firm utilizes franchising as a means of overcoming resource constraints in the early stages of its growth. These constraints are typically seen as being mainly in relation to financial resources, although as Thompson (1994) has argued, a scarcity of managerial talent may be an even greater constraint for the growing organization. The desire for rapid early growth is associated with the need to achieve a minimum efficient scale and to develop the brand name capital that is so vital for retail oriented operations (Combs and Castrogiovanni, 1994). The life-cycle model suggests that as the firm grows in size, resource constraints ease and the firm will ultimately acquire the more profitable units operated by franchisees (see Thomas et al., 1990). Those in low volume locations where there is a danger of 'free-riding' in the form of lower investment, poor maintenance of quality standards and so on, by franchisees (see agency theory below in relation to this particular issue) will also tend to be acquired by the franchisor. Full vertical

Hospitality, Leisure & Tourism Series

7

integration (i.e. full company ownership) will be avoided as greater economic benefits can be derived from quasi-vertical integration, albeit with a dominant percentage of company-owned units. Implicit in this view is that company ownership is the preferred mode of economic organization.

Hunt (1972) provided early empirical support for the Oxenfeldt and Kelly conjecture. He examined the US fast food industry and detected an aggregate trend towards company-owned units. Later research by Caves and Murphy (1976), which examined hotel, motel and restaurant sectors in the USA, reported similar findings. More recently, Anderson (1984) found evidence of a systematic increase in the percentage of franchisor-owned units over a ten-year period (Elango and Fried, 1997). None the less, subsequent reviews of this stream of research suggested that, while inter-esting, the empirical support for this ownership redirection thesis remains equivocal (see Dant *et al.*, 1992, 1996). Indeed, data gathered over the period 1975 to 1990 indicate a very steady ratio of 80:20 in favour of franchised units (Trutko *et al.*, 1993).

The resource scarcity thesis thus suggests that firms use franchising as a means of reducing financial and managerial constraints and to transfer a measure of risk from the firm to a franchisee. This latter issue of risk spreading is arguably a third theory of franchising in its own right (Combs and Cas-trogiovanni, 1994). Risk spreading could be particularly attractive to new firms with a relatively unproven concept and who require the rapid achievement of a sustainable critical mass (Gilman, 1990). It has been suggested that where units require a high level of initial investment or where high growth is being experienced, franchising is likely to be preferred to company ownership (Thompson, 1992). The importance to firms of the use of franchising as a growth strategy appears well supported by survey data (see Lafontaine, 1992b; Dant, 1994).

Rubin (1978), who suggested that raising funds from investors is more efficient, has questioned the use of franchising as a means of raising scarce capital *per se*. Accordingly, it is argued that there must be other reasons for franchising than simply that of access to capital. However, Lafontaine (1992a) has suggested that the existence of higher incentives at the single (franchised) unit than those found in a company-owned and managed chain, could produce a scenario whereby franchising was a more efficient source of capital than investors. This is an important issue, as clearly there are companies who do have access to capital markets, but who continue to prefer franchising as a mode of operation and consequently this behaviour cannot be explained by sole recourse to resource scarcity theory (Lafontaine and Kaufmann, 1994).

Agency theory

It is the apparent anomaly in resource scarcity theory described above that the second explanation for franchising seeks to address. Here researchers draw upon the theory of efficient capital markets which suggests that a franchisor would reduce the level of risk inherent in a given activity through direct ownership and thus achieve a lower cost of capital – and thus a reduction in capital scarcity – than could be achieved by franchisees. Consequently, there must be an alternative explanation for franchising and to this end researchers draw upon what is known as agency theory (Brickley and Dark, 1987; Mathewson and Winter, 1985; Rubin, 1978). The agency problem arises because of a divergence of goals between the managers (agents) that firms (principals) employ (Eisenhardt, 1989; Jensen and Meckling, 1976). Here it is argued that managers as agents, since they have their compensation fixed, will tend to shirk in their duties to the firm (the principal). A related danger is that agents will behave in an opportunistic fashion and pursue their own interests at the expense of those of the principal. A primary reason for this potential behaviour is that in an employment situation any surpluses generated by employees belong to the owner and thus they have no incentive to maximize their work effort in the interests of the firm. Since this is the case, the firm has to incur costs in order to monitor employee activities to ensure that they act in the best interests of their employer. The franchising arrangement is seen as being more efficient in this respect as the interests of both the franchisor and the franchisee can be more closely aligned through the effective design of the franchise contract and thus reduce the threat of potential opportunism (Elango and Fried, 1997).

From an agency perspective the argument is that rational franchisors will act to maximize the value of their system of operation through minimizing the cost of effective monitoring of the activities of units. Franchising, it is argued, can, given certain circumstances, provide a hybrid form of organization that delivers this desired outcome (Klein *et al.*, 1978; Rubin, 1978). The point at which franchising becomes superior to company ownership is the point at which the marginal cost of monitoring owned units becomes greater than the marginal cost of using franchise contracts (Norton, 1988b). It is claimed that in franchising there is a potential for greater goal convergence between agents (franchisees) and principals (franchisors) than in the employment arrangement as used in the case of company ownership (Combs and Castrogiovanni, 1994). In the case of the latter, monitoring costs are driven by a number of factors, including (Caves and Murphy, 1976; Rubin, 1978; Brickley and Dark, 1987; Martin, 1988; Norton 1988a, 1988b):

- the importance of local knowledge;
- spatial proximity of units to the head office and to one another;
- availability of trained managers;
- the population density at unit locales.

All of these factors act to determine the total costs of ensuring the effective monitoring of units.

The obvious question that arises at this juncture is why should franchising remove or reduce such costs? The primary reason cited is that the franchisee is motivated to maximize the present value of his or her own operation and this aligns with the interests of the franchisor. Since the franchisee has a significant personal investment in their own unit they will, if rational, act to maximize the returns from the operation. Through payment of an initial fee and the subsequent ongoing royalties to the franchisor, the franchisee has full residual claim on any profits that arise from the operation. The only way that the franchisee can maximize the present value of the unit and thus achieve an acceptable return on their investment (which also includes equipment and fitting out costs) is through engaging in effective day-to-day management practices (Alchian and Demsetz, 1972; Norton, 1988b; Carney and Gedajlovic, 1991). However, franchising itself is not without monitoring problems for the franchisor and thus it too has monitoring costs that must be considered.

A central issue for the franchisor is the attainment of system-wide goals and, at times, this may result in conflict between the franchisor and franchisees. For example, franchisees may resist pressure to make ongoing or additional investments in their operation given their high initial investment at start-up. While further investments may bring system-wide benefits they may provide little perceived additional value to the individual franchisee. Accordingly, a major challenge for the franchisor can be motivating franchisees to adopt more of a system-wide perspective of their individual activities. This can prove difficult where the franchisee discerns little or no tangible benefit from any additional investments requested by the franchisor. Typically, the franchisor will have to resort to the active selling of new initiatives and attempt to encourage a position of enlightened self-interest on the part of the franchisee. Success or otherwise in this endeavour is likely to depend upon the level of trust in the relationship rather than through invoking clauses in the franchise agreement or making veiled threats about future dealings with one another. In Chapter 4, Morrison explores this issue in more depth.

Empirical support for the agency theory of franchising has been provided by Brickley and Dark (1987), who found that high employee monitoring costs, low initial investment cost and a high frequency of repeat customers per unit favoured franchising over company ownership. The prediction of agency theory that both urban and larger units will induce company ownership has found support in research undertaken by Thompson (1992). Where franchising is deployed, the primary advantage from the franchisor's perspective is the high level of motivation among franchisees compared to paid managers (Lillis *et al.*, 1976). In short, owner–managers appear capable of working the assets deployed in a unit much more efficiently and effectively than employee–managers and at a lower cost to the franchisor. If the franchisor's operating system is configured to produce the optimum return from the business then the rational franchisee will be very strongly motivated for sound economic reasons to observe the system as prescribed by the franchisor.

Towards a 'unified' theory of franchising

While the two theories of franchising discussed above are often presented as competing explanations as to why companies franchise, there is perhaps merit in considering them as being complementary rather than distinctive perspectives. Some researchers have taken this approach and provided evidence that tends to support such a view. Martin (1988) found both resource scarcity (capital requirements) and agency (monitoring costs) reasons for franchising, in addition to competition and scale factors. The development of a path model of the franchising life cycle by Carney and Gedajlovic (1991) using data from Quebec, combined both franchising theories. Furthermore, research by Lafontaine (1992a) supported the prevalence of franchising as a solution to incentive problems, but also as a means of accommodating growth strategies. In the case of the latter issue, she highlights that the resource constraint to be confronted may well be other than that of a financial nature. Overall, it would appear that both perspectives on why companies franchise offer useful insights. The challenge that currently confronts academics is to draw these two sets of explanations together in a unified framework that resolves some of the apparent contradictions that remain.

Hospitality, Leisure & Tourism Series

Franchising and McDonald's

Seeking to further explain the popularity of franchising through adopting the perspective of the theory of the firm as a mode of economic organization, we now turn to McDonald's. This provides a basis for offering some sort of 'reality check', exploring the issues raised in the context of the evolution of this organization and its use of franchising. Chapter 11 augments this case study in investigating McDonald's from a company and operational perspective.

> What eventually separated McDonald's from the rest of the pack was Kroc's ability to marshal the efforts of hundreds of other entrepreneurs – his McDonald's franchisees – to work not merely for their selfish interests but for McDonald's interests. As Ray Kroc saw it they were one and the same. (Love, 1995, p. 66)

By any conventional measure, McDonald's represents an example of a highly successful firm. Though in recent years they have come under increasing competitive pressure in their domestic market, McDonald's maintains a 41.9 per cent share of US fast food market retail sales, compared to arch-rival Burger King's 19.2 per cent (Tomkins, 1997). While critics predicted a spectacular fall from grace during the 1990s, in 1995 McDonald's managed to post the biggest percentage rise (17 per cent) in profits since 1988. Through the first half of the 1990s the company's profits rose at a compound annual rate of 12 per cent per annum (Tomkins, 1996). Increasing market saturation within the USA has created significant pressure on McDonald's profits, however the company has managed to largely offset this with rapid international growth. One measure of the success of this strategy is that globally the McDonald's brand is valued at being worth about $20 billion, some £12.5 billion (Willman, 1997). Indeed, the McDonald's brand according to the 1996 Interbrand Survey has now ousted Coca-Cola as the world's best-known brand (Tomkins, 1997). By 1999, McDonald's had 25,000 units operating in 117 countries, of which 85 per cent are franchised. System-wide sales are about $36 billion and 60 per cent of revenues are derived from non-US sales (McDonald's Corporation, 1999). The actual strategic nature of McDonald's competitive advantage is discussed in detail elsewhere (see Taylor, 1998), but it is intimately linked to their approach to franchising, which is now discussed.

This short case study (which is drawn from Love, 1995) outlines the development of the franchising strategy at the

McDonald's Corporation in the 1950s. It was to prove a highly successful approach and was subsequently to become the basis upon which all franchising agreements in the hospitality services sector were to be modelled. It is a particularly good example of how the agency problem can be tackled through an effective franchising strategy and how this can align the goals of both the franchisor and franchisee to the mutual benefit of each party. Indeed, as Love (1995) pointed out, Ray Kroc's major contribution was not to invent the hamburger, or a new system for their production or the drive-in concept as many appear to believe. In fact, what Kroc did do, was to create a unique franchising system that differentiated McDonald's from all their early fast food competitors. One can theorize about franchising as long as one wishes, but a considerable amount can be gained by examining the actual franchising strategy upon what is arguably the most successful business format franchise in the hospitality services sector is based. This provides a powerful lens through which to revisit the theoretical explanations for franchising introduced earlier in this chapter.

As in so many cases, the McDonald's story is not one of overnight success, but rather one of a gradual evolution characterized by a process of problem solving. When Kroc struck his deal in 1955 with the McDonald brothers to franchise their 'Speedee Service System' he did so with a view primarily to increasing sales of the five spindle 'Multimixers' to which he held the national marketing rights. The brothers had already granted a number of licensees, but this 'amounted to little more than a rent-a-name scheme' (Love, 1995, p. 22). The arrangement with the McDonald brothers was, with hindsight, to prove to be a poor one from Kroc's perspective. As it stood, his original deal with the two brothers was to prove anything but financially lucrative. Indeed, it was in response to this very problem that McDonald's was ultimately to devise a new approach to franchising. For, as Love (1995, p. 151–2) observed: 'Kroc had been too generous to the McDonald brothers, too concerned about the success of his franchisees, and too honest in arranging for supplies'.

The original deal that Ray Kroc agreed with the McDonald brothers meant that his company's income was limited to an up-front fee of $950 and an ongoing 1.9 per cent service fee based on franchisees' food sales. However, McDonald's only retained 1.4 per cent of this as this agreement specified that 0.5 per cent went to the two McDonald brothers. The up-front franchise fee of $950 was by industry standards very modest and was only to raised to $1,500 in 1956 (by mid–1990s this was $45,000). Unlike many other franchisors, McDonald's received no significant income stream from equipment or supplies sales to franchisees. Based upon 1950s data, an average store had annual sales of $200,000 from which the company received $3,800 as an annual service fee and $1,000 of this went to the McDonald brothers. This was insufficient revenue to support the level of activity and support McDonald's provided to operators. On this basis, everyone made money – suppliers, operators, the McDonald brothers – everyone, that is, except the company.

The financial breakthrough for McDonald's came from an idea developed by Harry Sonneborn, who Kroc hired in 1956. As Kroc was to note not long before his death in 1984: 'Harry alone put in the policy that salvaged this company and made it a big-leaguer. His idea is what really made McDonald's rich' (quoted in Love, 1995, pp. 152–3). The 'Sonneborn Solution', as it became known, was essentially a very astute real estate strategy that leveraged the highly efficient McDonald's operating system and circum-navigated the financial constraints imposed by the original deal Kroc had made with the McDonald brothers. Ultimately, as well as being the critical source of revenue hitherto absent, it was also to provide substantial additional benefits to the company in terms of substantial assets in real estate and ultimate control over franchisees.

The strategy was deceptively simple. McDonald's would form a separate real estate company (called Franchise Realty Corpora-tion) and lease real estate (in the late 1950s it cost about $30,000 for the required half acre site) on which the landowners were required to build a new McDonald's outlet (costing about $40,000). The landowner would then grant McDonald's a fixed 20-year lease on this complete package. Franchise Realty Cor-poration would, in turn, sub-lease to franchisees at a premium rental. This was originally fixed at 20 per cent, but later increased to 40 per cent above McDonald's own rental costs. Such a figure covered the company's own leasing costs and provided it with an attractive return. In addition, franchisees were required to pay a security deposit (originally $7,500) on the lease and this meant that from the outset the real estate arm of McDonald's produced a positive cash flow that enabled it to start purchasing sites. This strategy was ultimately to lead to the company becoming one of the largest owners of retail real estate in the USA by the late 1990s. In effect, the property lease payments were the company's main revenue stream. These were ultimately tied to outlet revenues as the company inserted a clause in the rental agreement that stated rental payments would be either at this initial fixed rate (i.e. McDonald's own lease payments plus 20 per cent) or a rent based on a percentage of store sales, initially 5 per cent and currently now 8.5 per cent. The higher of these two figures would be the applicable lease payment for franchisees.

This strategy enabled McDonald's to increase the applicable 'royalty' to 6.9 per cent (5 per cent plus the original 1.9 per cent) of which they retained 6.4 per cent.

A significant advantage of the McDonald's leasing strategy was that it was an extremely effective means, more effective than a mere franchise agreement in the 1950s when their legal power was less established, of preventing opportunism on the part of franchisees. For instance, it prevented franchisees from simply replacing the franchisor's signage and withholding royalty payments. Sonneborn himself expressed the view that he didn't think 'the franchise contract was worth the paper it was written on [as] it could never stand up in legal action' (quoted in Love, 1995, p. 156). Any such legal ambiguities were absent in the case of leases as they were well established as a legal contract and would be readily enforced by the courts, if such a need were ever to arise. Accordingly, McDonald's compelled franchisee compliance to its operating standards by ensuring that observance of these was inserted as a legal condition of the property lease. Thus the franchise agreement and the lease became fused together to provide the company with a highly effective, enforceable mechanism of franchisee control.

Indeed, Kroc apparently was immediately attracted to the 'Sonneborn Solution', not by its ability to generate profits, but by the control it afforded over operators: 'I have finally found the way that will put every single McDonald's we open under our complete control' (quoted in Love, 1995, pp. 156–7). Under the new leasing strategy McDonald's could give thirty days notice to operators who violated operating standards. Thus, as Kroc reputedly reported back to the McDonald brothers, the company now had 'a club over them [the franchisees], and by God, there will be no more pampering or fiddling with them. We will do the ordering instead of going around and begging them to co-operate' (quoted in Love, 1995, p. 157).

While the additional control was vitally important, the primary impact of this real estate strategy was its ability to generate, for the first time, real profits for the company. Crucially, it was to prove to be a robust strategy. For, unlike other franchising 'tie-in' strategies, it did not require operators to purchase equipment and supplies. This approach was ultimately to be ruled against by the US courts in the 1960s and 1970s as being an illegal conflict of interest. Moreover, during the same period the courts consistently supported the right of franchisors to select and control restaurant locations as an integral part of their operations.

The importance of monitoring franchisees to ensure their compliance with prescribed standards was an early lesson learned by McDonald's. In the first year of his arrangement with the McDonald brothers, Kroc granted eighteen franchises, half of which were in California, nearly two thousand miles from McDonald's head office in Chicago. Given the lack of a suitable infrastructure and the geographic distance, the inevitable happened – the system got out of control. Between them, the Californian franchisees apparently deviated from every single operating requirement imposed by McDonald's. This involved violations in pricing, menu items and the carefully prescribed standards in relation to quality, service and cleanliness. This was an important early lesson for McDonald's and led to a temporary suspension of West Coast expansion and a focus on developing the system closer to home, initially in Illinois, then in adjoining states. From this point onwards McDonald's focused upon developing an organization that provided a comprehensive infrastructure to support and monitor their operating system.

Every requirement of this fast food operation needed to support the system, from suppliers to operators, was defined in detail and then closely monitored. Indeed, such was the exactness of McDonald's requirements that they not only revolutionized fast food restaurants, but also radically modernized farming methods (potato, beef and dairy), food processing and food distribution in the USA. Ultimately, it was this attention to detail, the ability to develop the necessary standards and then control them, that was McDonald's critical competitive advantage. No other competitor could match the company for its ability to be consistent across its rapidly expanding system. In retrospect, it would have been impossible for McDonald's to have developed as quickly and efficiently as they did unless they had utilized franchising. The building of the infrastructure that supported the restaurants consumed a vast amount of resources, both financial and managerial. The creation of a large chain of fast food outlets operated by highly motivated managers almost certainly could not have been achieved by a single organization in the same time scale.

The power of the McDonald's strategy was ultimately its ability to align a number of key elements in a highly synergistic fashion. The company would only really start to make money once a franchisee started to hit 'percentage rent'. Thus, unlike many other franchising arrangements, which were based upon mainly initial franchise fees and equipment sales, there was a very real incentive for McDonald's to help operators to achieve maximum sales revenues as quickly as possible. In effect it created an extremely strong goal congruence between McDonald's and its owner–operators and minimized the threat of opportunism – a classic win–win situation. Additionally, it ensured for the first time that Kroc's QSC (quality, service and cleanliness) formula gained real economic teeth for both parties to the franchise agreement. In the case of many other franchisors, their income was largely tied to the number of new franchises granted as they relied upon up-front franchising fees and new equipment sales rather than royalties. Alternatively McDonald's relied predominantly on the continuing sales revenues of existing franchisees as its major source of income. Accordingly, an ongoing interest in, and relationship with, franchisees was firmly supported by a very real economic imperative. This is the essence of any successful franchising strategy.

Summary

This introductory chapter has explored franchising from within the broader context of the literature concerning the theory of the firm. This facilitates the recognition that franchising is but one mode of organization from which hospitality firms can select to engage in economic activity. The two principal theories pertaining to this choice, namely resource scarcity theory and agency theory, were then introduced along with the associated arguments advanced to support their veracity. The research evidence examined suggests that each of the two theoretical explanations for the reasons why firms use franchising as a mode of organization would appear to have some explanatory power, that is, some validity. However, each explanation also offers a source of contradiction and a major challenge for academics is to develop a 'unified theory of franchising' that is capable of providing a more comprehensive explanation as to why and when firms franchise.

The second part of this chapter consisted of a case study of McDonald's, who pioneered and perfected business format franchising in food service in the USA in the 1960s. The franchising strategy developed by this organization was demonstrated as being a critical element of its subsequent capability to develop and expand its innovative approach to food service. It was seen that the approach developed by McDonald's was evolutionary in that is was arrived at through a process of trial and error in response to the challenges confronting the firm in its early stages of growth. While the use of franchising did provide McDonald's with a means of overcoming capital scarcity in its early stages, and this was clearly a major motivator in the firm's selection of this mode of organization, it also graphically highlights that agency considerations were highly influential. As one of McDonald's key strengths from a customer perspective was its ability to create standardization in its restaurants, they subsequently developed a franchising strategy, that minimized the threat of franchisee opportunism. Finally, the case study illustrates how McDonald's managed to reconcile the advantages and disadvantages of rapid growth through using a non-equity based strategy through the development of a highly effective franchising method.

Debate topics

- Theories associated with the firm as a mode of economic organization are inadequate to understand accurately the endurance of franchising as an organizational form.

- Franchising provides both parties (franchisor and franchisee) with the full range of resources, the combination of which guarantees mutual success.

- Through the franchising of operational units franchisors solve the human resource problems associated with the management of remote units.

Selected readings

Elango, B. and Fried, V.H. (1997) Franchising research: A literature review and synthesis. *Journal of Small Business Management*, July, pp. 68–81.

Fulop, C. and Forward, J. (1997) Insights into franchising: a review of empirical and theoretical perspectives. *The Service Industries Journal*, **17** (4), 603–25.

Love, J.F. (1995) *McDonald's: Behind the Arches*. Bantam Books.

References

Alchian, A. and Demsetz, H. (1972) Production, information costs and economic organization. *American Economic Review.* **62**, 777–95.

Anderson, E. (1984) The growth and performance of franchise systems: company versus franchise ownership. *Journal of Economics and Business*, **36**, 421–31.

Brickley, J. and Dark, F. (1987) The choice of organizational form: the case of franchising. *Journal of Financial Economics*, **18**, 401–20.

Carney M. and Gedajlovic, E. (1991) Theoretical integration in franchise systems: agency theory and resource explanations. *Strategic Management Journal*, **12**, 607–29.

Caves, R. and Murphy, W. (1976) Franchising: firms, markets and intangible assets. *Southern Economic Journal*, **42**, 572–86.

Coase, R. (1937) The nature of the firm. *Economica*, **4**, 386–405.

Coase, R. ([1937]1952) The nature of the firm. In Stigler, G.J. and Boulding, K.E. (eds), *Readings in Price Theory*. Irwin, pp. 331–351.

Combs, J. and Castrogiovanni, G. (1994) Franchisor strategy: a proposed model and empirical test of franchise versus company ownership. *Journal of Small Business Management*, April–June, pp. 37–48.

Conner, K. (1991) An historical comparison of resource based theory and the five schools of thought within industrial organization economics: do we have a new theory of the firm? *Journal of Management*, **17** (1), 121–54.

Conner, K. and Prahalad, C. (1996) A resource-based theory of the firm: knowledge versus opportunism. *Organization Science*, **7** (5), 477–501.

Dant, R. (1994) *Motivations for Franchising: Rhetoric versus Reality*. Working paper, Boston University.

Dant, R., Kaufmann, P. and Paswan, A.K. (1992) Ownership redirection in franchised channels. *Journal of Public Policy and Marketing*, **11** (1), 33–44.

Dant, R., Paswan, A. and Kaufmann, P. (1996) What we know about ownership redirection in franchising: a meta-analysis. *Journal of Retailing*, **72** (4), 429–44.

Eisenhardt, K. (1989) Agency theory: an assessment and review. *Academy of Management Review*, **14** (1), 57–74.

Elango, B. and Fried, V. (1997) Franchising research: a literature review and synthesis. *Journal of Small Business Management*, July, pp. 68–81.

Foss, N. (1996) Knowledge-based approaches to the theory of the firm: some critical comments. *Organization Science*, **7** (5), 470–6.

Fulop, C. and Forward, J. (1997) Insights into franchising: a review of empirical and theoretical perspectives. *The Service Industries Journal*, **17** (4), 603–25.

Gilman, A. (1990) Competitive growth with franchising. *Chain Store Age Executive*, January, p. 160.

Hunt, S. (1972) The trend toward company-operated units in franchise chains. *Journal of Retailing*, **49** (2), 3–12.

Jensen, M. and Meckling, W. (1976) Theory of the firm: managerial behavior, agency costs, and ownership structure. *Journal of Financial Economics*, **3**, 305–60.

Klein, B., Crawford, R. and Alchian, A. (1978) Vertical integration, appropriable rents, and the competitive contracting process. *Journal of Law and Economics*, **21**, 297–326.

Kogut, B. and Zander, U. (1992) Knowledge of the firm, combinative capabilities, and the replication of technology. *Organization Science*, **3**, 383–97.

Lafontaine, F. (1992a) Agency theory and franchising: some empirical results. *Journal of Economics*, **23** (2), 263–83.

Lafontaine, F. (1992b) How and why do franchisors do what they do: a survey report. In Kaufmann, P.J. (ed.), *Franchising: Passport for Growth and World of Opportunity. Proceedings of the Society of Franchising*, Lincoln, NE, International Center for Franchise Studies, University of Nebraska.

Lafontaine, F. and Kaufmann, P.J. (1994) The evolution of ownership patterns in franchise systems. *Journal of Retailing*, **70** (2), 97–113.

Lillis, C., Narayana, C. and Gilman, J. (1976) Competitive advantage variation over the life cycle of a franchise. *Journal of Marketing*, **40** (1), 77–80.

Love, J. (1995) *McDonald's: Behind the Arches*. Bantam Books.

Martin, R. (1988) Franchising and risk management. *American Economic Review*, **78** (5), 954–68.

Mathewson, G. and Winter, R. (1985) The economics of franchise contracts. *Journal of Law and Political Economics*, **28**, 503–26.

Minkler, A. (1990) An empirical analysis of a firm's decision to franchise. *Economic Letters*, **34**, 77–82.

NatWest/BFA (1998) *UK Franchise Survey*. British Franchise Association.

Norton, S. (1988a) Franchising, brand name capital, and the entrepreneurial capacity problem. *Strategic Management Journal*, **9**, 105–14.

Norton, S. (1988b) An empirical look at franchising as an organizational form. *Journal of Business*, **16** (2), 197–218.

Oxenfeldt, A. and Kelly, A. (1969) Will successful franchise systems ultimately become wholly-owned chains? *Journal of Retailing*, **44** (49), 69–83.

Penrose, E. (1959) *The Theory of the Growth of the Firm*. Wiley.

Price, S. (1997) *The Franchise Paradox: New Directions, Different Strategies*. Cassell.

Rubin, P. (1978) The theory of the firm and the structure of the franchise contract. *Journal of Law and Economics*, **21**, 223–33.

Stern, P. (1998) The two partners of franchising. *Franchise World Directory* 1999, pp. 1–7.

Taylor, S. (1998) Performance determinants in hospitality organizations: a competence perspective. Conference proceedings of the 7th Annual CHME Hospitality Conference. Glasgow, pp. 237–55.

Thomas, W., O'Hara, M. and Musgrave, F. (1990) The effects of ownership and investment on the performance of franchise systems. *American Economics,* **34** (1), 54–61.

Thompson, R. (1992) Company ownership versus franchising: issues and evidence. *Journal of Economic Studies,* **19** (4), 31–42.

Thompson, R. (1994) The franchise life cycle and the Penrose effect. *Journal of Economic Behavior and Organization,* **24** (2), 207–18.

Tomkins, R. (1996) McDonald's makes sceptics eat their words: Burger chain's continued growth confounds critics. *Financial Times,* 11 March, p. 19.

Tomkins, R. (1997) When the chips are down. *Financial Times,* 16 July, p. 21.

Trutko, J., Trutko, J. and Kostecka, A. (1993) Franchising's growing role in the US economy, 1975–2000. *Small Business Research Summary.* No.136. US Department of Commerce.

Williamson, O. (1975) *Markets and Hierarchies.* Free Press.

Willman, J. (1997) Perspective: managing global brands. *Financial Times,* 22 October, p. 4.

2

History and development

Christina Fulop

Key points

- Business format franchising entails a more integrated relationship between the parties involved, compared with the wide variety of business relationships which is loosely referred to as franchising/licensing.

- A growing number of large, well-established companies have entered franchising as a means of developing their businesses, and some firms that have traditionally relied upon looser forms of third party distribution have converted to franchising in order to exert a higher degree of support and control.

- Essentially a franchise is a partnership – albeit an unequal one – and it has been the difficulties of coping with the complexities of this arrangement, and the potential for conflict that may ensue, that has sometimes led to the failure of some franchise operations.

- Developments within the franchisor/franchisee relationship are altering the power distribution in favour of franchisees.

Introduction

Although the term franchising is often used very loosely to cover a wide variety of business relationships, and is also used interchangeably with the term licensing, the focus here is on *business format franchising*. The major distinguishing feature of business format franchising compared with other types of franchising/licensing is that it entails a more integrated relationship between the parties involved.

Thus, in business format franchising (hereafter referred to as franchising) the licensor (i.e. the franchisor) does not only grant permission for the licensee (i.e. the franchisee) to sell the franchisor's branded products or services, but should also provide a proven method of operating, support and advice on the setting up of the franchisee's business and ongoing support to the franchisee. Furthermore, the franchisee has invariably to pay an initial fee to the franchisor, some type of ongoing fee, and a marketing/advertising levy (see Chapter 6). Another distinguishing feature of franchising is that the franchisor and franchisee remain legally distinct, although the two parties work together and combine their efforts with the aim of creating a successful business format (Rubin, 1978; Mendelsohn, 1996). In the marketing literature franchising has been identified as a hybrid form of vertical marketing system and, as a consequence, as a method of marketing goods and services dependent on complex contractual arrangements (Williamson, 1975, 1991; Stern and El-Ansary, 1992).

Although business arrangements similar to franchising seem to have been in existence as far back as the middle ages, the more modern origins of this marketing technique date from the latter half of the nineteenth century. In the USA the arrangements between the Singer Sewing Machine company and the owners of outlets which sold its sewing machine spare parts and undertook repairs bore a certain resemblance to modern day franchising, including branding the outlets with Singer signage. The next discernible stage in the development of franchising occurred in the 1920s and 1930s when petrol companies and some wholesalers and retailers (Baillieu, 1988; Brown, 1988) developed similar licence/franchise arrangements.

Business format franchising began in the USA in the late 1940s and early 1950s when, for the first time, franchising was applied as a distinct way of starting a new business as opposed to merely a method of distributing an existing product. From the few franchisors who could be identified in 1946, by 1960 there were over 700. During that period many businesses which have since become household names were established, such as McDonald's,

Holiday Inn and Budget Rent-a-Car. Franchising was first established in the UK in 1955 when J. Lyons & Co. Ltd purchased the master franchise rights for the UK from the American Wimpy hamburger restaurants. In the UK franchising grew rapidly during the 1970s and 1980s and gained acceptance. Since the late 1960s and early 1970s franchising has spread throughout the world, where it is present in varying stages of development in an estimated 140 countries, many of which have a significant number of successful franchise systems (Arthur Andersen, 1995; Mendelsohn, 1996).

Cross-border franchising has also expanded on a large scale (for example, see Chapters 7 and 8). As franchisors have reached maturity in their domestic markets they have often seen the possibility of exploiting opportunities in foreign markets. Although, as might be expected, the USA has by far the largest number of cross-border franchisors – an estimated 400 – there has been a steady increase in the number emanating from other countries (Arthur Andersen, 1995). The entry strategy most widely used in cross-border franchising is the master franchise and that which is most often utilized by British franchisors. An overseas company (the master franchisor) granting the right to a domestic company (the master franchisee) to develop the concept in the latter's country typifies this arrangement. Unfortunately, there is some evidence that the purchase of a master franchise as a quick 'off the peg' method of establishing a franchised operation has often encountered problems. Examples of how this strategy has failed some franchise systems are provided in Chapter 7, relative to the importation of US catering concepts into the UK. In particular, this relates to differences in the social, economic and cultural environment of the two countries, which frequently necessitated substantial adaptations and modifications to the original product, systems and marketing.

The main impetus to the development of franchising has been from newly emerging businesses that have utilized this method of marketing goods and services as a means of expansion with less risk. A growing number of large, well-established companies have also entered franchising as a means of developing their businesses. Some established retail chains, too, have introduced franchising alongside their managed outlets for a variety of reasons. For example:

- to achieve a more rapid rate of market penetration than would have been possible through their company-owned operations alone;

- to raise capital by converting existing branches;

- to improve the performance of some of their marginally profitable outlets by converting them to franchising.

Nevertheless, the rate of success of such a dual distribution system (the operation of franchised and managed outlets within a network) has been very variable. It has often proved difficult to reconcile the decentralized organization and operating methods implicit in the franchising concept with the centralized decision-making, management and culture of a corporate concern (Forward and Fulop, 1996).

Many firms that have traditionally relied upon looser forms of third party distribution such as dealers, licensees or tenants have also adopted a franchise format. The principal reason for the conversion of these looser distribution arrangements into franchises has been to facilitate a higher degree of support and control. This closer relationship should ensure:

- better quality and more uniform customer service;
- more consistent operational standards across the system;
- improved performance at outlet level with reduced operating costs.

In a more dynamic market environment many business persons who would formerly have set up in business by themselves have preferred to become franchisees in order to obtain the support and assistance of a large organization (Fulop and Warren, 1992).

Although franchising is found mainly in the retail and service sectors, it is also utilized by:

- some manufacturers in order to secure outlets for their products;
- some wholesalers as a means of obtaining outlets for products and in order to make more economic use of storage and distribution facilities.

Why franchising has come about

Franchising has expanded over the past fifty years as a preferred marketing and distribution channel option for many firms over alternative business formats because it has advantages for both franchisor and franchisee. These advantages have been reinforced by socio-economic influences and the active involvement of interested third parties.

Advantages of franchising for franchisors

For the franchisor the prime motivation for franchising is usually lack of capital or, alternatively, unwillingness to take on the risk of borrowing, as is discussed in Chapter 6. Since franchisees provide the capital, which is invested in the outlet, expansion should be achieved for the following reasons:

- a lower capital input is required from the firm;

- some of the business risks are passed from the firm to the franchisee;

- there is the potential for more rapid growth than would otherwise be possible;

- the franchisor needs fewer staff than if the outlets were all company owned;

- relatively lower capital investment of the franchisor should lead to higher returns on capital employed.

On the other hand, there is some evidence that the cost in money, time and manpower of developing the franchise system in the early stages is often underestimated by franchisors (Forward and Fulop, 1993). This finding has prominence in Chapter 6, where it is discussed in detail.

Moreover, at the outlet level the operation of a franchise should enable firms to acquire some of the characteristics of a small business operation such as local knowledge, and flexibility as emphasized in Chapter 4. And since franchisees who have invested their own wealth in the business are generally highly motivated individuals, this should lead to improved outlet performance when compared to outlets operated by company managers. The high motivation and entrepreneurial attitude of the franchisee can be a particular asset in business activities where it is difficult to monitor employees, e.g. mobile operations. Lashley focuses on this aspect in Chapter 5 within the construct of franchisee empowerment.

There is another aspect of franchising that has made it attractive to firms which have been experiencing difficulty in finding suitable staff, namely, that it should prove easier to attract quality franchisees than quality managers because of the benefits pertaining to the franchise format, such as:

- the opportunity of being their own boss;

- having the backing of a successful organization;

- the supply of products that are sometimes exclusive and/or at favourable prices.

As a consequence, where a firm may have found itself unable to recruit the required calibre, or specific expertise, of an outlet manager, franchising may ease its staffing problems (Forward and Fulop, 1996).

Advantages of franchising for franchisees

A potential small businessman or woman may prefer to become a franchisee rather than operate an independent small business because in such an arrangement they hope to gain the advantages of both a large and small business (Baron and Schmidt, 1991). While franchisees have to be prepared to relinquish some independence, in return they gain support and assistance from a format with an established name and reputation. This considerably reduces the risk inherent in establishing a new business. Thus franchisees gain the freedom to operate in a controlled, assisted and supported environment, while at the same time gaining the benefits of a brand name, professional management and the economies of scale of a larger organization. Finally, but by no means least, the franchisee has a business which has the possibility of being sold at a profit.

Respondents in the Fulop (1996, 39–40) survey summed up these motivations for becoming a franchisee rather than becoming an independent businessperson as follows:

'It's not a 100 per cent way to make money, but it's certainly less risky than starting up a normal business from scratch.'

'The beauty of franchising is that in terms of marketing and advertising you gain all the benefits of being part of a large company. A one-man (woman) operation could never obtain the same advantageous rates.'

'I was looking to work for myself . . . I liked the basic idea of the franchise network – the system of support from a head office even though we're fairly autonomous.'

Socio-economic influences and interested third parties

Several environmental factors have facilitated the expansion of franchising. The most important long-term influence has been the shift in the economy towards the service sector. This is where franchising is concentrated because the input of a committed and highly motivated franchisee should encourage a high quality of service. Secondly, over the past thirty years the greater emphasis on an 'entrepreneurial culture' has stimulated the growth of franchising because of its reputation for being an easier and less risky entry into business. At the same time, the purchase of franchises has been facilitated by a high incidence of unemployment. This made a great deal of redundancy money available and, at least in the 1970s and 1980s, rapidly rising house prices created equity which could be released to fund the purchase of a franchise. Thirdly, franchising has benefited from the increased interest in the expansion of small firms by central government, and its willingness to facilitate the supply of finance to viable small firms where conventional loans are not available due to a lack of security. The European Union (EU) has also acknowledged the value of franchising as a means of stimulating the creation and viability of small businesses, and this view led to the exemption of franchise agreements in 1988 from EU competition legislation (Mendelsohn and Harris, 1992). Finally, franchising in the UK, but to a lesser extent in other countries, has benefited from the active recognition and support of the clearing banks. Franchisees are considered to have a lower risk of failure than other small businesses when they join an ethical franchised network that has been investigated thoroughly by the banks (see Chapter 6). While the recession in the early 1990s undoubtedly affected all areas of business in the UK, there were less problems in the franchise sector than in others. As a consequence, UK banks are usually prepared to offer higher than conventional gearing ratios and possibly lower interest charges to prospective franchisees. This is because, while the latter may have little or no previous business experience, the franchisor is operating a proven business concept (Stern and Stanworth, 1994).

The British Franchise Association (BFA), the trade association of franchisors, established in 1977, has also assisted the growth of franchising. It is the only voluntary accreditation body for franchising in the UK. Its remit is to develop and continuously improve the standards of good practice in franchising and to accredit franchisors that meet these standards. For franchisors, membership takes the form of full, associated or provisional members, and franchise professionals are accepted as affiliates. As part of the European Franchise Federation the BFA is able to lobby the European government on behalf of its members. In particular, it has raised the 'profile' as well as the standards of franchising through its Code of Ethics.

The downside of franchising

Despite the many benefits which franchising may provide for both franchisor and franchisee, it is by no means an easy concept to manage. The franchisee may bring motivation, commitment and initiative, together with an input of capital to a business. However, the expense and difficulty of ensuring, in such a decentralized operation, the maintenance of uniform standards of service and a consistent public image across the network may offset these valuable assets. This aspect is investigated within the theoretical frameworks of entrepreneurship and empowerment in Chapters 4 and 5.

Franchisees can be highly motivated but can also be very demanding of the time and effort of the franchisor's senior management. To some degree, this is due to the fact that the business of the franchisee is legally separate from that of the franchisor. As a consequence, compared to managed outlets, the scope for issuing commands is limited. The fact that it is necessary to 'persuade' franchisees compared with the ability to 'tell' company managers has led some observers (Williamson, 1991) to conclude that franchised firms are less capable of adapting to change than fully integrated companies. Essentially, a franchise is a partnership, *albeit* an unequal one, and it has been the difficulties of coping with the complexities of this arrangement, and the potential for conflict that may ensue, that has led to the failure of some franchised operations.

For the franchisor the biggest challenge is to manage successfully the relationship with the franchisee in all its aspects. For the franchisee the most important concerns are:

- the quality of the franchisor;
- how rigorously the business concept has been tested;
- the ability of the other franchisees in the network;
- how well the franchisor will continue to develop the business and provide a sustained and high level of ongoing support.

Measuring the size of the franchise industry

The annual surveys commissioned by the British Franchise Association (BFA) and sponsored by NatWest Bank since 1984, are the main source of statistics on franchising in the UK. According to these trade statistics, the overall turnover of the franchise industry rose between 1984 and 1990 from £0.84 billion to £5.2 billion. The average *annual* percentage increase during these years was 36 per cent, admittedly from a low base. In comparison, in the following five years from 1990 to 1995 the average *annual* increase in turnover of the franchise industry was 3 per cent, which includes changes of 8 per cent (1990–1991) and 11 per cent (1992–1993). The number of franchise systems rose between 1987 and 1991 from 253 to 432. Then from 1992, and employing a stricter definition, the number of systems increased from 373 to 474 by 1995, the latter showing a 14 per cent increase over 1994. By 1997 the number of business format franchises had reached 568 with an estimated turnover of £7 billion (NatWest/BFA, 1998).

Although these trade surveys are valuable to the understanding of the scope and growth of franchising they have certain limitations. This is an important theme taken up and developed by Price in Chapter 3. Not only are the response rates low, for example, but a higher proportion of respondents are members of the BFA, and these tend to operate franchised networks which are well established compared with the networks of non-members. Furthermore, while franchising has become a mature industry in the United States and is well established in the UK and many other countries, it is not easy to measure accurately its scope in any one country. It is even more difficult to make comparisons between countries from the available statistics because these are often unreliable and imprecise due to the wide variations in definitions of franchising and limitations in methods of data collection (Forward and Fulop, 1993; Stern and Stanworth, 1994). Since 1998 the NatWest bank has sought to address this issue by commissioning an annual European franchise survey.

Franchisor/franchisee relationship

Since the success of a franchise network is determined largely by the ability of the franchisor to resolve, or at least minimize, potential conflicts concerning power and control, and to promote a co-operative environment, it is not surprising that the complexities and contractual nature of the franchisor/franchisee relationship has attracted the attention of many researchers. These investigations have considered the:

- nature and behavioural aspects of the franchisor/franchisee relationship;
- power distribution within the franchise network;
- extent of franchisee autonomy when compared to other independent small businessmen or women.

The following considers some of these key aspects associated with franchising.

The contract, control and balance of power

There are several aspects of the franchisor/franchisee relationship which are liable to cause friction. For example, these may include:

- the level of support may not come up to the expectations of franchisees;

- the franchisee may consider that the franchisor has misrepresented the projected sales and profit levels;

- franchisees may resist the imposition of changes in systems;

- disputes may develop over the product mix and stock control procedures, or over the quality of products.

In an investigation undertaken by Fulop (1996) three causes of friction outweighed all others among those franchisees who had experienced difficulties:

- not enough training support;

- too many changes to the system;

- too many restrictions.

Since it is the contract that defines the formal relationship between the franchisor and the franchisee, and sets out comprehensively and specifically the obligations of franchisees, it is the extent to which the contract is the main source of power, control and conflict that has been the main subject of investigation (Brandenberg, 1989; Felstead, 1990, 1993; Stanworth, 1991; Pilotti and Pozzana, 1991; Stern and El-Ansary, 1992).

According to Sanghavi (1990, p. 19): 'There are many examples of contract clauses which are unfair to the franchisee.' It has been pointed out, for example, that the franchisee signs the franchise contract before they see the franchise manual in detail. Furthermore, the contract obliges the franchisee to put into operation any changes made to the operating manual over the period of the franchise. Termination clauses and restrictions on post-termination activities are also sometimes regarded as leaving franchisees disadvantaged. In addition, the financial arrangements (see Chapter 6) usually stipulated in the contract are considered as an inherent cause of friction because while franchisors usually receive a fee based on the franchisee's turnover, franchisees are reliant on the profits of the outlet. Adverse consequences of this payment system may include a reluctance by franchisees to change menus or to refurbish their premises. It has also been suggested that territory clauses can lead to a conflict of interest. On the one hand, franchisees often resent the infringement on their independence imposed by the territorial limits laid down by the franchisor; yet, conversely, they frequently seek territorial protection from the establishment of new franchisees in order to maintain profits (Hoy, 1994)!

There is, however, an opposing view to the above which maintains that the specific nature of the contract is unavoidable if uniformity is to be achieved across the system. Such homogeneity is seen as an advantage not only for the franchisor, but as beneficial to all franchisees, because it diminishes the likelihood of wide variations in service and offering which may well lead to dissatisfied customers, and penalize all franchisees, not only those who breach the rules (Mendelsohn, 1996). Moreover, on all these contentious issues there is evidence that many franchisors are aware of such potential pitfalls and take steps to avoid them. For instance, many termination clauses either lay down that the franchise can only be bought back by the franchisor at an independently assessed 'market value', or in line with a specified formula. In addition, the view that the contract allows the franchisor to exert a considerable degree of control, which effectively curtails the actions of franchisees and thereby their autonomy has been disputed. This is because the majority of franchisees seem prepared to renew their contracts, express little desire to change the contents, and many are able to negotiate certain clauses with their franchisor prior to signing. It would, therefore, seem that franchisees do not regard the contract as a severe curtailment on their autonomy.

Finally, the assumption that independence is a top priority for franchisees and that they resent clauses in the contract which diminish this autonomy seems at variance with the main *raison d'être* for becoming a franchisee. Namely, this is that the franchise route has been chosen deliberately, as emphasized by Morrison in Chapter 4. It provides the opportunity of working within an interdependent environment under the umbrella of a large organization in order to diminish business risk (Baron and Schmidt, 1991; Fulop, 1996). Indeed, a government publication on franchising specifically warns small business people who wish to retain their independence that franchising may not be suitable for them (DTI, 1995).

The management of conflict

Given the many potential pitfalls in the franchisor/franchisee relationship, how do franchisors exercise power in order to diminish levels of conflict? In practice, experience in franchising, as in other third party distribution relationships, has shown that management by persuasion and example (non-coercive power) rather than by threat and sanctions (coercive power) is more likely to lead to channel co-operation (Ennew *et al.*, 1993). This approach is progressed by Lashley relative to empowerment in Chapter 5. There are many sources of non-coercive power available to the franchisor. These include: the training programme which, if formal, authoritative and detailed, will influence the franchisee to operate in line with the franchisor's guidelines; provision of comprehensive detail in the franchise manual; and regular communication with franchisees. Finally, and not surprisingly, co-operation has been forthcoming from franchisees if the level of ongoing support and assistance is perceived as satisfactory (Fulop, 1996).

At the same time as acknowledging the beneficial effects of non-coercive power measures in diffusing conflict between franchisor and franchising, it has also been pointed out that the balance of power in the franchisor/franchisee relationship is not as one-sided as it is often portrayed. This is because there exist several sources of franchisee power, which often tend to be underestimated. For instance, franchisors:

- are dependent upon their franchisees to operate as stipulated, to implement changes in the operation, and not to bring the franchisor's name into disrepute;

- may also be reluctant to challenge disgruntled franchisees for fear of provoking court cases, adverse publicity and increased legislation;

- the growth of multi-outlet and area franchises in many networks has enhanced the power of franchisees, as has the widespread introduction of Franchise Advisory Councils (FACs) during the past decade, especially in the United States. Such FACs have strengthened the power of franchisees when potential areas of disagreement arise, such as changes in products, operating methods and territory size (Dandridge and Falbe, 1994).

With a company-owned network this dependence on a person who is not an employee would not exist. Due to the interdependence, therefore, of the franchisor and the franchisee both parties have to accept some trade-off in terms of loss of independence in return for the advantages they receive. Finally, as some empirical findings have demonstrated, perhaps the most important factor which leads to the reluctance of either party to exercise power is the recognition that it is in their mutual interest to keep disagreements to a minimum. This can be achieved by making the necessary commitment and compromises, which will enable the network to operate successfully (Manaresi and Uncles, 1995).

Franchisee protection

Although the exercise of non-coercive power helps to lessen conflict in the franchisor/franchisee relationship, it is generally recognized that franchising requires a regulatory framework on account of the inherently complex relationship between franchisors and franchisees which makes some degree of conflict inevitable. The acceptance of this viewpoint has led to the introduction either of legislation, as in the United States (and France), or self-regulation, as in the UK (Mendelsohn, 1995) to ensure that franchisors conduct their affairs in a manner which is not 'unfair' to franchisees.

Legislation tends to be favoured when the franchisee is regarded as being significantly disadvantaged (Terry, 1991). Legislation aimed at inducing appropriate disclosure of information prior to the signing of the franchise contract is prevalent in the USA. France has also introduced trademark licensing disclosure laws, which include franchising. In the USA two methods have been adopted to ensure that the contents of the disclosure document are appropriate. The first requires a franchisor to register their disclosure document with the state authorities for approval on a continuous basis. The second, included in American Federal legislation, lays down guidelines on the information which should be included in a disclosure document, but no registration of the document is necessary.

On the other hand, Mendelsohn (1995) and Calvani (1990) regard voluntary codes of ethics as an equally efficient means of 'policing' franchising but with the added advantage of avoiding what they claim have been the undesirable consequences of legislation in the United States and which are cited as:

- higher costs which disproportionately adversely affect smaller and younger franchise systems;

- in many instances the disclosure of less information rather than more as intended;

- some evidence that legislation has acted as a barrier to entry, and has slowed down the rate of expansion of franchising.

Moreover, the proponents of self-regulation maintain that:

- the small occurrence of unscrupulous actions by *bona fide* franchisors does not warrant legislation;

- dissatisfied franchisees have existing avenues open to them for seeking redress;

- prospective franchisees have an obligation to thoroughly investigate any business proposition before entering the relationship.

By contrast, the advocates of legislation maintain that:

- Codes of conduct/ethics constitute a very weak form of protection since they are only applicable to members of the relevant trade body and that these comprise a minority compared with non-members (Baillieu, 1988);

- disclosure requirements are too vague and general (Abell, 1995);

- legislation should not result in substantially higher costs because a competent franchisor should be offering such information to a prospective franchisee even if legislation did not exist.

Since there are drawbacks in both the regulation of franchising by legislation and a code of ethics/practice, some countries have tried to find a more satisfactory regulatory regime. As one example, and after experimentation with a variety of legislative, quasi-legislative and non-legislative regimes, the Australian franchise industry finally adopted a 'voluntary' code of practice, which is in effect mandatory. The Australian code specifies:

- compulsory registration of all franchises;

- it has the backing of the Government, the banks and the press;

- contravention of the code can lead to a ban on advertising.

Other countries, such as Canada, have introduced similar measures, as a means of providing a compromise solution to the regulation of franchising which satisfies both the proponents and opponents of legislation.

Hospitality, Leisure & Tourism Series

Future trends in franchising

There are a number of conflicting trends which are likely to affect the size and the rate of expansion of the franchise industry. Some of these influences are external to franchising; others are internal to the operation and organization of the franchise itself. External factors that will impinge on the rate of growth range include the:

- degree of economic activity;
- shift towards the service sector;
- rate of entry into franchising of large established firms;
- extent of cross-border franchising.

There are also internal trends within the franchise format, which are likely to intensify, and these will affect future development. These include:

- the need to widen the recruitment base of potential franchisees and make available alternative non-traditional sources of funding;
- the growth in number and importance of multi-unit franchisees and of franchisee association/councils.

External influences

Undoubtedly, the two most important external factors which will determine the rate of expansion of franchising are the buoyancy or otherwise of the economy (Fulop, 1996), and the continuing shift towards the service sector in which franchising tends to be concentrated. The expansion of the service sector is a long-term trend that at the end of the 1990s in the UK accounts for more than two-thirds of the output of the economy. There is scope for franchising to penetrate further than has so far occurred into professional and financial services. The expansion plans of the growing number of multiples in these sectors will depend on the recruitment of highly qualified staff to operate their outlets. Conversely, the increasingly competitive environment in many of these sectors may make many professionally qualified people who would formerly have set up in business by themselves consider franchising as an alternative option. This would provide them with the opportunity to gain the benefits of working under the umbrella of a large organization, while still operating as a small business.

A further factor favourable to the expansion of franchising is the willingness of an increasing number of large organizations to develop their businesses through franchising. This is viewed as a means of assisting them in the implementation of their diversification and/or market penetration strategies, the requirement of some of them to recruit qualified and skilled staff, and the need of other such firms to maximize the potential output of the outlet.

Finally, the movement by franchisors into foreign markets is likely to accelerate as an increasing number of franchise systems reach maturity in their domestic markets. In particular, US franchise systems will increasingly seek out other markets, of which the UK will probably continue to appear the most attractive, because of the widespread belief that we share a common language, but with the intention of then moving into the rest of Europe. The use of the UK as a 'gateway' to Europe for US hotel companies is clearly illustrated by Taylor in Chapter 8. Thus, while British franchisors will be seeking to develop abroad, particularly to Eire, France, Germany and Spain, they will at the same time face severe competition from foreign entrants into their domestic market across most industry sectors.

Cross-border franchising is also likely to expand because some large-scale retailers, who do not franchise in their domestic market, utilize this marketing technique as a mode of entry into overseas markets where population size or per capita expenditure may be insufficient to support a major programme of expansion. In addition, some retail organizations employ the franchise format as a means of test marketing in foreign countries prior to establishing a full-scale operation, and thus reduce the financial risk of moving abroad.

Internal influences

A constraining influence on the rate of expansion of franchising has been, and is likely to continue to be a lack of high calibre applicants with sufficient money to invest. Although by no means new, the difficulty in recruiting suitable franchisees was highlighted during the economic downturn in the early 1990s. At that time, it became evident that many of the franchisees who were unable to cope with adverse trading conditions had sometimes been accepted simply because they had sufficient finance. Alternatively, it was because the firm wanted to get the franchise system up and running quickly, or through over-eagerness to recoup the costs incurred in developing the system. Consequently, the recruitment of unsuitable franchisees led to serious problems later on. As a result of their experiences many franchisors subsequently adopted more rigorous selection procedures which have led them to prefer a slower rate of growth rather than lower their selection standards. Since franchisors put down many of their problems to poor franchise selection, more stringent selection criteria would considerably diminish many sources of current friction, although it could at the same time slow down the rate of expansion of a franchise system.

Many franchisors have also become increasingly aware that their projected rate of expansion may be constrained unless sources of funding can be made available to suitable potential recruits who do not have the required finances. To date, only a minority of franchisors have been prepared to offer 'easy entry' financial schemes to such potential franchisees. Such packages usually take one of two forms. First, the franchisor may finance the start-up costs of the franchisee with the loan being repaid at a later date from the profits from the business. Secondly, if an existing manager has been identified who would make a suitable franchisee, then an outlet may be made available and the 'manager-cum-franchisee' paid partly by salary and partly by commission. In this arrangement, commission payments will be left to accumulate to form the down payment for the franchise. In Chapter 11 Lashley provides an example of the financing schemes offered by McDonald's.

The trend towards a higher proportion of multi-unit franchisees, and the growing importance of franchisee associations, are both developments within the franchise network which are likely to continue, and which will alter the power distribution within the franchisor/franchisee relationship in favour of the franchisee. The expansion of multi-unit franchisees has been evident for some time in the USA. This is mainly due to the earlier maturity of franchise systems in that country. In the UK it seems inevitable that successful franchisees will also seek to expand by acquiring additional outlets within the same system, as has already happened in the fast food trade. To date, many franchisors express misgivings about this possible development on account of the operational difficulties multi-unit franchisees pose, and the potential power they might wield (Fulop, 1996, p. 56): 'Multi-outlet franchisees can become too powerful. Then the tail begins to wag the dog.'

As a result of these fears, at the present time many franchisors, including McDonald's, impose severe restrictions on the number of outlets any one franchisee is allowed to own. However, it is increasingly appreciated that successful franchisees could become frustrated if they are not permitted to operate more than one outlet, and that this frustration might equally lead to conflict. In addition, the number of franchisee associations in the UK is likely to increase appreciably. During the 1990s the growth in their rate and influence accelerated. In the main this was due to the pressure/lobbying exerted by franchisees that had become dissatisfied with the performance of franchise systems during the economic downturn. It is anticipated that this trend is likely to continue, as happened in the 1980s in the USA, where some 74 per cent of franchise systems now boast a franchisee association/council. Although these associations aim to reduce conflict by better and more regular communication and to harness the entrepreneurship of franchisees, at the same time they strengthen the power of franchisees when potential areas of disagreement arise regarding changes in products, operating methods, and territory size.

Summary

Within the term 'business format franchising' is hidden a complexity of typologies, which encompass a wide range of market entry and product/service distribution strategies. Furthermore, there exists a significant range of organizational arrangements that may be adopted, such as, a mix of company-owned units, single and multi-unit franchisees, master franchise and multi-brand. A number of environmental factors have supported the expansion of the franchise organizational form. These include: the shift in the economy to the service sector; the widespread acceptance in society of entrepreneurship and business investment; government support for business start-up and franchising specifically; and a proactive approach to financing franchising by banks. Further legitimization of franchising is provided by the British Franchise Association, which advocates and enforces a strong ethical stance.

Intrinsic to business format franchising is the symbiotic relationship between the franchisor and franchisee, within which tensions tend to arise concerning command and control, entrepreneurship and empowerment. In practice, the potential for friction can be minimized by the exercise of non-coercive power, namely, persuasion and example, which can lead to the development of a mutually rewarding partnership. Also implicit in the franchise concept is a decentralized organization and operation which distances the franchisor from the maintenance of uniform and consistent standards essential for the reputation of the brand. Again in practice, this potential pitfall can be overcome by ensuring that franchisees adhere, as stipulated in the contract, to standardized processes and procedures. By these means it is possible to avoid wide variations in service and dissatisfied customer which would have an adverse impact on all the franchisees in the system. However, although the contract defines the formal relationship between franchisor and franchisee, it is the informal relationship that evolves between the two parties which is all-important; in particular, the recognition that it is in both their interests to keep disagreements to a minimum by commitment and compromise.

In view of the advantages, which franchising offers to both franchisor and franchisee, franchising has expanded, and will continue to expand. This is in spite of the inherent difficulties encountered in a hybrid organizational format dependent on complex contractual arrangements, which are liable to lead to conflicts in the franchisor/franchisee relationship. Internal factors identified as likely to affect the size and rate of expansion of the franchise industry centre on: the availability of suitable recruits; access to funding; a move to multi-unit franchisees; and the enhanced power of franchisees through professional associations and/or councils. External factors that will impinge on the rate of growth are the degree of economic activity; shift towards the service sector; rate of entry into franchising by established firms; and extent of cross-border franchising.

Debate topics

- The development of franchising has been dependent upon organizational and socio-economic factors, which have led many firms to prefer franchising to alternative business formats.

- The growth of franchisee associations and multi-unit franchisees is likely to make the management of a franchise even more complex and difficult.

- Franchising represents a legal minefield, which no sane business person would willingly enter.

Selected readings

Bradach, J. (1998) *Franchise Organizations*. Harvard Business School Press.

Department of Trade and Industry (1995) *Small Firms: An Introduction to Franchising*. DTI Small Firms and Business Link Division.

Fulop, C. (1996) *Overview of the Franchise Marketplace 1990–1995*. Centre for Franchise Research, City University Business School.

References

Abell, M. (1994) Question of disclosure. *Franchise World*, July–August, pp. 35–8.

Abell, M. (1995) Comment: Athena rescue. *Franchise World*, March–April, pp. 24–7

Arthur Andersen (1995) *Worldwide Franchising Statistics*. Arthur Andersen, London & World Franchising Council.

Baillieu, D. (1988) *Streetwise Franchising*. Hutchinson.

Baron, S. and Schmidt, R. (1991) Operational aspects of retail franchises. *International Journal of Retail and Distribution Management*, **19** (2), 13–19.

Bradach, J. (1998) *Franchise Organizations*. Harvard Business School Press.

Brandenberg, M. (1989) Franchising into the Nineties. *Accountancy*. **103** (1146), 143–5.

Brickley, J.A., Dark, F.H. (1987) The choice of organizational form – the case of franchising. *Journal of Financial Economics*. **18**, 27–35.

Brown, S. (1988) Business format franchising. In *Handbook of Retailing* (West, E., ed.), Gower, pp. 73–90.

Burt, S. (1995) Retailer internationalisation: evolution of theory and practice. In *International Retailing: Trends and Strategies* (McGoldrick, P. and Davies, G., eds), Pitman, pp. 51–71.

Calvani, T. (1990) Is there a case for franchising legislation? *International Journal of Franchising and Distribution Law*, **5** (2), 116–52.

Commission of the European Community (1991) *Towards a Single Market in Distribution*. COM (91) 41.

Cressy, R. and Storey, D. (1995) *New Firms and Their Bank*. National Westminster Bank plc.

Dandridge, T.C. and Falbe, C.M. (1994) The influence of franchisees beyond their local domains. *International Small Business Journal*, **12** (2), 39–49.

DTI (Department of Trade and Industry) (1995) *Small Firms: An Introduction to Franchising*. DTI Small Firms and Business Link Division.

Ennew, C., Unusan, C. and Wright, M. (1993) Power and control in distribution channels: the case of automobile distribution in Turkey. *Journal of Marketing Management*, **9**, 393–403.

Felstead, A. (1990) What's in a franchise contract?, *Business Franchise Magazine*, **4** (2), 46–8.

Felstead, A. (1993) *The Corporate Paradox*. Routledge.

Forward, J. and Fulop, C. (1993) Elements of franchising: the experiences of established firms. *Service Industries Journal*, **13** (4), 159–78.

Forward, J. and Fulop, C. (1996) Large established firms entry into franchising: an exploratory investigation of strategic and operational issues. *International Review of Retail, Distribution and Consumer Research*, **6** (1), 34–52.

Fulop, C. (1996) *Overview of the Franchise Marketplace 1990–1995*. Centre for Franchise Research. City University Business School.

Fulop, C. (1999) Franchising. In *International Encyclopaedia of Business and Management* (Baker, M. ed.), International Thomson Business Press, pp. 613–23.

Fulop, C. and Forward, J. (1997) Insights into franchising: a review of empirical and theoretical perspectives. *Service Industries Journal*, **17** (4), 603–25.

Fulop, C. and Warren, K. (1992) The marketing of a professional service: opticians. *International Journal of Advertising*, **11**, 287–305.

Hoffman, R. and Preble, J.F. (1991) Franchising: selecting a strategy for rapid growth. *International Journal of Strategic Management*, **24** (4), 74–85.

Housden, J. (1983) *Franchising and Other Business Relationships in Hotel and Catering Services*. Heinemann.

Hoy, F. (1994) The dark side of franchising, or appreciating flaws in an imperfect world, *International Small Business Journal*, **12** (2), 26–38.

Lafontaine, F. and Kaufmann, P.J. (1994) The evolution of ownership patterns in franchise systems. *Journal of Retailing*, **70** (2), 97–113.

Macmillan, A. (1996) *Aspects of Franchise Recruitment*, Special Studies Series No. 8, International Franchise Research Centre. University of Westminster Press.

Manaresi, A. and Uncles, M. (1995) Retail franchising in Britain and Italy. In *International Retailing: Trends and Strategies* (McGoldrick, P. and Davies, G., eds), Pitman, pp. 151–66.

Mendelsohn, M. (ed.) (1992) *Franchising in Europe*. Cassell.

Mendelsohn, M. (1995) *The Ethics of Franchising*, 2nd edn. British Franchise Association.

Mendelsohn, M. (1996) *The Guide to Franchising*. Pergamon Press.

Mendelsohn, M. and Harris, B. (1992) *Franchising and the Block Exemption Regulation*. Longman.

NatWest/BFA (1991–98) *Franchise Survey*. British Franchise Association.

NatWest (1998) *European Franchise Survey Supplement*. NatWest Retail Banking Services.

Pilotti, L. and Pozzana, R. (1991) *Report Study on Franchising Contracts in the European Community*. Universita Bocconi.

Price, S. (1997) *The Franchise Paradox: New Directions, Different Strategies.* Cassell.

Rubin, P. (1978) The theory of the firm and the structure of the franchise contract. *Journal of Law and Economics*, **21**, 223–33.

Sanghavi, N. (1990) *Retail Franchising in the 1990s.* Longman.

Sibley, S. and Michie, D. (1982) An exploratory investigation of co-operation in a franchise channel. *Journal of Retailing*, **58** (4), 26–38.

Stanworth, J. (1991) Franchising and the franchise relationship. *International Journal of Retail Distribution and Consumer Research*, **1** (2), 175–99.

Stanworth, J., Curran, J. and Hough, J. (1984) The franchised small business: formal and operational dimensions of independence. In *Success and Failure in Small Business* (Lewis, J., Stanworth, J. and Gibb, A., eds), Pitman, pp. 223–30.

Stern, L. and El-Ansary, A. (1992) *Marketing Channels*, 4th edn. Prentice-Hall.

Stern, P. and Stanworth, J. (1994) Improving small business survival rates via franchising – the role of the banks in Europe. *International Small Business Journal*, **12** (2), 15–25.

Terry, A. (1991) Policy issues in franchise regulation: the Australian experience. *International Journal of Franchising and Distribution*, **6** (2), 77–90.

Williamson, O.E. (1975) *Markets and Hierarchies.* Free Press.

Williamson, O.E. (1991) Comparative economic organization: the analysis of discrete structural alternatives. *Administrative Science Quarterly*, **36** (June), 269–96.

Zeidman, P.F. and Loewinger, A.P. (1993) Pre-sale franchise disclosure: a review and comparison of disclosure requirements in France, the United States and Canada. *Journal of International Franchising and Distribution Law*, **7** (1), pp. 21–36.

• • • •

CHAPTER 3

Franchising research: a failed literature?

Stuart Price

Key points

- Extant franchise academic literature has failed to assess whether franchising delivers as much as it promises in terms of economic performance and financial returns.

- A success rhetoric dominates franchising and is now culturally embedded, leaving important ethical questions unresolved because of a lacuna of debate.

- To some observers, the lack of government and regulatory body intervention and/or a requirement to sound a caveat in regard to the success rhetoric suggests that they condone the message of success.

- There is a persistent failure to consider issues that lie at the heart of examining whether there is foundation to the belief that franchising is both boundary-less and has a boundless future.

Introduction

MACBETH:	*If we should fail,*
LADY MACBETH:	*We fail!*
	But screw your courage to the
	sticking place,
	And we'll not fail.

William Shakespeare, Macbeth, I: vii

Extant franchise academic research has failed. It has failed because it has not answered empirically or holistically the central and only question that pre-occupies the franchise fraternity, the investment community and regulators. Is franchising all it's cracked up to be? Of course, this begs the obvious question: exactly what is franchising cracked up to be? However, it also begs two others: in which specific areas has the franchise literature failed to assess whether franchising delivers as much it promises, and, what can be done to address the franchise literature's failure? This chapter posits tentative answers to all of three of these questions.

Sampling both the academic and populist franchise press (see Illustrations 3.1 and 3.2) one would expect there to be a sharp divergence of views concerning the economic performance of franchising and the available financial returns. After all, there appears to be the potential for a rich debate – empirical or otherwise – examining the degree to which franchising delivers as much it promises. Indeed, according to Brown (1969) franchising is a 'Trap for the Trusting', and Lord Roskill believes that 'Fraudsters induce investors to buy franchises, . . . holding out the prospect of large returns on investment. But once the payment has been made, the franchise proves worthless' (Lord Roskill, Fraud Trials Committee, 1986, quoted in Abell, 1999, p. 53).

In a similar vein, Kursh (1968, p. 128) contends:

> There is perhaps no business, no industry, no aspect of life, that is entirely free of phonies, frauds, assorted swindlers, ingenious 'con' men, and borderline operators who walk and talk in the shadow of the law. The franchising field is no exception. It has its share of fast-buck wheelers and dealers. How many? Nobody knows. But from my experience, from the moment I started research into franchising in 1956, I would say that franchising, perhaps because it has been mushrooming, attracting the 'little guys', has more than its fair share of

gyps. The crooks that have invaded and exploited the zooming interest in franchising are among the nation's vilest thieves. They will think nothing of separating anyone from his legacy or life's savings.

Unfortunately, in spite of such sentiments, the only divergence appears to be the one between expectation and reality. There seems to be a single recurring message within the franchise literature. It is this: franchising offers potential investors a fast and safe route into business that would otherwise be fraught with risk and uncertainty. Aspiring entrepreneurs are encouraged to choose the franchise path in order to improve the chances of their success and survival, especially during the formative years, rather than alternative forms of self-employment. The typical message here is that the franchisee is in business for him/herself, but not by him/herself (Izraeli, 1972; Banning, 1996; Stanworth and Kaufmann, 1996; G. Williams, 1999). In this vein, Dewar-Healing opines: 'The failure rate is very low and if you ask me what is the main cause of failure in franchising I would say lack of two-way communication between the franchisor and franchisee' (quoted in G. Williams, 1999, p. 33). Similarly, Fulop (1996, p. 14) suggests: 'Most franchisees are seeking an interdependent relationship with a franchisor in order to reduce business risk and gain the advantages of belonging to a large established organization'.

According to Housden (1984) and Felstead (1993), such messages have a ready audience amongst potential franchise investors. They contend that some people become franchisees because they are attracted to the franchise's brand name and the product itself. Housden observes that franchisees realize significant savings in time and costs resulting from the use of a tried and tested system, the availability of technical and operational expertise, and the benefits of attaining freedom from working for an employer.

As far as the franchisor is concerned, Dickinson (1981) amongst others, suggests that franchising is a suitable strategy for reducing small business failure, and, also holds the promise of fulfilling the 'American Dream' of 'making it big'. An entrepreneur with only a small retail establishment could build a large and profitable organization on the original concept (Hunt, 1977; Pollock, 1986). The opportunity to realize such ambitions is made further attractive by the possibility of funding expansion and surmounting a variety of inhibiting factors which, individually or in tandem, otherwise preclude the realization of such ambitions (Rubin, 1978; Martin, 1988, 1996; Thompson, 1994; Bronson and

Morgan, 1998). As such, the franchisor is seen to be as dependent on the franchisee, at least for capital and promise of increased efficiency, as the franchisee is reliant on the franchisor. The implication from this position is that franchising represents a form of alliance between two independent parties with mutual interests (McIntyre *et al.*, 1994; Bradach, 1998). Of course, the mutuality of benefits does not necessarily imply equality of benefits, but rather that all parties to the alliance will receive benefit in proportion to the contributions made.

Like most good propaganda, this message is based on a simple tenet and reinforced in related ways. As far as franchising is concerned, the reinforcing process is invariably conducted by reference to research of the loosest type. This 'research', which has rarely benefited from empirical testing and/or the application of appropriate research methodologies, usually refers to one or more of the following three topics.

- The large scale and rapid growth of franchising (Illustration 3.1);

- The opportunity for both parties to generate excess financial returns;

- The low rates of failure vis-à-vis other types of small business (Illustration 3.2).

Unlike Lady Macbeth's response to her husband's thought of failure, the franchise literature appears quite unequivocal in tone. Though it is possible to interpret Lady Macbeth's response in a variety of ways, from resignation to anger, incredulity and indignation, potential franchisees are invariably reassured that they are latter-day Dick Whittingtons, on a route paved with gold. Powers (1995, p. 2) for example, observes: 'for you and other 21st century entrepreneurs, it's . . . buying a franchise that offers the best chance of turning independence into reality.' He is not alone. Curry *et al.* (1966) suggested that history has shown that franchising has reduced 'financial' failures considerably, and the examples in Illustration 3.2 show that this opinion has not changed much since Curry *et al.*'s statement. Note that there seems to be some failure – it has never been made explicit whether this failure is intentional or not – by the authors to distinguish between whether their subject is the franchisee or franchisor. The suggestion here is that franchise system and franchisee failure rates are identical and interchangeable. This represents somewhat of a confusion that infers that franchising *per se*, rather than particular franchise businesses, is a sure-fire path to

Hospitality, Leisure & Tourism Series

success in business (Purvin, 1994) and offers the opportunity to yield supra-normal returns.

Consider also the titles of books, articles and pamphlets such as:

- *Partners in Profit* (Curry *et al.*, 1966);

- *Franchising for Profit* (Pollock and Golzen, 1985);

- 'Franchising – a profitable partnership' (Stern, 1998);

- *The Best of Relations* (Gerstenhaber, 1998);

Illustration 3.1 Quotes on the size and growth of franchising

Franchise selling has been flourishing in recent years; and in 1960 franchising companies established their own trade group, the International Franchise Association. The Association estimated in 1962 that over 400 companies in 80 different fields franchised over 100,000 people. (Konopa, 1963, p. 35)

Franchising has expanded rapidly in North America and around the world during the 1970s and 1980s. Total franchise sales for the United States and Canada in 1981 were estimated to be about $376 billion, about one-third of all retail sales. There are nearly 500,000 franchised business establishments in North America, which account for approximately five million jobs, and the numbers are growing daily. An estimated 7,500 franchisors offer franchises in the United States, and more than one thousand Canadian franchisors administer over 2,500 franchise units in Canada. (Knight, 1984; p. 53)

Franchising ... is an important and growing phenomenon in the US economy. The Department of Commerce estimates that the number of ... franchisors increased from 909 in 1972 to 2,177 in 1984. Total nominal sales through outlets of ... franchisors grew by 442 per cent between 1972 and 1986, with the number of outlets growing by 65 per cent in the same period, from 189,640 to 312,810. (Kaufmann and Lafontaine, 1994, pp. 417–18)

Over 500,000 franchise outlets in the US generated more than $750 billion in combined retail sales in 1991 ... This estimate represents approximately one-third of all US retail sales activity ... Growing at a substantially faster pace than GNP – an estimated 10% and 125% growth in the number of franchised establishments and sales volume, respectively, over the past decade alone – franchising employs over 8 million plus workers in the US today ... (Dant, 1996, p. 1)

For many, franchising represents an opportunity to achieve the American Dream. Escapees from corporate America, entrepreneurs and moms-and-pops are flocking to the industry like never before. (Nucifora, *San Francisco Times*, 1 June, 1998)

Illustration 3.2 The populist approaches to franchise failure

It certainly appears to be the case in the USA that the failure rates for franchised businesses are substantially less than the failure rates for non-franchised businesses. The most frequently stated figures in the USA suggest a 90% failure rate for non-franchised new businesses over a five year period compared with a 10% failure rate in the case of franchised new businesses over the same period ... these figures are not regarded by many as being completely reliable, and the failure rate for non-franchised businesses was said, at a recent IFA [International Franchise Association] symposium, to be 65% over a five year period. However, there is certainly a vast contrast between the failure rates of non-franchised businesses compared with those which are not franchised. (Mendelsohn, 1982, p. 13)

Putting success into the context of small business, commercial failures in franchising are considerably lower than the 42% defaults in the Government Loan Guarantee Scheme; and considerably less than the 43% closures within three years under the Enterprise Allowance Scheme or the general small business closure rate of 34% in the same time. The position in the UK is fast approaching that recorded in the US where nearly 38% of individual start-ups go out of business after the first year of operation, 57% after the second year; 67% after the third year; and 73% after the fourth year ... By stark contrast ... only 3% of franchises are discontinued in the US after one year; 6% after the second year; and 7% after the third and fourth years. After five years, 92% of franchises are still in operation ...(Brandenberg, 1989, p. 143)

Whilst an increasing number of other countries also have thriving franchise industries, we remain the envy of many, because of the overall performance achieved here. I don't want to dwell on statistical data, which is available from reliable sources such as the British Franchise Association and the banks. Suffice to say, however that the UK franchise industry has a record of continuing healthy growth with few failures. (Williams, 1999, p 36)

Run a ——— pub as one of our Business Partners and we'll give you the key to a very bright future. That's because, as pioneers of pub franchising, ——— can offer you a proven formula for success. You'll benefit from our total support, award-winning training and expert advice from everything from business planning and accountancy to catering. So if you have £15,000 to invest, contact ——— (Anon (1996), Advertisement, *Business Franchise Magazine*, March, p. 34)

Franchising, one of the most successful business systems created by the mind of man and woman, is still relatively unknown throughout the world. That is because it is transparent, i.e. you cannot tell whether that shop on the main street or the vendor who provides a certain service is a franchisee or an independent business person. But, generally speaking, the firm you do business with will reveal itself as a franchised business because it will be around a lot longer. That is the key to franchising – it is far and away more successful almost all of the time ... The old franchise axiom that 'you're in business for yourself but not by yourself' works for more than 95% of the time. And that number generally represents the closure or non-closure rate for franchising . . . only 3–5% close each year (and most of these are transferred to other owners or to the franchisor) and after five years 85% of those opened are still doing business under the original ownerships. (Cherkasky, 1996, p 5)

Reputable franchising of the kind represented by the British Franchise Association has a nearly 95 per cent success rate in establishing franchisees in business. This is not surprising. Surveys show that the vast majority (85 per cent) of people becoming franchisees want to be in business on their own account. They also show that most of them find the reassurance they expect from their franchisor. (Sir Bernard Ingham, President of the British Franchise Association, *Franchise World Directory*, 1997)

A franchise is not a short cut to riches, but it can be a safer way of establishing your own business. With a properly constructed and viable franchise operation, the risk of failure can be considerably less than would be for someone setting up a similar business on their own. (Stern, 1998, p. 9)

The prospect of branching out on you own in the business world can be daunting. However, it doesn't have to be. The world of franchising creates a more secure environment in which to start your own business, and minimizes the risk of failure. The 1999 NatWest/British Franchise Association survey results are very encouraging. An impressive 89% of franchisees record profits compared to 70% previously. But it doesn't stop there. As many as 81% of franchises which have been trading for less than two years are claiming profitability – a fine illustration for success for a franchised business. (*BFA*, March, 1999)

- 'Improving small business survival rates via franchising' (Stern and Stanworth, 1994);

- 'If you want a rewarding experience: consider franchising' (BFA leaflet, 1999)

Note that none of these titles has a question mark in them, an omission which seems to underline the belief that franchising delivers excess returns to all of its incumbents as a statement of fact. However, we do not truly know whether such a sentiment is, in fact, warranted.

How has the franchise literature failed?

For all the franchise fraternity's success rhetoric and the propaganda, the inescapable fact is that the extent to which franchising is all it's cracked up to be remains largely unproved

– at least scientifically. Lafontaine and Bhattacharyya (1995, p. 39), for example, state: 'One of the major selling points of franchising to franchisees over the years has been the statistics vehiculated by the trade press on the very low failure rates of franchised businesses compared to independent operations. These statistics never had real scientific basis.' Accordingly, it is not possible to determine conclusively whether failure rates among franchised businesses are lower than among independent businesses (Cross, 1998). Such is the state of research that when the US House Committee on Small Businesses looked at franchise failure in 1992, they found little rigorous statistical evidence. As such, it had to resort to opinions made by the incumbents and observers of the franchise fraternity. The committee rejected the often used uniform 5 per cent failure rate, instead preferring a two-tiered system of failure in which the best systems have a low failure rate with a much higher rate in lesser quality systems.

Arguably, there are two main reasons for this situation and one outcome. First, there has been a distinct lack of contribution by academics. For example, though the management of the operational dynamics is critical to the success or failure of an individual franchise unit, there are very few studies examining the operational dynamics within franchises. In this vein, Elango and Fried (1997, p. 76) conclude that the 'lack of research on implementation is very disturbing . . . the manner in which franchising systems actually work to create value has been ignored'. Second, there has been a tendency for researchers to use inappropriate methodologies – such as non-linear product life cycle techniques (Easingwood *et al.*, 1983) – to examine the dynamics of franchising.

The outcome is that the franchise fraternity's success rhetoric potentially leaves ethical issues that have yet to be resolved. After all, there has been a lack of regulation to keep such contentions in check. Any research, whether empirically founded or not, with contrary findings to the propaganda has failed to have a significant impact on potential franchisee's investment decisions. In the UK, at least, there simply is no franchise-specific legislation. Unlike investments in stocks and shares, pensions, endowments, and other financial products, there seems to be no requirement for franchisors or their supporters to caveat their marketing efforts.

Franchise relationships are also not required to conform to labour law, or consumer law, but rather a patchwork of statutes and legal precedents and those generated by the European Community (EC) contained within the Treaty of Rome and the Block Exemption. These parallel legal systems are very different. Franchises are covered in UK laws by such mechanisms as the Restrictive Trade Practices Act (1976), Competition Act (1980), the Fair Trading Act (1973) and the Retail Prices Act (1976). Unlike EC law, which seems to have little focus on the form of a transaction but concentrates on its effects, UK law is concerned with how a transaction is structured and is absorbed with the form of agreements (Abell, 1990). It is not necessarily concerned with what anti-competitive effects are achieved.

Lack of academic contribution

Though there are strong motivational forces at work which provide an explanation for the continuing interest in franchise research (Kaufmann, 1996), and a large number of research issues worth exploring in the area of franchising (Lafontaine, 1996), the fact is that few academics have taken up the challenge. Even fewer have examined the propensity of franchise businesses to survive and/or deliver excess returns. For example, Stanworth (1995) describes the subject of franchisor attrition as a 'very quiet debate' because of the dearth of research exploring this topic. That said, this has since been redressed through the contributions of Chater and Fernique (1990), Lafontaine (1996), Lafontaine and Shaw (1996), Price (1996, 1997), Shane (1996), I.F. Consulting (1997); Stanworth *et al.* (1997).

Franchise researchers have instead shown a tendency to favour a particular perspective and a tight focus on typically pragmatic issues, such as 'encroachment', location and franchise fee policies, or more theoretical discourse on transaction cost analysis, ownership redirection etc. However, practitioners and some researchers claim that the academic literature is too fragmentary and oblique to be of direct use to investors (Thompson, 1968). As such, it is debatable whether this focus serves to answer, directly or otherwise, the underlying issue of whether and/or to what degree franchising is all it's cracked up to be.

Of course, the validity and accuracy of franchising's propensity to deliver the 'American Dream' have been challenged by the more journalistic end of the research spectrum (Burck, 1970; Purvin, 1994). There also exists a plethora of case studies, press reports and details of legal proceedings against wayward franchise businesses (see, for example, Giugni and Terry, 1998). If the conclusions of this latter stream of research are to be believed, franchising's promise is an empty one. For instance, Bucklin (1971, p. 39) likens franchising to Russian roulette:

> To devotees of the sport of gambling, Russian roulette is the supreme game . . . Franchising may be just this kind of game, except that five of the bullet chambers are loaded instead of just one. Fortunately, the cartridges are packed with only such niceties as seventy-two hour work weeks and a minimum-wage-busting pay scale, rather than with gun-powder. The empty chamber consists of that long awaited pile of riches at the end of the rainbow.

To those that subscribe to such a perspective, investors are the victims of spurious success claims, who often lose more than their life savings in the process, and have fallen foul of the significant vested interests in the franchising fraternity. However, as Kursh (1968, p. 51) points out: 'Franchising cannot afford a truly high rate of "financial" failures. If that were the case, it would be the end of franchising. The fact that the successful franchise is "packaged success" lies at the very heart of the franchise boom.'

Indeed, favourable and uncorroborated attrition statistics may, for example, prove useful to franchisors when attracting new franchisees. Castrogiovanni *et al.* (1993, p. 106) observe that: 'individual franchisors may be reluctant to "air their dirty laundry" by reporting excessive failure rates . . . it is in the best interests of the franchise sector as a whole to convey the appearance that franchising is a relatively safe form of business ownership.'

For the franchise trade bodies, consultants, solicitors and accountants, the benefits derive from the revenues spent on feasibility studies, contracts and the increased economic significance of franchising (Bradach, 1992). The inference here is that the statistics on franchise failures are being created, misused, abused, and/or misinterpreted (Walker and Cross, 1988; Cross, 1994) and that the activity has higher rates of failure and lower levels of financial success than has been either openly admitted or acknowledged.

According to Thompson (1968, p. 84) the fact that there exists so much anecdotal evidence questioning the extent of franchising's success and that some elements of the franchise fraternity have employed dubious practices, is partly responsible for the lack of academic contribution:

> Over the past decade, the emphasis in marketing literature as a whole has shifted from the procedural and operational to the conceptual and analytical. With no cohesive group of marketing people or scholars engaged

in the study of franchising, this topic does not reflect the trend. One plausible explanation is that the low esteem in which franchising has been held in the past by the popular press may have deterred more formally trained researchers who preferred to direct their interests to higher status areas.

Similarly, Phan *et al.* (1996, p. 380) suggest:

Although there have been over 225 articles published under the auspices of the Society of Franchising, and more than 80 academic articles published in the last 10 years among entrepreneurship researchers, the franchisee has been one of the least studied entrepreneurial types. This lack of interest reflects the fact that entrepreneurship researchers may view franchising as a programmed mode of entry, which they perceive to be non-entrepreneurial.

If true, this situation not only suggests that the academic fraternity appears to be possibly as self-serving as its franchise counterparts but also important ethical questions remain unresolved because of the lacuna of debate. For instance, possibly due to the lack of empirical evidence, there has been a tendency for the franchise fraternity and its supporters to dismiss the failures as mere aberrations. For example, Hayes (1994, p. 53) states:

Critics of franchising will list a dozen reasons why you should be fearful of investing in a franchise. They can tell you numerous horror stories about failed franchises . . . It's true that some of the nearly 3,000 franchise companies in America deliver less than they promise. It's true that some of the nearly 600,000 franchised outlets in the USA fail. But if the majority of these businesses prosper (whereas most non-franchised businesses fail) there must be more that's right with franchising than wrong with it.

Watson (1999, p. 60) contends: 'But for the most part franchising has an enviable track record. Successes continue to outweigh the small number of failures. Franchisors in general suffer less than a 3 per cent failure rate, compared with 33 per cent in the non-franchised venture.' Furthermore, possibly related to the belief that franchise failures are an aberration and the belief that franchising both generates economic wealth and reduces the wasted resources that comes from organizational failure, it is also seen to have a 'boundless future'. For example, Burck (1970, p. 152): 'Franchisors and their trade organizations insist that things aren't all that bad in the business. They regard the critics as overzealous, often misinformed, and sometimes dated in their understanding of current franchise practices ... Despite the problems and abuses, most people in the industry see a boundless future for franchising.' Patterson augments this (1998, p. 134) when he assures that 'Franchising is suitable for practically every type of business ...'.

However, are Burck's and Patterson's comments true? Despite the abundance of anecdotal evidence to the contrary, we simply do not know. What is apparent is that franchising has become associated with success in spite of the anecdotes to the contrary. According to Izraeli (1972), the combination of the persistent success propaganda and the lack of regulation has resulted in the cultural-embeddedness of franchising's success rhetoric. He posits that the American public are regularly treated to success stories of people who have 'made it' through franchising. These success stories are also increasingly prevalent in the UK press through certain newspapers and a variety of specialist franchise magazines.

As in the USA and elsewhere, the messages of success are presented not as the unusual case or exception to the rule, but rather as typical of the possibilities open to all people no matter how lowly the starting point. As such, in spite of there being substantially different levels of risk across different franchise 'sectors' (Lafontaine, 1996) a potentially misleading message is compounded by the application of one failure statistic across different economies and industries. This practice is misleading as it infers that all franchises, irrespective of economic context and the status of the franchise itself, are more or less equally safe and that franchising has a boundless future.

The situation suggests that there has been significant conditioning of prospective franchisees prior to the offer by a specific franchisor, and that there is an implicit hollowness to the franchise fraternity's contention that self-regulation serves to protect such people. To some observers, the lack of intervention and/or a requirement to modify this success rhetoric with any note of caution suggests that the UK (and European) government and regulatory bodies condone the franchise fraternity's messages of success. This situation, so franchising's critics claim, is ethically deficient and should be remedied. Despite the franchise fraternity's counter-arguments, according to Storholm and Scheuing (1994, p. 188), it is more a question of how than if. They contend that the regulation process should occur through competitive dynamics rather than through legislation:

> The entrepreneurial spirit, which permeates the franchising industry, has frequently led to unethical practices, which ignore law and the fine line that exists between embellishment and deceit will continue to play a large part in the exploitation of investors. Questionable practices in franchising will never be expunged entirely, but competitive pressures may help more than mandates.

For this to happen, however, one has to have the belief that market dynamics will resolve the ethical issues. Unfortunately, this might be more indicative of wishful thinking than hard reality. Surely, if efficient markets such as equities and investment have had to be regulated, what hope can there be for imperfect markets? The franchise market is less than perfect, precisely because incumbents have a vested interest in not disclosing information and, consequently, investors are making, and will continue to make, decisions on the basis of biased 'research' and expectations. Of course, this lack of disclosure also presents problems for researchers.

For instance, one especially pertinent franchise research desert is the dearth of independent research specifically examining franchisee financial performance. Yet, this lacuna persists even though the promise of excess returns is a recurrent theme in the popular franchise press. Some of that which does exist (see, for example, Price, 1993; Kaufmann and Lafontaine, 1994; Bates, 1995, 1998) is problematic because of the lack of specific consideration of accounting practices that potentially reduce comparability of performance among franchisees and between franchisees and non-franchised concerns. Indicative of this situation, Lafontaine and Slade (1998) contend that while the extant franchise literature evaluates performance in survival, service quality and profitability, much more work is required in assessing the profitability of franchise firms. The same cannot be said of the service quality dimension (Curran and Stanworth, 1983; Stanworth *et al.*, 1984; Anand, 1987; Felstead, 1991, 1993; Stern and El-Ansary, 1992; Strutton *et al.*, 1993). Such is the dominance of this aspect that it is often the only aspect considered in assessments of the relative benefits of franchising.

But resolving this lacuna is not an easy task. Researching the financial performance of franchise organizations has not been helped by the lack of transparency of financial statements. It is no secret that the majority of franchise organizations tend to be small firms that take full advantage of the accounting restrictions afforded to them by the respective accounting standards.

Furthermore, even though the US Federal Trade Commission required franchisors to divulge specific information about their prospective franchise to potential franchisees, such as through a Uniform Franchise Offering Circular, the vast majority of franchisors choose not to include earnings claims (Stadfeld, 1992; Sherman, 1994). Kaufmann and Lafontaine (1994) suggest that this practice exists for three reasons:

- the claims must be relevant to the location of the prospective franchisee;

- all assumptions must be disclosed;

- the franchisor must retain and produce on request to the prospective franchisee, the Federal Trade Commission, and the state administrators all the data necessary to substantiate them.

In the UK, even though firms in general are more financially transparent than they are in the USA, there is no requirement to divulge similar information. As such, prospective franchisees are not free to compare and contrast competing franchise offerings on a like-for-like basis. This lack of disclosure places the burden of researching the viability firmly onto the prospective franchisee's shoulders. Unfortunately, this burden is made heavier by the fact that both the franchisor and the existing franchisees (should there be any) are small businesses and may not file complete financial statements.

However, the lack of transparency cannot be solely responsible for the inadequate questioning of franchisee or, for that matter, franchisor financial performance. Surely, if extant strategic management thought (Porter, 1980, 1985) is correct, the promises of financial success and supra-normal returns are somewhat incongruous with the relatively low financial barriers to entry into franchising (Price, 1997; Stanworth and Purdy, 1999). According to Porter (1985), industries characterized by low entry barriers do not yield above average returns. But, unfortunately, even general observations appear to be the exception to the rule in the extant franchise literature. Unfortunately, therefore, not only have the beliefs about franchising's ability to deliver the 'American Dream' and assumption about the activity's boundless future been perpetuated by the franchise fraternity's success rhetoric, but also by what can only be described as inadequate testing through the application of inappropriate research methodologies.

Inappropriate research methodologies

The application of inappropriate methodologies can be demonstrated in two inter-related ways. First, extant methodologies within the ownership redirection discourse purport to evaluate the degree to which franchisee outlets are being bought back by their franchisors. Such action has ethical implications because the franchisor, by undertaking such action, not only expropriates the goodwill developed by the franchisee, but also buys the units back at a fraction of their economic value.

Yet, in order for researchers to test whether such activity is occurring in a collective manner or, for that matter, within a particular franchise system, one would expect them to be explicitly modelling for the nature of interaction between franchisee- and franchisor-owned outlets. The employed methodologies do no such thing. Equally, one might expect researchers to model for the word-of-mouth effects that go with such activity. After all, if franchisors were indeed buying back franchisee-operated outlets en masse, one would expect there to be an increasing word-of-mouth effect, as the number of franchisors undertaking the activity increased. Alas, there is no such test in the extant ownership-redirection research.

The second example is related to the first. In general, there is a lack of understanding concerning why firms decide to franchise and why aspiring franchisees decide to take the plunge and invest more than their life savings in this form of investment. These decisions are not just important at the micro-level in helping the franchise fraternity to market their products more effectively and efficiently, but are also important at a macro-level for what they imply about the nature and shape of franchising's diffusion curve. As Price (1997) observes, examining the nature and shape of the diffusion curve is not a matter of merely being pedantic. The shape of the diffusion curve is important because, for example, it suggests where significant barriers to adoption may occur and it permits some general comments to be made about the illiberality of competitive conditions and the prospect of excess returns (Donaldson, 1985; Porter, 1980, 1985). It is the persistent and overt failure to consider this issue which lies at the heart of examining whether there is foundation to the belief that franchising is both boundary-less and has a boundless future (Patterson, 1998) and also provides some indication and/or broad hypotheses concerning the rate failure.

For example, Illustration 3.1 shows that both the academic and populist franchise writers refer to the scale and growth of franchising in the opening sentences of their work. However, population ecologists contend that there is a degree of inter-relatedness between such rhetoric, the scale and growth of an activity and the survival propensity and performance of its incumbents (Lomi, 1992; Carroll and Hannan, 1995). The critical contention here is that industries illustrate specific carrying capacities, which refers to the situation where the growth rate is zero. If a population is below carrying capacity, it will increase and the growth rate will be positive, and if it has exceeded its carrying capacity, the population will begin to decline.

Thus, in the commercial arena, the population of a particular organizational form will increase when the rate of entries exceeds the number of withdrawals/failures. It decreases when the withdrawal/failure rate exceeds the entry rate. The carrying capacity is therefore the stable equilibrium, and from the statements made in Illustration 3.1, one could conclude that the franchise sector is still on a growth trajectory and, as such, the rate of failure is less than the rate of entry. The important observation, however, is that there could be variation in carrying capacities, and therefore variation in the rate of withdrawals, of franchises across different industries. For example, using the population ecology framework to examine the dynamics of the rise of hotel chains in the United States between 1896 and 1980, Ingram (1996, p. 134) concludes that:

> Franchising . . . appears to be an important environmental change in the hospitality industry. Founding rates increased and failure rates decreased as a function of the aggregate level of franchising. Franchising started relatively late in the period I examine . . . The first hotel chains to be franchisees [sic]) did not appear until 1960. Franchising grew quickly between 1960 and 1980, and has grown even more quickly since 1980. In fact, franchising might be characterized as representing a second era of environmental change, after the changes I examined, that is critical to the evolution of hotel chains since 1980. The effect of franchising on hotel chains is made more interesting because the chains that are directly involved in franchising suffer higher rates of failure.

So it would appear that, on the whole, those academics who are sufficiently interested to pursue research activity within the domain of franchising have not yet fashioned and implemented appropriate methodologies. We can see this by reference to research examining franchisee financial performance. For example, due to restrictions on small company reporting rules in the US, Bates (1998) uses net income as a proxy to evaluate whether franchisee firms out-perform their non-franchised counterparts. In contradiction to Kaufmann and Lafontaine's (1994) analysis of financial performance in the McDonald's network, they found that franchisees generate below average profits compared to independent firms. Yet, in this comparison, two factors need further consideration. First, one has to wonder – it is not explicit – about the degree of comparability of the respective financial statements on which these conclusions are based. After all, accounting policy factors, such as variations on the depreciation policies, can serve to reduce comparability: if one company aggressively depreciates its assets, it will record lower operating profits and net income than a company that depreciates its assets over a long period and/or at a lower rate. In short, if property has been depreciated at a high level then this would serve to depress new income (Bate's only proxy for performance). In franchising, it is usual for the franchisee to treat the initial franchise payments as goodwill and to amortise them over the period of the franchise contract (McCallum, 1993). As non-franchisees do not have to incur such added investment, so they may have a lower depreciation charge, which then inflates operating profits and goodwill. Incidentally, Price (1997) finds that UK fast food franchisees often have higher levels of depreciation than non-franchised companies because they tend to amortise the initial franchise expenses to reduce their tax burden. Second, the usual constraint of inter-company financial analyses is the adoption of different accounting standards, which reduced the comparability of key accounting rations and insolvency analysis (Lincoln, 1984). Research shows that there is an increased potential for the lack of comparability the more the management feel the exigencies of under-performance. Sharma and Stevenson (1997) posit that management of failing companies adopt a greater number of favourable accounting policies than management of non-failing firms. They also show that failing firms are more likely than non-failing firms to adopt discretionary accounting policy changes for a combined material net favourable effect on income and total assets.

This seeming lack of overt consideration of such factors is concerning in an area which is suffering from something of a 'drought' of well-founded, focused and rigorous research. Consequently, we are no closer to challenging the dominant success rhetoric, which desperately needs analysis of the central question: Is there foundation to the belief that franchising is both boundary-less and has a boundless future?

Summary

It has been argued that extant franchise academic literature has failed to assess whether franchising delivers as much as it promises, in terms of economic performance and available financial returns. In particular, there are few studies that examine the operational dynamics within franchising, most favour a particular perspective and tight focus on a typically pragmatic issue. Furthermore, those that do exist have frequently used inappropriate methodologies. An outcome of this 'failed literature' is the dominance of a success rhetoric that tends to neglect a range of ethical questions that remain unresolved because of the lacuna of debate. Moreover, the combination of persistent success propaganda and the lack of formal regulation have resulted in the cultural-embeddedness of the success rhetoric. This is concerning given its inadequate testing through the application of appropriate research methodologies.

Debate topics

- There is an urgent requirement for government and regulatory bodies to introduce franchising specific legislation to assist in improving the investor's research process.

- The claim that research methodologies employed to study franchising's success to date are largely inappropriate is unfounded.

- As an organizational form, franchising is both boundary-less and has a boundless future.

Selected readings

Bronson, J. and Morgan, C. (1998) The role of scale in franchisee success: evidence from the travel industry. *Journal of Small Business Management*, **36** (4), 33–42.

Castrogiovanni, G. and Justis, R. (1998) Franchising configurations and transitions. *Journal of Consumer Marketing*, **15** (2), 170–190.

Shane, S. (1998) Making new franchise systems work. *Strategic Management Journal*, **9** (7), 697–707.

References

Abell, M. (1990) The legal regulation of franchising in the United Kingdom. In Campbell, D. and Lafili, L. (eds.), *Distributorships*,

Agency and Franchising in an International Arena: Europe, The United States, Japan, and Latin America, Kluwer, Deventer, pp. 115–124.

Abell, M. (1999) Should steps be taken to regulate franchising? In *Franchise World Directory,* Franchise World Publishing, pp. 53–7.

Anand, P. (1987) Inducing franchisees to relinquish control: an attribution analysis. *Journal of Marketing Research,* XXIV (May), 215–21.

Anon (1996) Advertisement. *Business Franchise Magazine,* March, p. 34.

Banning, K. (1996) *Opportunities in Franchising Careers.* VGM Career Horizons.

Bates, T. (1995) A comparison of franchise and independent small business survival rates. *Small Business Economics,* **7**, 377–88.

Bates, T. (1998) Survival patterns among newcomers to franchising. *Journal of Business Venturing,* **13**, 113–30.

Bradach, J. (1992) The organization of the franchise relationship: the roles of the franchise consultant. Working Paper. Harvard University.

Bradach, J. (1998) *Franchise Organizations.* Harvard Business School Press.

Brandenberg, M. (1989) Franchising into the Nineties. *Accountancy,* **103** (1146), 143–5.

BFA (British Franchise Association) (1999) Leaflet on franchising and the British Franchise Association. British Franchise Association.

Bronson, J. and Morgan, C. (1998) The role of scale in franchisee success: evidence from the travel industry. *Journal of Small Business Management,* **36** (4), 33–42.

Brown, H. (1969) *Franchising: Trap for the Trusting.* Little Brown and Company.

Bucklin, L. (1971) The Economic Base of Franchising. In Thompson, D. (ed.), *Contractual Marketing Systems,* Heath Lexington Books, pp. 33–62.

Burck, C. (1970) Franchising's troubled dream world. *Fortune,* pp. 116, 148, 150 and 152.

Carroll, G. and Hannan, M.(1995) *Organizations in Industry: Strategy, Structure, and Selection.* Oxford University Press.

Castrogiovanni, G. and Justis, R. (1998) Franchising configurations and transitions, *Journal of Consumer Marketing,* **15** (2), 170–190.

Castrogiovanni, G., Justis, R. and Julian, S. (1993) Franchise failure rates: an assessment of magnitude. *Journal of Small Business Management,* 31 (April), 105–15.

Chater, R. and Fernique, F. (1990) *The Financial Performance of Top 100 UK Business Format Franchising Companies*. CAMC Publications.

Cherkasky, W. (1996) Franchising: a key to business success. *Franchising Research: An International Journal*, **13**(1), 1–12.

Cross, J. (1994) Franchising failures: definitional and measurement issues. In *Proceedings*, Society of Franchising Conference, Las Vegas.

Cross, J. (1998) Improving the relevance of franchisee failure rates. In *Proceedings*, Society of Franchising 12th Annual Conference, Las Vegas.

Curran, J. and Stanworth, J. (1983) Franchising in the modern economy – towards a theoretical understanding. *International Small Business Journal*, **2** (1), 8–26.

Curry, J., Morris, T. and Larkworthy, J. (1966) *Partners for Profit: A Study of Franchising*. American Management Association Inc.

Dant, R. (1996) Motivations for franchising: rhetoric versus reality. *International Small Business Journal*, **14** (1), 10–32.

Dewar-Healing, L., quoted in Williams, G. (1999) Franchising's low failure rate. *Business & Finance*, April, p. 33.

Dickinson, R. (1981) Business failure rate. *American Journal of Small Business*, **6** (2), 17–25.

Donaldson, L. (1985) Organization design and the life-cycles of products. *Journal of Management Studies*, **22** (1), 25–37.

Easingwood, C., Mahahan, V. and Muler, E. (1983) A non-uniform influence model of new product acceptance. *Marketing Science*, **2** (3), 273–95.

Elango, B. and Fried, V. (1997) Franchising research: a literature review and synthesis. *Journal of Small Business Management*, **35**, 68–82.

Felstead, A. (1991) The social organization of the franchise: a case of 'controlled self-employment'. *Work, Employment and Society*, **5** (1), 37–57.

Felstead, A. (1993) *The Corporate Paradox: Power and Control in the Business Franchise*. Routledge.

Fulop, C. (1996) *Overview of the Franchise Marketplace 1990–1995*. Centre for Franchise Research, City University Business School.

Gerstenhaber, M. (1998) *The Best of Relations. Franchise World Directory*. Franchise World Publishing, pp. 7–9.

Giugni, D. and Terry, A. (1998) Factors in franchise failure: lessons from the Cut Price Deli Litigation. *Proceedings*, Society of Franchising 12th Annual Conference, Las Vegas.

Hayes, C. (1994) Taking the fear out of franchising. The Internet Presence and Publishing Corporation. http://www.ip.net/legal.html

Housden, J. (1984) *Franchising and Other Business Relationships in Hotel and Catering Services.* Heinemann.

Hunt, S. D. (1977) Franchising: promises, problems, prospects. *Journal of Retailing,* **53** (3), 71–84.

I.F. Consulting (1997) *UK Franchise Performance Review.* London.

Ingham (1997) Foreword. *Franchise World Directory.* British Franchise Association.

Ingram, P. (1996) *The Rise of Hotel Chains in the United States, 1896–1980.* Garland Publishing.

Izraeli, D. (1972) *Franchising and the Total Distribution System.* Longman.

John, G. (1984) An empirical investigation of some antecedents of opportunism in a marketing channel. *Journal of Marketing Research,* **XXI** (August), 278–89.

Kaufmann, P. (1996) The state of research in franchising. *Franchising Research: An International Journal,* **1** (1), 4–7.

Kaufmann, P. and Lafontaine, F. (1994) Costs of control: the sources of economic rents for McDonald's franchisees. *Journal of Law and Economics,* **37** (2), 417–53.

Knight, R. (1984) The independence of the franchise entrepreneurs. *Journal of Small Business Management,* **23** (April), 53–61.

Konopa, L. (1963) What is meant by franchise selling? *Journal of Marketing,* April, 75–101.

Kursh, H. (1968) *The Franchise Boom: How Can You Profit from It?* Prentice Hall.

Lafontaine, F. (1996) The economics of franchising: some thoughts on research issues. *Franchising Research: An International Journal,* **1** (1), 29–32.

Lafontaine, F. and Bhattacharyya, S. (1995) The role of risk in franchising. *Journal of Corporate Finance,* **2**, 39–74.

Lafontaine, F. and Shaw, K. (1996) *Franchising Growth and Reality in the U.S. Marketing: Myth and Reality.* University of Michigan/ Carnegie Mellon University.

Lafontaine, F. and Slade, M. (1998) Incentive Contracting and the Franchise Decision. Working Paper No. 6544. National Bureau of Economic Research.

Leibowitz, M. (1997) Franchise margins and the sales-driven franchise value. *Financial Analysts Journal,* November/December, pp. 43–53.

Lincoln, M. (1984) An empirical analysis of the usefulness of accounting ratios to describe levels of insolvency risk. *Journal of Banking and Finance,* **8**, 321–40.

Lomi, A. (1992) Density dependence and spatial duality in founding rates of Danish commercial banks, 1846–1989. London Business School. January.

Martin, R. (1988) Franchising and risk management. *American Economic Review*, **78** (5), 954–68.

Martin, R. (1996) The market for franchise opportunities. *Bulletin of Economic Research*, **48**, 97–114.

McCallum, R. (1993) *Franchising: an Accounting, Auditing and Income Tax Guide*. John Wiley.

McInytre, F. and Huszagh, S. (1991) Internationalisation of franchise systems. *Journal of International Marketing*, **3** (4), 39–56.

McIntyre, F., Young, J. and Gilbert, F. (1994) Franchising: a strategic alliance perspective. Presented at Society of Franchising Conference: Understanding and Accepting Different Perspectives . . . Empowering Relationships in 1994 and Beyond, Las Vegas.

Mendelsohn, M. (1982) *The Guide to Franchising*, 3rd edn. Pergamon Press.

Nucifora, A. (1998) *San Francisco Times*, 1 June.

Patterson, G. (1998) Count your chickens . . . *The Franchise Magazine*, July/August, pp. 134–5.

Phan, P., Butler, J. and Lee, S. (1996) Caressing mother: entrepreneur-franchisee's attempts to reduce franchisor influence. *Journal of Business Venturing*, **11**, 379–402.

Pollock, A. (1986) Sell the business format and grow bigger. *Accountancy*, October, 90–91.

Pollock, W. and Golzen, G. (1985) *Franchising for Profit, A Guide for Professional Advisers & Businessmen*. The Institute of Chartered Accountants in England and Wales.

Porter, M. (1980) *Competitive Strategy: Techniques for Analyzing Industries and Competitors*. Free Press.

Porter, M. (1985) *Competitive Advantage: Creating and Sustaining Superior Performance*. Free Press.

Powers, M. (1995) *How to Open a Franchise Business*. Avon Books.

Price, S. (1993) *The UK Fast-Food Industry 1993*. Cassell.

Price, S. (1996) *Behind the Veneer of Success: Propensities for UK Franchisor Failure*. Small Business Trust, Open University.

Price, S. (1997) *The Franchise Paradox: New Strategies, Different Directions*. Cassell.

Purvin, R. (1994) *The Franchise Fraud: How to Protect Yourself Before and After You Invest*. John Wiley.

Rubin, P. (1978) The theory of the firm and the structure of the franchise contract. *Journal of Law and Economics*, **21**, 223–33.

Shane, S. (1996) Hybrid organizational arrangements and their implications for firm growth and survival: a study of new franchisors. *Academy of Management Journal*, **39**, 216–34.

Shane, S. (1998) Making new franchise systems work. *Strategic Management Journal*, **19** (7), 697–707.

Sharma, D. and Stevenson, P. (1997) Impact of impending corporate failure on the incidence and magnitude of discretionary accounting policy changes. *British Accounting Review*, **29**, 129–53.

Sherman, A. (1994) Hard data on franchises. *Nation's Business*, **82** (February), 54.

Spinelli, S. (1996) The pitfalls and potential of franchising. *Financial Times, Mastering Enterprise Series*, **4**, 8–9.

Spinelli, S. and Birley, S. (1996a) Toward a theory of conflict in the franchise system. *Journal of Business Venturing*, **11**, 329–42.

Spinelli, S. and Birley, S. (1996b) An examination of the effects of exit and switching costs on trademark valuation and franchisee satisfaction. In Reynolds, P. (ed.), *Frontiers of Entrepreneurial Research*, Babson Entrepreneurship Research Conference, pp. 316–326.

Stadfeld, L. (1992) Comment on proposed US franchise legislation: a search for balance. *Common Law Journal*, **97** (4), 540–66.

Stanworth, J. (1995) The franchise relationship: entrepreneurship or dependence? *Journal of Marketing Channels*, **4** (1–2), 161–76.

Stanworth, J. and Kaufmann, P. (1996) Similarities and differences in UK and US franchise research data: towards a dynamic model of franchisee motivation. *International Small Business Journal*, **14** (3), 57–70.

Stanworth, J. and Purdy, D. (1999) *Succeeding as a Franchisor*. Business Link London Central and International Franchise Research Centre.

Stanworth, J., Curran, J. and Hough, J. (1984) The franchised small business: formal and operational dimensions of independence. In *Success and Failure in Small Business* (Lewis, J., Stanworth J. and Gibb, A., eds), Pitman, pp. 223–30.

Stanworth, J., Purdy, D. and Price, S. (1997) Franchise growth and failure in the US and the UK: a troubled dream-world revisited. *Franchise Research: An International Journal* **2** (2), 75–94.

Stern, L. and El-Ansary, A. (1992) *Marketing Channels*, 4th edn. Prentice-Hall.

Stern, P. (1998) Franchising – a profitable partnership. The British Franchise Exhibition. Wembley Conference & Exhibition Centre. Visitor Information Pack and Exhibition Guide, p. 9.

Stern, P. (1999) Introduction to franchising. The British Franchise Exhibition, Wembley Conference & Exhibition Centre. Visitor Information Pack and Exhibition Guide, p. 3.

Stern, P. and Stanworth, J. (1994) Improving small business survival rates via franchising – the role of the banks in Europe. *International Small Business Journal*, **12** (2), 15–25.

Storholm, G. and Scheuing, E. (1994) Ethical implications of business format franchising. *Journal of Business Ethics*, **13**, 181–8.

Strutton, D., Pelton, L. and Lumpkin, J. (1993) The influence of psychological climate on conflict resolution strategies in franchise relationships. *Journal of the Academy of Marketing Science*, **21** (3), 207–15.

Thompson, D. (1968) The literature on franchising: a selected, classified bibliography. *Journal of Retailing*, **44** (4), 84–8.

Thompson, R. (1994) The franchise life-cycle and the Penrose effect. *Journal of Economic Behavior and Organization*, **24** (2), 207–18.

Trade Union Congress (1997) The small firm myths: a TUC analysis of the small firm sector within the UK economy. Economic & Social Affairs Department. January.

Walker, B. and Cross, J. (1988) Franchise failures: more questions and answers. In *Proceedings*, Society of Franchising Conference, Las Vegas.

Watson, R. (1999) Lateral thinking for prospective franchisees. *Business Franchise*, April, pp. 60–1.

Williams, D. (1999) Why do entrepreneurs become franchisees? An empirical analysis of organizational choice. *Journal of Business Venturing*, **14**, 103–24.

Williams, G. (1999) Franchising's low failure rate. *Business and Finance in Scotland*, April/May, pp. 33–6.

CHAPTER 4

Entrepreneurs or intrapreneurs?

Alison Morrison

Key points

- Franchisors can be regarded as entrepreneurs in that they instigate an entrepreneurial event in the creation of a new business concept that has significant market potential.

- Persons who voluntarily choose to enter into a franchising contract are not entrepreneurs but intrapreneurs, working within an interdependent organizational environment.

- Franchisors and franchisees combine into a system within which the ensurance of integrity and the capacity for innovation and organization renewal are key dimensions, and the driving dynamics are autonomy and control.

- Managed intrapreneurship can be applied to increase the capacity for innovation and organizational renewal which requires to be bounded by carefully prescribed limits to action in order that it be constructive, rather than destructive.

Introduction

This chapter specifically concentrates on the relationship between individual-operator franchisees and franchisors, and investigates the interface of franchising with entrepreneurship, intrapreneurship and organization theory. The aim is to develop a deeper understanding of the dynamics, management modes, and organizational structures associated with franchise system integrity, and innovation and organizational renewal. Fulop and Forward (1997) have identified these aspects as central to franchise systems. Emergent issues and themes are illustrated through the use of service sector-specific examples, as summarized in Table 4.1.

These examples have been specifically selected for the strength of their illustrative ability, and have been sourced from the promotional materials of the range of franchise organizations. The organizations have been categorized as: supplier forward integration into a retail franchise system; UK and international franchise systems with integrated value chains; and entrepreneur originated concepts with unproven franchise systems. The chapter is structured into four sections. First, the relationship between entrepreneurship, intrapreneurship and franchising is investigated. Second, the role and characteristics of owner–operator franchisees as *intrapreneurs* is explored. Third, franchisors as drivers of organizational innovation and system renewal are investigated. Finally, arising management issues are identified and developed relative to the ensurance of system integrity, and innovation and organizational renewal, within franchise systems.

Entrepreneurship, intrapreneurship and franchising

There exists substantial debate as to whether becoming an individual-operator franchisee represents a genuine form of entrepreneurship, collective or otherwise (Felstead, 1991; Price, 1997). What is proposed in this chapter is that those individuals who voluntarily choose to enter into a franchising contract are not entrepreneurs, but **intrapreneurs**. It is believed that this is justified given that franchising represents a complex organizational arrangement that combines elements of both entrepreneurship and employment.

Despite definitional conflicts, entrepreneurship, in essence, involves the process of creating value by bringing together a unique package of resources to create or exploit a market opportunity (Morrison, 1998). Under this guise, the entrepreneurship construct has three implicit dimensions: innovativeness,

Hospitality, Leisure & Tourism Series

Franchise company	Description	Type of system	Issue(s) illustrating
Caffee Roberta	Italian cafe	Supplier forward integration into retail franchise system	• In-bound master franchise
Bombolini's	Speciality coffee cart	Supplier forward integration into retail franchise system	• Innovative spark of entrepreneurs in originating new concept
Domino's Pizza	Home delivery and takeaway pizza	International franchise system with integrated value chain	• Innovation and organizational renewal • Insurance of system integrity • Culture of mutual respect and trust
Don Miller Bakery	Traditional bakery produce fast food outlet	International franchise system with integrated value chain	• Innovation and organizational renewal
McDonald's	Quick service food restaurant	International franchise system with integrated value chain	• Interdependence of franchisor/ franchisee relationship • Constructive franchisee entrepreneurship
Nestlé	Branded national coffee house	Supplier forward integration into retail franchise system	• New concept separation and piloting
Pancake Place	Restaurant specializing in sweet and savoury pancake based dishes	Entrepreneur originated concept and unproven franchise system	• Mature stage of business life-cycle
Pierre Victoire	French restaurant serving freshly made produce at exceptional value	Entrepreneur originated concept and unproven franchise system	• Franchisor difficulties in enforcing contractual obligations
The Tapas Tree	Mediterranean restaurant serving one-price tapas dishes	Entrepreneur originated concept and unproven franchise system	• Entrepreneurial creation of a new business concept with market appeal
Wimpy International Ltd	Family hamburger restaurant	International franchise system with integrated value chain	• Duality of management of bounded autonomy and control • Socialization of franchisees into the system

Table 4.1 Service sector illustrative examples

risk-taking, and proactiveness. However, explicit in the franchise contract are control mechanisms which constrain the degree of innovativeness, risk-taking and proactiveness to which franchisees are party. Given this transparent control mechanism, it is puzzling that much franchising literature (for example, Siropolis, 1990; Hall, 1995) discusses supposedly resulting relational tensions between franchisors and franchisees, in the vein of a 'conspiracy theory'. There is nothing underhand or hidden. At the point of signing the contract, the degree of control required by the franchisor over the franchisee, in order to ensure the integrity of the system, should be explicit and legally binding. The franchisee therefore enters into the agreement voluntarily, accepting the established level of constraint relative to innovativeness and proactiveness, in return for perceived reduced risk-taking in comparison to independent entrepreneurship. For example, the British Franchise Association (BFA, 1996) asserts that a franchisee is five times more likely to succeed than a comparable independent business. Furthermore, according to Barclay's Bank (Levene, 1998), approximately 50 per cent of independent small businesses survive to at least the three-year point, which is 40 per cent less than franchisee businesses. However, these positive inferences are tempered by Stanworth *et al.* (1998), who claim that failure rates of franchised small businesses are at least as high as non-franchised ones. This issue and the associated ambiguity and controversy are addressed in Chapters 3 and 6.

Within a franchising system, individuals contribute to the process of intrapreneurship, which refers to the collective entrepreneurial endeavour of franchisees within the franchise system. This is a form of internalized entrepreneurship (Lloyd, 1987). Lessem (1987) describes it as organizational members devising innovative solutions to traditional problems, and new and imaginative means to deal with changes in the environment. In the service sector innovation is largely concerned with new and creative ways of satisfying customers. Thus, intrapreneurship is directed at continuous strengthening of the integrity of the system, while also developing a sustainable competitive advantage through organizational innovation and renewal. The concept is inclusive of a wide range of creative processes and could incorporate numerous franchisor and franchisee initiated actions. These may be minor or major, have incremental or significant effects, and be positive or negative relative to the achievement of system objectives at tactical, operational, business and strategic levels. In this respect, the more encompassing view of intrapreneurship overlaps with approaches to employee empowerment (see Chapter 5). With empowerment, it has been demonstrated that the scope for discretion is bounded by carefully prescribed limits to action (Lashley, 1997). It is proposed (Morrison *et al.*, 1998) that this should also be the case with intrapreneurial behaviour and represents the central tenet in the final section of this chapter.

Franchisee as intrapreneur

The foregoing has moved discussion from consideration of owner–operator franchisees as entrepreneurs to that of being intrapreneurs. The ways in which they differ from employees, the relativity of their independence within a franchise system, and the impact of antecedent factors on individual and system behaviour are now discussed.

In considering franchisees as intrapreneurs, we must question how they differ from entrepreneurs. One of the key differences is that franchisees have chosen to work collectively within the established dynamics of the franchise system, and as such, they are affected by organizational variables such as structure, processes, procedures and culture. Lessem (1987) claims that, as a consequence, intrapreneurs have to place more emphasis on integration and co-ordination than entrepreneurs do. Further-more, Ferguson *et al.* (1987) claim that intrapreneurs do not have the temperament or desire to take their entrepreneurial instincts onto the open market. The franchisee perceives personal eco-nomic risk to be reduced through franchising and has selected to work within an organization, which has set boundaries, albeit with the illusion of a certain degree of flexibility and autonomy. In this respect, Levene (1998) refers to franchisees as 'refugees' from the small business sector. Quite simply, many persons become franchisees because they lack the expertise and courage to go it alone (Hoy, 1994). However, successful intrapreneurs tend to possess the entrepreneur's ability to take action-oriented decisions and implement them. In fact, franchisees do share many of the personal characteristics and behaviours associated with entrepreneurs, such as, commitment to work, market opportunity alertness and a motivation to excel. It is the 'sheltered' and interdependent context and organizational setting that is different rather than the individual and what they do.

One particular feature of the franchise context and setting emphasized by Felstead (1991) is that the level of independence enjoyed by franchisees is fragile. The word franchising comes from the French *franchir* which means 'to free'; originally it meant 'to free from slavery', so it is interesting that Knowles (1996) describes the franchisor/franchisee relationship in terms of master and servant. Furthermore, Hall (1995) asserts that, in tightly controlled franchise systems, there is very little difference from working for a company that operates a system of payment by results. This is supported by Felstead (1991), who argues that a franchisee is an employee in all but name and with none of an employee's advantages. However, Fulop and Forward (1997) sensibly point out that it seems to be implicitly assumed that independence is a top priority of franchisees. The counter-argument is that while potential franchisees may harbour a desire for independence, the franchise option has been chosen deliberately. It has been deemed to provide the opportunity of working within an interdependent environment under the umbrella of a large organization, which has the potential to reduce business risk, and enable reward based on franchisee performance. The nature of this relationship is often reflected in the language used in franchisors' promotional materials. For example, McDonald's states that as a franchisee you'll be working for yourself, but can be assured that you won't be on your own.

In reality, the nature of the franchisor/franchisee relationship is one that is highly interdependent, co-operative and with limited autonomy (Hoy, 1994; Mendelsohn, 1996) and Felstead (1991, p. 83) reminds us that interpretations of 'independence' are relative concepts:

> The ability to exercise independence, 'be your own boss' or 'mind your own business' are not dichotomous notions, but rather relative concepts with some small firms enjoying more, and some less, than others. A similar argument applies to the sub-set of franchised businesses.

Clearly, franchisors want people who are sufficiently independent and self-reliant to run their own business, and who accept that they are required to work within a legislated framework (West, 1996). Therefore, the prospective franchisee must be independent enough to be able to manage a business on his or her own, but also be dependent enough to want to work within the rules of the franchise and not continually be challenging the franchisor and seeking an excuse to break away (Mendelsohn and Acheson, 1996). This leads Siropolis (1990, 134) to suggest that 'The ideal franchisee is the sergeant type – midway between the general who gives the orders and the private who merely follows them.'

Inevitably, such persons entering into a franchise contract will have been influenced by a number of antecedent variables, including self-efficacy expectations, as discussed by Lashley in detail in Chapter 5. These expectations refer to an individual's belief in their abilities to perform particular behaviours success-fully, and are developed from their experiences of their own past behaviours (Waldinger *et al.*, 1985). These expectations may be based on their closure from certain occupations and derive from prior educational, ethnicity, work and/or personal experiences. Price (1997) identifies three sets of antecedent factors, which appear to influence the decision to become a franchisee as: prior employment experience; nature of networks; and individual factors. For example, Price points out that few persons choose franchising as a first career choice. It generally represents a second career route driven by redundancy, early retirement, decentralization, merger and acquisition activity, or failed self-employment.

Thus, franchisees' response within a franchise system will be individualized relative to their subsequent socio-economic con-ditioning; this in turn will impact on the type of work ethos and commitment they inject into their franchise. Furthermore, once part of the system, franchisees are involved in fragmented and personalized learning which occurs as they interact within their own social networks (Reve, 1990). Consequently, the franchisor needs to recognize that the grouping of franchisees under any one-umbrella brand is heterogeneous in nature and that con-sistent behavioural responses cannot be guaranteed. This was experienced by the Pierre Victoire restaurant franchise organiza-tion, which following initial substantial success went into voluntary receivership in 1998. It found that it was insufficient for a franchisor to have as a contractual obligation that franchisees share any innovations that they may come up with. The reality was that some franchisees volunteered and shared their innova-tions while others behaved in a secretive manner and attempted to hide innovations. Therefore, of greater significance to the degree of intrapreneurship in a franchise system is the manage-ment of the relational conditions deriving from the franchise contract at an individual franchisee level.

Franchisor, innovation and organizational renewal

The franchisor can be considered as fitting the mould of what is generally accepted as being an entrepreneur. The justification for this is that in the beginning the founding entrepreneur performs a creative, catalytic role in instigating the bringing together of a business concept, resources, franchisees and customers into a system. At this introduction stage, franchisors are genuinely innovative in linking the necessary components into an entrepre-neurial event, namely the creation of a new business concept, which has significant market potential. This is the case with Jake and Sophie Findlay. On their return from three years living and working in the south of France, a restaurant idea was born. Their concept was to create a new eating experience incorporating the warm atmosphere of the Mediterranean and at the same time allowing dishes from all around the globe to be enjoyed through the freedom and selection which is tapas. They successfully piloted (see Chapter 6) the concept in two Tapas Tree company-owned units and are currently actively seeking franchisees to expand the operation.

Thereafter, innovation and organizational renewal are dependent on factors such as life-cycle requirements, the nature and degree of organizational learning and resultant franchisee behaviours. Furthermore, Castrogiovanni and Justis (1998) state that franchise organizations tend to lose their entrepreneurial abilities sooner than non-franchise, although some franchise systems disprove this. For instance, Domino's Pizza states that you don't get to be the world's leading pizza delivery operation by sitting next to the phone and waiting for it to ring. You go out and make things happen, which is exactly what the company has been doing since 1960, when entrepreneur Tom Monaghan founded the company. It is dedicated to research and development, and many of Domino's innovations have been adopted by the industry as standard.

By providing this innovatory spark, franchisors are active in advocating the attractions that 'pull' many persons considering self-employment into a franchise system (Felstead, 1991). This may take the form of creating a new concept, as was the case with the Tapas Tree, adapting a concept to the local market as with Mongolian Barbeque, or importing a proven concept through a master franchise agreement as did two Glasgow-based entrepreneurs. They noted the success of Glasgow's rejuvenated tea rooms and believed that an Italian coffee house might be a similar draw. They contacted the head office of Caffe Roberta, Italy's fourth largest coffee roaster. It was looking to expand the company's chain of coffee houses abroad. After some negotiation, the entrepreneurs secured the master franchise rights for the UK.

One way of better understanding this issue of innovation and organizational renewal is to use the concept of a business life-cycle, which Delahunt (1998) found to have significant influence on franchisor activity (see also Chapter 7). As a franchise organization evolves along a life-cycle trajectory, from entrepreneurial embryo to a mature corporate entity, decline or collapse, it changes in nature and needs. This can be illustrated in the case of the Pancake Place. Established in 1973, it represents a relatively mature franchise concept and system. Within this organization, the introduction phase focused on establishing the business concept, creating a market and seeking growth potential. The growth period was characterized by the opening of new company-owned outlets in Scotland, identification of potential sites in England and Wales, and harvesting opportunities by seeking franchisees to develop new markets. Maturity coincided with rationalization and a new management ethos, which may have led to the loss of entrepreneurial abilities. Consequently, the franchisor's current strategy seeks to find replacement products for the Pancake Place to halt decline and potential collapse (Delahunt, 1998).

Macmillan (1996) provides further definition of life-cycle behaviour. He found that franchisor expansion, where driven by founding entrepreneurs new to franchising systems, tends to follow a general behaviour pattern of:

- initially shooting in the dark, influenced in large part by the competition and perceived wisdom in the industry;
- to getting a little arrogant, a feeling of having got things under control and a belief that franchising is relatively easy;
- to a period of re-examination and loss of confidence, as the mature franchisees get more powerful and begin to flex their muscles and cause disruption in the network;
- to uncertainty over future recruitment policies and indeed recruitment candidates.

This life-cycle approach emphasizes the recognition of an organizational learning curve. Decisions taken by franchisors that are relatively new to franchising are often based on imperfect learning and knowledge. In the short-term, the consequences may be regarded as irrational, and potentially damaging, business behaviour. However, in the long term franchisors' learning increases. For example, they could develop the ability to identify and retain the most profitable franchisees. In turn, this may encourage a movement towards 'buy-back' franchising of the most profitable units, in the belief that further profit enhancement can be achieved. This has been the case with Pizza Express, and is a theme that Ball addresses in Chapter 7. Alternately, Houston (1984) points to the 'transitional' advantages of franchising for those of an independent nature. Short/medium-term 'apprenticeship' as a franchisee provides a mechanism by which to gain business expertise and self-efficacy for the transformation in the spin-off of franchisees into their own ventures. This was clearly illustrated by the Pierre Victoire restaurant chain. When it went into voluntary receivership in

1998 the company was broken up. Thirty-seven of the viable restaurants were sold for £4 million to a consortium of franchisees. The deal included the right to the Pierre Victoire brand name. The buy-in consortium, named Voila!, acquired fourteen restaurants run by its own members along with a further nineteen operated by other franchisees (Morrison, 1999).

Thus, it would appear that the life-cycle model has some currency relative to franchising. The model presented in Figure 4.1 is open and dynamic, demonstrating a constant process of change and development designed to create self-perpetuating innovation. At each stage intrapreneurial learning takes place from both negative and positive effects. Organizational impact and individual franchisor/franchisee assessment of negative and positive learning will continuously occur, relative to the organization and the environment. This may be further individualized as a result of the differing local/micro-level competitive conditions, which each franchisee will experience. It is proposed that franchisors, who seek constantly to learn and innovate, will have more control over the life cycle of the system as new ideas and learning are consolidated constantly to improve and develop the

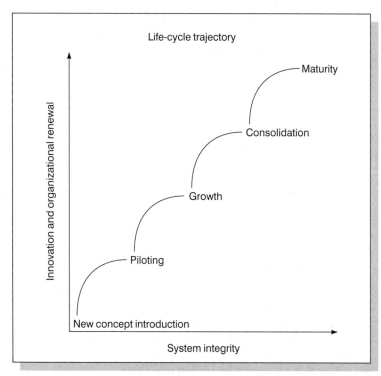

Figure 4.1 Life-cycle trajectory (adapted from Hall, 1995, p. 122)

Hospitality, Leisure & Tourism Series

product offering. This requires an organizational climate and culture which incorporates both openness to change, encouragement of managed risk-taking, recognizes franchisees' need for self-efficacy, and the trust necessary to bind all parties interdependently towards the achievement of mutually beneficial rewards. McDonald's endorses this approach. The company recognizes that its success is inextricably linked to the success of each and every franchisee, so they can be confident of receiving the full backing of all the McDonald's team – the company, suppliers and other franchisees.

Management of intrapreneurship

From the above discussion, which links intrapreneurship, franchisees and franchisors, a key question emerges. How do franchisors effectively engage franchisees in the process of intrapreneurship? Furthermore, it has been recognized that intrapreneurship requires to be managed within carefully prescribed limits to action. This is designed to ensure system integrity and support innovation and organization renewal that will contribute to the sustainability and competitive advantage of the franchise organization over its life cycle. Relative to system integrity, Domino's Pizza have identified that fundamental to their success, both in the UK and internationally, is the way the Domino's brand has come to stand for uncompromising quality, unbeatable value for money, friendly and efficient service, impeccable hygiene and unerring consistency. The company considers these to be priceless brand values. The issue of innovation and organization renewal is addressed by the 'Don Miller' bakery brand. The company regards itself as a 'pioneer' in new developments in the sector, epitomized when it first launched the 'Hot Bread Kitchen' format twenty-five years ago. Currently, it is ready to go national with its latest concept – 'Don Miller's Express Bakery'. This concept draws on the traditional baker values of the Don Miller brand but repositions them in the growth fast food sector.

Figure 4.2 summarizes the range of common and contrasting franchisee, franchisor and system characteristics that have been identified. It can be seen that both the franchisee and franchisor bring their own unique sets of antecedent variables, self-efficacy expectations and an action orientation approach to business. Thereafter, the characteristics contrast reflecting the nature of the relationship. These combine to form the franchise system, within which the effective management of integrity and organizational innovation and renewal are paramount.

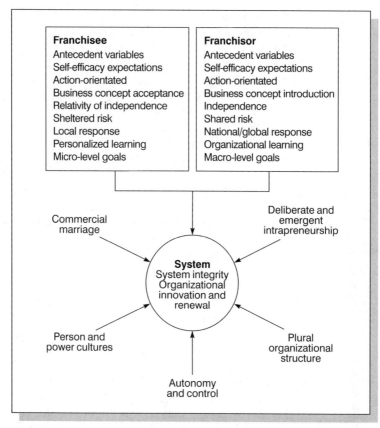

Figure 4.2 Common and contrasting franchisee, franchisor and system characteristics

From the foregoing, it has been identified that the nature of the franchise system demands certain policies and procedures relative to: commercial marriage; person and power cultures; autonomy and control; deliberate and emergent intrapreneurship; and plural organizational structure. These are now discussed.

Commercial 'marriage'

It has been identified that the management of a franchise system is complex due to the recognition that each individual franchisee will bring their unique set of antecedent variables and expectations to the system. Furthermore, once part of the system, their responses will be highly personalized relative to their subsequent socio-economic conditioning. Therefore, if the franchisor is to manage effectively the process of intrapreneurship the franchisor needs to understand fully the 'human' aspects and the importance of building and maintaining relationships between individual franchisees. Indeed, the metaphor most frequently used to describe the relationship is borrowed from the closest and most complex of human partnership: marriage (Bradach, 1998). Bradach emphasizes that personal and emergent dynamics embody the commercial relationship.

The franchisor/franchisee relationship commences development during the franchisee recruitment process. Criteria that may be used include previous successful business experience, empathy with the franchise business concept, full family support, personality characteristics, commitment to work, and, of course, the necessary financial capital. For example, McDonald's is rigorous when selecting new franchisees, taking great care to make sure that they and the franchisee are absolutely right for the business. As they are going to be partners for twenty years a mistake will be costly to both parties. It franchises only to individuals, not to partnerships, absentee investors or families, and those individuals must have their own liquid funds to commit to the business. McDonald's looks for a strong business track record, coupled with people skills, integrity, initiative and the tenacity that will be needed to make a McDonald's restaurant a success. In contrast, some other franchise companies are only interested in whether or not the potential franchisee has sufficient financial capital.

Dewhurst and Burns (1993) highlight the consequences of poor franchisee recruitment. Certainly, in the early stages of new franchise system roll-out, decisions are frequently taken to recruit wholly inappropriate franchisees in order to maintain cash flow, (see Chapter 6). In the longer term, this almost always proves to be a mistake, due to the potential impact on the total system. For example, it may take the form of franchisee low interest, refusal to follow systems, inability to run the business, defrauding the franchisor, breakdown of relationships, reputation damage and/or market confusion due to dilution of the concept (Dewhurst and Burns, 1993). Thus, it is essential that the recruitment process is designed to achieve a 'strategic fit' (Morrison, 1996) between the business and personal objectives of both the franchisor and franchisees in order to achieve a long and happy commercial 'marriage'.

However, Macmillan (1996) questions the use of the term 'recruitment', in that it has connotations of hiring company employees. The franchisor is in fact selling a product. Thus, the relationship is much more one of willing buyer and willing seller. In this respect it may be a sound proposition that franchise systems take on the form of strategic alliances defined as: co-operation between one or more businesses, whereby each partner seeks to add to its competencies by combining some resources with those of its partners (Morrison, 1996). This moves the relationship from one of 'master and servant' to explicit partnership, albeit asymmetrical in nature, where terminology includes 'working with' franchisees and 'selling them' policies rather than 'management' and 'enforcement' (Bradach, 1998). For the partnership to work, there has to be a relationship that encourages joint involvement in the decision making processes. Furthermore, it is proposed that the franchisor must adopt a management style that respects and trusts the franchisees (Hoy, 1994; Mendelsohn, 1996). Domino's Pizza endorses the partnership approach. It provides a full range of support services, including site location, design, training, marketing, business administration plus a highly efficient food supply and distribution service. In return, franchisees provide better-detailed knowledge than the franchisor of such things as local real estate, business practice and the consumer. In this way, Domino's views the franchisor/franchisee relationship as a business partnership. Thus, one of the most important aspects of franchise management is that franchisors regard the franchisees as strategic human assets. They require to engage them as partners in managed intrapreneurship, and not merely to view franchisees as passive agents or distributive mechanisms within the system.

Divergent tendencies: autonomy and control

The handling of this partnership approach is complicated, given two divergent tendencies in franchise business management (Forward and Fulop, 1993), as illustrated in Figure 4.3. One tendency stretches towards centralization, standardization and control, the other catapults in the direction of decentralization, innovation and autonomy. Here we are faced by the complex reality of franchise management. Furthermore, Price (1997) asserts that the inability to appreciate this symbiotic relationship has been the undoing of a number of franchised operations.

Thus, if it is accepted that the two key dimensions of franchise organizations are ensurance of system integrity, and organizational innovation and renewal, then the two driving dynamics must be autonomy and control. They represent inseparable dynamics of franchise system managerial action. Furthermore, Bradach (1998, p. 185) states that:

> Integrity and innovation are not dichotomous dimensions. Each benefits from the presence of the other. All units need the capacity to maintain uniformity, respond

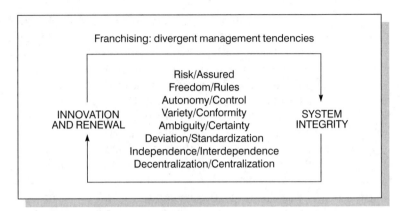

Figure 4.3 Divergent management tendencies

locally and be adaptable on a system-wide basis in order to escape the natural tendency of internal arrangements to ossify over time.

According to Fieldman (1989), innovation in organizations requires the simultaneous regulation of autonomy and control in order to promote creativity and experimentation, to produce positive business performance.

Thus, autonomy and innovation through intrapreneurship can never be regarded as ends in themselves, but always depend on a context for control and their relevance to the organization. When not in balance, it is clear that a vicious circle can develop which undermines commitment to organizational goals. Thus, intrapreneurship in organizations requires participants to have a highly developed sense of legitimate possibilities of autonomy. In particular, the need to ensure the brand relative to the consistency of service delivery makes the managed control of intrapreneurship within prescribed parameters and systems essential. If not, innovation may develop negative connotations, spiralling the franchise system into anarchy and eventual self-destruction.

Accordingly, franchisees are empowered (see Chapter 5) to be intrapreneurial with a defined degree of responsible autonomy that is explicit within the operational guidelines, negotiated franchisee business objectives and legal contract. Thus, a foundation set of certain specific service and product standard thresholds is established and agreed which bound the degree to which franchisees are free to act intrapreneurially. Therefore, within franchise organizations there is a requirement formally to prescribe and effectively communicate the boundaries to franchise autonomy, as it is likewise for franchisor control. This is explicitly done by Wimpy. The company states that a Wimpy franchisee is expected to be dedicated to the high quality and standards that the franchisor believes in, and accept the Wimpy franchise disciplines. However, in addition, most of all the franchisee will need ambition, enthusiasm and drive to be able to realize their dreams.

Deliberate and emergent intrapreneurship

It is apparent that intrapreneurship can be the result of a deliberate organizational policy and procedures to support innovation. Alternatively, it can occur as an emergent activity through the actions of franchisees, perhaps acting opportunistically outside the agreed standardized procedures and processes (Reve, 1990). In the latter case, the franchisor needs to assess the potential value and implications of intrapreneurial outcomes to the system and the degree of support and championing that they wish to invest. Burgleman (1983) recognizes these different processes, referring to induced behaviour as being the outcome of deliberate strategy, whilst autonomous emergent innovation results from operational level participants seeing opportunities that exceed the opportunity set proffered by central management. Thus, innovation can be unpredictable and influenced by factors not necessarily in the control of the franchisor.

In terms of deliberate organizational policy and procedures, some franchisors create separating mechanisms, in order to manage intrapreneurship more effectively (Falbe and Dandridge, 1992). This enables clearer differentiation between ongoing management of the existing operation and the development of means of innovation and renewal. Once a new concept has been successfully worked up, justified by initial market research and piloted in a unit, it may be introduced to the system. For example, company-owned outlets within the franchise organizational structure represent an important aspect of such an approach. They can act as test beds for both new products, services and business support systems, and a means of monitoring the marketplace. Potentially, this separation gives advantages in terms of consistent management and operation of the existing units, and the avoidance of detrimental effects that may be caused by the premature introduction of untested, or unplanned, innovations. Nestlé adopted a separation approach when it made a decision to franchise a chain of cafes based on Nescafé instant coffee. First, the company successfully trialled the concept in Kingston and Leeds then rolled it out to new franchisees. In addition, the company is committed to continuous product development. The menu is continually revised and reviewed, including the introduction of new coffee drinks, which are tested in the company-owned units prior to being made available to franchisees.

Another aspect of bounded, deliberate intrapreneurship is for the franchisor to offer franchisees a portfolio of proven innovative ideas from which to select what is most appropriate to their local needs and markets. For example, Marks & Spencer does this. For its international franchisees, the company has devised a menu of creative material from which the franchisees can freely choose which allows them to reflect their own local requirements, but within a clearly prescribed corporate framework.

The emergent approach to intrapreneurship is a result of the outpourings of creative effort by franchisees engaged in often disorderly or chaotic experimentation and exploration at a local level. This may take the form of one of two divergent forms of 'opportunism': shared and constructive to the system as a whole; and dysfunctional and destructive to the system as a whole. It may be a consequence of frustrated entrepreneurial initiative, and/or franchisees provided with little opportunity to participate in strategy formulation for their businesses (Dandridge and Falbe, 1994). Alternatively, it may emerge from the franchisee's closeness, and responsiveness, to the marketplace. McDonald's views emergent intrapreneurship positively. It states that fundamental to the company's long-term success story has been the innovative ideas and contribution of its franchisees. Without them, McDonald's believes that it would not be what it is today, as is emphasized by Lashley in his account of McDonald's in Chapter 11.

If franchisee intrapreneurial behaviour is undirected and not given a forum to emerge and express its innovative capacity, undoubtedly some franchisees may be motivated to engage in dysfunctional and destructive opportunistic behaviour. Thus, although the franchisor may not necessarily want uncontrolled intrapreneurship, it is inevitable. Furthermore, in certain contexts it has been recognized that it can make an extremely positive contribution to the system. The challenge for the franchisor is to capture, harness and convert the best of opportunistic behaviour into system-wide adaptation and renewal.

Person and power cultures

From the foregoing, it would appear that management of the franchisor/franchisee relationship requires to achieve a balance between the following two modes, which should not be regarded as mutually exclusive:

- system integrity mode with detailed contracts and standard operations procedures that articulate a strong power culture, extensive monitoring, explicit regulations, business systems, quality assurance and control;

- innovation and organizational renewal mode in the development of a partnership with a strong person culture, extensive socialization, shared values, open communication, quality improvement, involvement in decision making and planning.

These two modes clearly blend person and power cultures. The power culture drives the disciplines and controls, which are essential parts of the mechanisms by which the success of franchise system standardization is achieved (Dewhurst and Burns, 1993). This dictates a system closely tied to central monitoring and decision making with a clearly defined hierarchy and delineated authority and responsibility. The person culture emphasizes individual autonomy and interpersonal relationships. Control is exercised through mutual accountability, and the aim is to maximize individual discretion and innovation (Fieldman, 1989). This supportive environment has the potential to result in the development of franchisees, each of whom requires strong self-efficacy and self-confidence to become a productive system and market satisfier. One company that subscribes to this approach is the Inn Partnership owned by Namura. It recognizes that critical to the success of the system is the quality and skills of 'independent' business people (franchisees) who are committed to realizing commercial opportunities. The franchisees acknowledge and accept the centralized control function necessary for the company to continue to be at the forefront of pub retailing in the UK. It has specific policies in place aimed at instigating, rewarding and supporting intrapreneurial spirit and enthusiasm. The company's philosophy centres on business growth but in a controlled and well-managed way, which maximizes business satisfaction and develops the franchisees.

It can be observed that policies and management styles can be deliberately designed to impact positively on the franchisees' feelings, attitudes and behaviours, engaging them on an emotional level to be motivated, interdependent system players. Especially within service sector organizations this emotional engagement is essential in the cloning of customer satisfaction in the manner conceived in the original, proven, franchise business concept. Consequently, the franchise system must be viewed as an integrated social system, with arrangements held together by formal contracts and informal relationships, formed into a federal structure (Bradach, 1998). An important aspect of this is the deliberate socialization of franchisees into the system. In doing so, the franchisor is making an attempt to control, or socially engineer, franchisees' behaviour in a proactive manner.

The aim is to encourage shared and constructive innovation, and avoid dysfunctionality and destruction of the system. In this manner, the franchisees may not feel the need to act opportunistically outside the standardized procedures of the franchise system. This process can be enhanced through the identification and enlistment of key franchisee influencers to assist in socialising franchisees into the system. Price (1997) advocates that such an integrated social system approach can lead to economic effectiveness, learning and innovation. The development of shared values, soft contracting and trust provide the opportunity for powerful win–win relationships and heightened innovation levels. So important is this aspect, that it is considered vital that the process of socialization is commenced by franchisors at recruitment and induction stage and sustained over the life of the franchisee's contract. This can take a number of forms, such as the 'hard' stipulation that potential franchisees must work in the company unpaid for nine months prior to opening their own franchise (see Lashley in Chapter 11). An example of a 'softer' approach is that of Wimpy. It organizes an annual programme of social, team and charity events for its franchisees and their employees. For example, the top performing fifteen Wimpy franchisees in the Customer Service Awards took part in an outdoor team-building event. The winners were split into teams for the day's activities, which included rally driving, Honda Pilots, clay pigeon shooting, archery, pistol shooting and fly fishing. The teams competed against each other and the winners won a Concorde trip to Paris.

Plural organizational structure

As a consequence of divergent management tendencies and cultures, a plural organizational structure requires to be carefully constructed to enable the effective implementation of appropriate system integrity and organizational innovation and renewal modes. This can result in many types of configuration; for example, McDonald's formally restricts franchisees to a maximum of four restaurants. This is in order to avoid the franchisee sub-organizational structure becoming like a company in structure and control, and the potential loss of intrapreneurial capability. According to Bradach (1998), the attraction of a plural form of organizational structure is its capacity to provide uniformity and system-wide adaptation, control and innovation. It has two key features: balancing the amount of similarity and difference between the two arrangements; and building processes that link both arrangements.

This takes cognisance of the fact that part of the structure requires to be more fluid and individualistic in nature, while more functional, routine activities can be managed in a standardized and formalized manner. The challenge, therefore, is to provide appropriate organizational constructs, which are open, receptive and dynamic, allowing sufficient accessible channels as outlets for franchisees' entrepreneurial energies. Thus, provided well-developed intrapreneurial systems and prescribed areas of empowerment discretion are established, it should be possible for all franchisees to contribute their ideas and expertise. Of course, this is supposing that they are sufficiently committed to the sustenance and success of their business and the franchise system. However, it would be wrong to regard it as a static partnership. Changes occur as parties, and the business itself, grow and develop along a life-cycle trajectory (Johnson and Kemp, 1994).

Figure 4.4 incorporates the above dimensions, demonstrating the forward momentum of the franchise organization. It provides a plural structure in that it separates the management of system integrity and innovation and renewal, but links the two arrangements through a 'bouncing ball' approach. This enables the injection of innovation, appropriate to the stage in the life-cycle trajectory of the franchise system, while ensuring the integrity of the system.

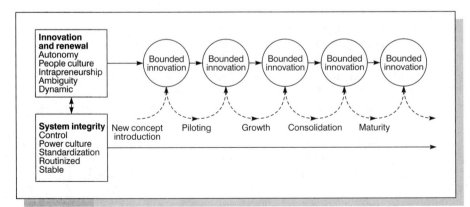

Figure 4.4 The 'bouncing ball' organizational structure

Summary

In this chapter it has been proposed that the ensurance of system integrity and the capability for innovation and organizational renewal are key dimensions of franchise systems, within which the driving dynamics are autonomy and control. Consequently, franchise systems represent a blend of two management modes: integrity and power culture, and innovation and people culture. Franchisors need explicitly to recognize this and develop appropriate policies and management styles which are designed deliberately to 'socially engineer' franchisees with strong self-efficacy and self-confidence, and emotionally to connect them in the system, to become productive system and market satisfiers.

Specifically, the management of innovation and organizational renewal has been considered within the context of one strand of entrepreneurship theory, that of intrapreneurship. It has been identified that intrapreneurship may be deliberate and induced by franchisors' policies and practices. Conversely, it may be autonomous and emergent from the creative efforts of franchisees, requiring the implantation of a mechanism to capture, harness and convert the best of opportunistic behaviour into system-wide adaptation and renewal. This requires a filtering process to be applied to the innovations arising from intrapreneurship. To ensure the integrity of the system some form of separation or isolation mechanism is necessary until the point when the franchisor is confident that the innovation can be successfully transferred system-wide to contribute to organizational renewal.

It is concluded that there is a need formally to prescribe and communicate the boundaries of constructive intrapreneurial behaviour. Furthermore, it is clear that central to the management of intrapreneurship in franchise systems are the relational conditions established and nurtured between the partners in the relationship – the franchisor and the owner–operator franchisees. In this respect, it is essential that franchisors view their franchisees as strategic human assets, partnered in the process of managed intrapreneurship, however relative the term 'partner' may be. These assets merge with the franchise system in a plural organizational structure that builds bridges between the two arrangements designed to ensure system integrity and innovation and organizational renewal as it progresses through its life-cycle trajectory.

Debate topics

- The relationship between the franchisor and franchisee cannot truly be regarded as a 'commercial marriage' given its asymmetric nature.

- A person selecting to enter into a franchise contract as a means of business entry does not possess the traits and characteristics generally associated with entrepreneurs.

- Without emergent innovation originating from the franchisees, franchise systems will not sustain a competitive advantage in the long term.

Selected readings

Lessem, R. (1987) *Intrapreneurship*. Gower.

Morrison, A., Rimmington, M. and Williams, C. (1998) *Entrepreneurship in the Hospitality, Tourism and Leisure Industries*. Butterworth-Heinemann.

Price, S. (1997) *The Franchise Paradox*. Cassell.

References

Bradach, J. (1998) *Franchise Organizations*. Harvard Business School Press.

British Franchise Association (1996) *Considering Franchising*. British Franchise Association.

Burgleman, R. (1983) Corporate entrepreneurship and strategic management: insights from a process study. *Management Science*, December, pp. 1349–63. Quoted in Kuratko, D., Montagno R., Hornsby, J. (1990) Developing an entrepreneurial assessment instrument for an effective corporate entrepreneurial environment. *Strategic Management Journal*, **11**, 49–58.

Castriogiovanni, G. and Justis, R. (1998) Franchising configurations and transitions. *Journal of Consumer Marketing*, **15** (2), 170–90.

Court, Y. (1998) *DTI: Franchising in Central Europe*. Healey and Baker.

Dandridge, T. and Falbe, C. (1994) The influence of franchisees beyond their local domain. *International Small Business Journal*, **2** (12), 39–49.

Delahunt, M. (1998) Franchising: a Strategy for Innovation or Standardization? MBA project unpublished, University of Strathclyde.

Dewhurst, J. and Burns, P. (1993) *Small Business Planning, Finance and Control*. Macmillan.

DTI (1998) *Franchising in Central Europe*. Healey and Baker.

Falbe, C. and Dandridge, T. (1992) Franchising as a strategic partnership: issues of co-operation and conflict in a global market. *International Small Business Journal*, **3** (10), 40–52.

Felstead, A. (1991) Facing up to the fragility of 'minding your own business' as a franchisee. In *Paths of Enterprise* (Curran, J. and Blackburn, R., eds), Routledge, pp. 68–87.

Ferguson, D., Berger, F. and Francese, P. (1987) Intrapreneuring in hospitality organization. *International Journal of Hospitality Management*, **6** (1), 23–31.

Fieldman, S. (1989) The broken wheel – the inseparability of autonomy and control in innovation within organizations. *Journal of Management Studies*, **25** (2), 83–102.

Forward, J. and Fulop, C. (1993) Elements of franchising: the experience of established firms. *Service Industries Journal*, **13**(4), 159–178.

Fulop, C. and Forward, J. (1997) Insights into franchising: a review of empirical and theoretical perspectives. *The Service Industries Journal*, **17** (4), 603–25.

Goss, D. (1991) *Small Business in Society*. Routledge.

Hall, G. (1995) *Surviving and Prospering in the Small Firm Sector*. Routledge.

Houston, J. (1984) *Franchising and Other Business Relationships in Hotel and Catering Services*. Heinemann.

Hoy, F. (1994) The dark side of franchising or appreciating flaws in an imperfect world. *International Small Business Journal*, **2** (12), 26–37.

Johnson, D. and Kemp, A. (1994) Strategies for expansion – franchising, acquisition and management contracts. In *Food and Beverage Management* (Davis, B. and Lockwood, A., eds), Butterworth-Heinemann, pp. 60–75.

Knowles, T. (1996) *Corporate Strategy for Hospitality*. Longman.

Lashley, C. (1997) *Empowering Service Excellence: Beyond the Quick Fix*. Cassell.

Lessem, R. (1987) *Intrapreneurship*. Gower.

Levene, T. (1998) Shop around for the best way to earn. *Scotland on Sunday*, 20 September, p. 11.

Lloyd, S. (1987) *New Forms of Enterprise: From Intrapreneurship to Spin-off*. Small Business Research Trust.

Lovelock, C. (1991) *Services Marketing*. Prentice-Hall.

Macmillan, A. (1996) *Aspects of Franchise Recruitment*. International Franchise Research Centre, Special Studies Series No. 8, University of Westminster Press.

Mendelsohn, M. (1996) *How to Evaluate a Franchise*. The Royal Bank of Scotland.

Mendelsohn, M. and Acheson, D. (1996) *How to Franchise Your Business*. The Royal Bank of Scotland.

Morrison, A. (1996) Small Firm Strategic Alliances: the UK Hotel Industry. Unpublished PhD thesis, University of Strathclyde.

Morrison, A. (ed.) (1998) *Entrepreneurship: an International Perspective*. Butterworth-Heinemann.

Morrison, A. (1999) Pierre Victoire – the drama. *Hospitality Review,* **1** (1), 3–10.

Morrison, A., Rimmington, M. and Williams, C. (1998) *Entrepreneurship in the Hospitality, Tourism and Leisure Industries*. Butterworth-Heinemann.

Price, S. (1997) *The Franchise Paradox*. Cassell.

Reve, T. (1990) The firm as nexus of internal and external contracts. In *Reindustrialization and Technology* (Aoki, M., Gustafsson, B. and Williamson, O., eds), Longman, pp. 133–161.

Siropolis, N. (1990) *Small Business Management*. Houghton Mifflin.

Stanworth, J. (1995) A European perspective on the success of franchise relationships. Presented at the Ninth Annual Conference of the Society of Franchising, San Juan, Puerto Rico, January.

Stanworth, J. (1998) *National Westminster Bank/BFA Survey*. British Franchise Association.

Waldinger, R., Ward, R. and Aldrich, H. (1985) Ethnic business and occupational mobility in advanced societies. *Sociology,* **19** (4), 586–97.

West, S. (1996) Avoiding pitfalls on the path to fiscal success. *Scotland on Sunday,* 14 April, p. 7.

CHAPTER 5

Empowered franchisees?

Conrad Lashley

Key points

- Many branded hospitality service organizations have experienced growth through the use of techniques borrowed from the manufacturing industry to establish predictable and standardized brands that lend themselves to being franchised.

- During the twentieth century human resource managerial concern shifted from employee relations and the reduction of industrial conflict to globalization and international competition, within which franchising has a significant role to play.

- Inherent in the franchisor/franchisee relationship are certain organizational arrangements to which franchisees will respond in a personalized manner relative to the degree to which they perceive the arrangements to be a benefit or a liability.

- The meaningful and valued empowerment of franchisees within a franchise system represents one management approach designed to build on a sense of personal efficacy and engage franchisees on both an emotional and business level.

Introduction

Service organizations, particularly those offering high volume consumer services, have developed distribution networks which are delivered through multi-unit organizations where the units are located close to their customers. Although they operate on a scale generally larger than independent firms, most fast food, themed restaurant and public house businesses have limited opportunities to gain from economies of scale because units need to be within easy reach of customers. Traditionally, this type of organization runs hundreds or thousands of establishments, and there has been a corresponding growth in organization structures – narrow span of control and multi-tiered bureaucracies.

Over recent years many of these organizations have gone through at least two phases. In the first phase, organizations increased control over the organization's activities, and in the second they have attempted to maintain that control whilst looking for ways to give unit managers more freedom to develop the business at local level. One senior executive of a major brewery chain explained: 'In the 1970s and 1980s we looked for ways of increasing our control of what went on in the pubs. Now we realize that we have reached the limit. Future profit growth will only come from tapping the talents and abilities of those closest to the business and its customers.'

This has resulted in organizational managers looking to the redesign of the traditional structure to what Goffee and Scase (1995) call 'adhocracies' – organizations that attempt to be both large and small, centralized in strategic direction but decentralized in tactical operation, global and local. Whilst there are many different terms to describe these organizations and many different forms that the redesign can take, franchising business units and 'empowering' local entrepreneurs to make more business related decisions is a common feature within service firms. Indeed, the British Franchise Association's annual directory for 1999 shows that all the key categories of franchises relate to service franchises. Catering and hotel service franchises are the second largest grouping, accounting for 19 per cent of all franchise operations in the UK. Table 5.1 summarizes the level of British franchise activity by industry category.

Franchisees are encouraged to act as 'independent' entrepreneurs, making the necessary 'nips and tucks' to the service offer to match local conditions. It is, thereby, hoped that franchisees' experiences and immediate unit knowledge will assist the organization to respond more quickly to both current and future service needs. Like other initiatives that aim to manage tensions between autonomy and control (see Chapter 4), franchisees in

Business category	No. franchise systems	No. franchisees
Building and maintenance services	47	1080
Catering and hotels	65	3675
Cleaning services	27	1775
Commercial and industrial services	81	1595
Direct selling, distribution, etc.	78	3995
Domestic, personal and caring services	40	1680
Employment agencies, training	24	8300
Estate agents, business transfer agents	20	430
Parcel, courier and taxi services	21	1520
Printing and copy, graphic design	12	600
Retailing	106	4785
Vehicle services	39	2035

Source: NatWest/BFA Franchise Survey (1998)

Table 5.1 British franchise business categories

service organizations have to manage their business in a way that is constrained by a framework determined at senior levels within the franchisor organization. The nature of the brand being offered to customers, and the need to provide a standardized offer, limits the individual's freedom to meet customer requirements. Standardized systems, centrally determined sources of product supply, and rigid operating procedures may also create restriction. The individual's response to these tensions is likely to be a key factor in determining whether franchisees see these arrangements as a benefit or liability. To be successful franchisees need to develop a sense of self, or personal efficacy and be convinced that they can make a difference to the performance of the business.

The franchisor context

Many of the current nostrums for organizations in the twenty-first century have a much longer tradition than the updated terminology suggests. There has been a strand of criticism of organizations designed on principles of 'Scientific Management', and legal rational authority resulting in the growth of large industrial bureaucracies and monopoly capital (Braverman, 1974), stretching back to the beginning of the twentieth century and the origins of Taylor's (1947) approach. By the 1990s the focus of managerial concern had shifted from employee relations and the reduction of industrial conflict to globalization and international competition. A key concern was the organization structure. The very strengths of the formal and mechanistic organization structure were now seen as its weakness in allowing firms to compete in the fast changing competitive international market. There has been a recognition that the down-side of economies of scale adopted by the massive commercial organizations which dominate production and distribution in many Western economies is the growth of inflexibility and a sense of powerlessness amongst managers. The diseconomies of scale resulting from the growth of bureaucracy, longer lines of communications, a lack of customer orientation and organizational atrophy can limit the benefits enjoyed by large organizations.

Many firms have adopted a range of organizational strategies which are designed to 'maximize flexibility and minimize costs' (Goffee and Scase, 1995: xiii):

- sub-contracting out activities that were previously done in-house;

- management buy-outs of non-core activities;

- the establishment of shell corporations co-ordinating the activities of complex networks of small suppliers;

- the encouragement of 'intrapreneurship';

- franchising

are all examples of responses to a perception that greater competitive advantage can be gained from removing the restrictions of bureaucratic structures. In manufacturing, for example, particularly in the electronics sector (in Silicon Valley), organization forms have developed which are 'characterized by semi-permeable boundaries where strategic alliances and collaborative partnerships are a crucial component of the system; organizations break from centralized hierarchies to become federations and constellations of multiple business units' (Mabey *et al.*, 1998, p. 182). Ferlie and Pettigrew (1998, p. 200) stress the importance of the examples of Italian textile industrial districts as models of future organization:

> 'Certainly many large organizations are unbundling themselves into loosely coupled flotillas of smaller organizations.'

As stated above, the service sector underwent early development by adopting organizational forms and ideas that had been borrowed from the manufacturing sector. As large service brands and multi-unit businesses were established, the organization structures and management thinking were largely those in which the management 'take on the persona of military personnel' (Ferlie and Pettigrew, 1998, p. 200). The operating procedures, decision making structures and organizational rules were designed to enhance control and compliance to 'one best way' of doing things. The growth of companies like McDonald's Restaurants bear witness to the success of what Levitt (1972) has described as the 'production line approach to service' and the 'industrialization of services' (Levitt, 1976, p. 63). The tendency of service firms to adopt highly rigid organization structures and principles informed by a need for efficiency, calculability, predictability, controllability, was picked up by Ritzer (1995) when he identified the 'McDonaldization of Society'. For Ritzer, all service organizations were following the principles adopted by the eponymous original. Both customers and organizations wanted efficiency, calculability, and predictability because it allowed customers on the one hand to know what the service encounter was going to deliver, the time it would take and the other benefits to be provided. For the service organization, these characteristics helped planning and limited the use of resources. The McDonaldized approach delivered greater control of the encounter. Ritzer's somewhat doom laden account of the development of services is interesting because it does highlight some important principles which were applied to the development of some service organizations.

The problem with both Ritzer's comments and this general approach is that it has limited utility. Whilst some services lend themselves to the 'production line' or 'McDonaldized' approach, other services need a more flexible front-line dependent approach. Medical and other professional services clearly require services to be provided which reflect individual service users' needs and they do not lend themselves so readily to the standardized and mass produced service. In hospitality services, there are obviously some services which are *uniformity dependent* and standardized, like McDonald's. Other services, are more *choice dependent* or *relationship dependent*. In both these latter cases, service organizations need to adopt management structures and processes that match their specific needs and are different from the traditional military structure. For example, relationship dependent services need to engage front-line staff in developing appropriate relationships with customers, and 'flatter' structures that devolve autonomy and authority. Where services are choice dependent, the organization has to encourage front-line personnel to act as 'consultants' and the organization has some characteristics of the traditional structure, but which are more consultative of service deliverers.

Even the uniformity dependent organizations have re-examined their approach to organization structures, because the local units need to be responsive to the specific requirements of local customers and has to be more flexible to respond as opportunities arise. Some organizations, even McDonald's Restaurants, have tried to flatten their structures by empowering managers to act in a more entrepreneurial way. The problem has been that managers are not entrepreneurs and that the organizations find it difficult to manage autonomy in a culture or control. The initiative under discussion in this text involves franchising units so that *'entrepreneurs'* become more empowered as a means of creating a more flexible and responsive organization. The aim being that franchisees have the autonomy to build the business in a way that is relevant to their customer base.

The decision to franchise hospitality service units is, therefore, motivated by a desire to encourage franchisees as entrepreneurs. 'Independent' business owners, close to their markets, are best able to develop those markets and run the business in a flexible way to meet business demands. Many organizations feel that franchisees at local level will be better able to spot opportunities, develop relationships with key market segments, reflect customer tastes and needs, and manage costs more effectively. This corresponds to agency theory as discussed in Chapter 1.

Resource allocation theory (see Chapter 1) suggests that franchising can reduce operating costs, as there are fewer overheads on any given level of output. The franchisees are now responsible for delivering a bottom line rental or other payment and the organization does not need to be involved in the detailed running of the unit. In many cases ownership of the franchise unit premises reverts to the franchisor if the relationship ends or the franchisee's business fails. In other cases, the franchisor is the landlord to whom the franchisee pays rent. The ownership or title to the unit premises is an important consideration in hospitality services, particularly where the key to success is often said to be *'location, location, location'*. Franchising represents, therefore, a relatively low cost way of expanding the hospitality service brand using the franchisee's capital, expertise and effort, with limited risk to the franchisor. However, Morrison in Chapter 6 questions the proposition that franchising truly represents a low cost expansion strategy. Table 5.2 confirms the importance of this motive to franchisors operating both managed and franchised

Franchising is my company's primary means of expanding the business	44%
Franchising is of major importance in expanding my business	40%
Franchising plays some role helping my business expand	11%
Franchising is of little importance in helping my business expand	1%
Franchising does not figure in my future plans	4%

(Base: franchisors operating company owned and franchised units)
Source: NatWest/BFA Franchise Survey **(1998)**

Table 5.2 Relative importance of franchising in business development

units. The survey by the National Westminster Bank and the British Franchise Association showed that 84 per cent of the firms in the study regarded franchising as a major means of expanding the business.

In summary, many branded hospitality service organizations have experienced growth through the use of techniques borrowed from manufacturing industry to establish uniform, predictable and standardized brands. Although these frequently offered customers limited choice, they did help to provide customers with recognisable service offers which were consistent. The growth in size of these organizations has not been without problems as the cultures and bureaucratic procedures through which to manage predictability and efficiency have stifled flexibility and initiative. Alternative organization forms as a way of overcoming some of the difficulties inherent in these approaches have brought success. Franchising is one approach that offers the franchisor organization many benefits including:

- a flatter structure more responsive to customers and changes in service needs;
- new ideas, products and services through the innovative and creative franchisees;
- attention to service quality and customer needs at the point closest to customers;
- reduced operating costs through flatter structures and reduced administration costs;
- increased business activity with lower capital risk;
- improved purchasing power with suppliers through increased sales volume.

The franchisor organization

Most franchisor organizations require the franchisees to work to a standardized branded offer. The brand gives it presence in the market place. However, the brand represents a degree of conformity that constrains the supposedly independent franchise, and franchisor organizations therefore cannot absolve themselves from monitoring the franchisee operation. The Pierre Victoire franchised restaurant company, which went into receivership in 1998, clearly illustrated that an organization that forgets this principle will soon find itself in difficulties with its service and customers. In other words, customers expect a brand to deliver standardized, predictable and calculable service experiences, and the franchisor organization has to ensure that customers both know what to expect and have their expectations met. McDonald's very tight restrictions on the allocation of franchises. Even ex-employees must have reached the level of area supervisor before they may become a franchisee. Applicants from outside the company must undertake 2000 hours of work in a McDonald's restaurant before they are allowed to buy a franchise (see Chapter 11).

Leading from this, a particular problem for many franchise organizations is that they have to manage the tension between standardization and control, with entrepreneurial freedom and flexibility. The two examples mentioned earlier provide some insights into the difficulties. In the Pierre Victoire case, the organization was successful in attracting would be restaurateurs to the business, but had little by way of a standardized brand and operating system. The outcome was local entrepreneurship and freedom, but with an ill-conceived brand offer. Customers started to experience service variation and inconsistency between restaurants. Individual franchisees began to lose custom and had difficulties generating repeats. In contrast, the McDonald's brand provides a highly structured, 'tight' operating system, but which is controlled to a point that allows limited flexibility and variation by the franchisee. Hence the very high barriers to entry. In the McDonald's case, the franchisor wants to make sure that the franchisee will behave in a way consistent with the company's systems and procedures.

All franchisor organizations have to balance several opposing tensions. The brand requires centralized and standardized operating systems which customers know and understand. Potential customer confusion is reduced when all units in the franchise system deliver a common set of products and services. Yet the franchise organization has to be **decentralized** sufficiently to encourage creativity and franchisee responsiveness to local service needs. The franchise organization requires to be **stable** so that all members – both direct employees and franchisees – know the organization's mission and objectives, yet it needs to encourage **dynamism** so that the services reflect and respond to changes in customer needs and environmental circumstances. Clearly many hospitality service organizations offer brands that are uniform and meet customer security needs, but increasingly services require to reflect customers as individuals. Hence they need to manage **diversity**, reflecting individual and regional variations and tastes.

Hospitality franchisor organizations have formulated brands in traditional organization structures which developed strong command and control cultures; this was a bi-product of establishing the brand. The problem is that these cultures experience tensions when franchising is introduced, because they have to retain brand standards and control, yet the organization is no longer a single entity. They have to manage the tensions inherent in the relationship between franchisees and franchisor organization. Table 5.3 lists some of the differences in organization structures when an organization introduces franchising.

Franchisor organizations do not have a single centre of power and decision making. Unlike the traditional command and control organization, franchise organizations have multiple centres, because individually franchisees have rights and obligations within the relationship that limit the ability of the franchisor to command and control. At the very least, franchisees have a degree of tactical control, which puts some limits on the franchisor's ability to impose uniformity. It is, perhaps, not surprising that Stanworth reports (1999, p. 43): 'franchisors did indicate problems in maintaining what they felt was a satisfactory level of control over franchisees'. Collectively,

Traditional model	Franchise model
Single centre	Multiple centres
Self-contained	Steeples of expertise
Independent activities	Interdependent units
Vertical integration	Multiple alliances
Uniform structure	Diverse structure
Emphasis of efficiency	Emphasis of flexibility

Table 5.3 A comparison of organization attributes

franchisees can exercise more significant influence on the franchisor. The recent decision of some Pierre Victoire franchisees to buy the brand name (see Chapter 7) is a useful example of the way franchisees can join forces and operate with, or against, the franchisor organization.

Although the franchisor organization initially contains system expertise and can support franchisees with guidance and advice, franchising involves steeples of expertise rather than centralized self-contained experts found in the traditional structure. Franchisees have immediate knowledge of the conduct of the business on the front-line. They have knowledge of the array of business functions as these impact on their business. There is therefore a symbiotic relationship in which both the franchisor and the franchisee are experts. Theoretically, both seek and give advice.

Strictly speaking, the franchise system represents an interdependent relationship. Unlike the relationship an organization might have with its suppliers or customers, the franchisor cannot operate as an independent business in relation to the franchisees. The franchisee is both a client as a source of income, and a partner in expanding and operating the business. The franchisor has to balance immediate self-interest with the need to support and encourage the partner organization – the franchisee. Stanworth (1999) suggests franchisors recognize that a consequence of franchising requires that franchisors exercise a more negotiated and persuasive approach to franchisees than might be applied in directly managed units.

Multiple alliances develop between franchisees, and between franchisees and the franchisor organization. The organization needs to develop a sense of mutual purpose, objectives and rewards. Again, difficulties arise because of the tensions inherent in the relationship, where income for one organization is cost for the other, or where brand standards for one constrain and limit the actions of the other. Stanworth's study reports that some 40 per cent of franchisees felt that a national body representing the interest of franchisees was needed (see Chapter 2), though a majority seemed more concerned with the potential further impact on their freedom of action.

Diversity in the structure in the organization aids the ultimate health and survival of all the parties. Yet diversity taken too far leads to confusion in the marketplace. Where do local responsiveness and creativity and the encouragement of diversity end and market confusion, variable standards and chaos begin? In many cases, the franchisor retains a high degree of operational and strategic control of franchisee actions through the contract, issued by the company with few opportunities for franchisee amendment (Stanworth, 1999).

The management of franchise organizations in hospitality services requires, therefore, the management of several tensions. These tensions have been summarized in Figure 4.3. If the franchisee has to work within the standards of the brand offer, they have to be prepared to experience limits and boundaries to enterprise. As Morrison argues (Chapter 4), the franchisee represents a form of restricted entrepreneur, which she argues is in fact an 'intrapreneur'. Some other commentators have described the franchisee as occupying a point midway between the independent entrepreneur and the large corporate manager. The supposedly independent business is enmeshed within the larger organization. As we have seen, the organization is often motivated to franchise its units as a way of overcoming the rigidities experienced by the growth of service organizations. That said, the tensions and contradictions do not disappear, and the success or failure of the franchise relationship will depend in large part on the ability of both parties to live with the ambiguities and tensions inherent in the relationship.

Managing the tensions

The tensions between the rigid operating system of the brand, and the constrained independence of the franchisor has led some commentators to pose the question 'Your own boss or supervised employee?' (Stanworth, 1999, p. 40). The formal independence in the relationship can be explored through the legal contract between the franchisor and franchisee, 'some of the provisions seemed to closely circumscribe the franchisee's actions as an independent businessman' (Stanworth, 1999, p. 41). In some cases, the contract restricts the sale of the business without first refusal to the franchisor. In other cases, details of confidential business transactions have to be shared with the franchisor, and 'in one franchise in the study, the franchisor was entitled to 10 per cent of the sale price of an outlet when it changed hands' (Stanworth, 1999, p. 41). Furthermore, the same study indicated that over 50 per cent of the franchisees felt that the contract favoured the franchisor whilst 40 per cent felt that it was neutral and just 4 per cent felt it favoured the franchisee.

Franchisees are prepared to put up with constraints on their freedom because they receive other benefits from the relationship. The franchisee buys into a business format that has already been tested. This in part reduces the risk to the franchisee compared with starting a new business. The NatWest European Franchise Survey (1997) reports that in the UK just under 9.5 per cent of franchisees withdraw from the franchise each year, 5.3 per cent of these are forced to withdraw because of business failure or through the actions of the franchisor. The same survey reports that 90 per cent of UK franchisees are profitable. However, Price (Chapter 3) challenges the very premise of these calculations.

The franchise has established a brand name, and the franchisee gets the benefit of this plus the large-scale advertising and promotional campaigns which support it. In many cases, franchisees are provided with both operational and business management training by the franchisor. Similarly, site selection and general business start-up assistance is available to the franchisee. Pre-opening staff training, detailed operating manuals and on-going advice are all typically supplied by the franchisor. Unlike the independent entrepreneur, the franchisee has the support of the larger, experienced franchisor to call on. Even though there are some conflicts and tensions between the two parties, it is in the franchisor's interest to see franchisees succeed.

In many ways the franchisee is operating in an empowered context. Like empowered managers or employees, the franchisee has to be prepared to work within a system designed by the franchisor's management, and accept the constraints and limits set. Participative and delayered forms of empowerment require the empowered employee to accept the system devised by management (Lashley, 1997). They must be prepared to work within the boundaries set, and develop a clear understanding of both their responsibilities and their authority.

Franchisees are in principle independent businesses and for the franchisor the direct supervision of subordinate managers is not possible. Area managers have a more consultative role and spend less time with each franchisee. In McDonald's Restaurants the company role responsible for working with clusters of franchisees is called the Operations Consultant, emphasizing the change in the role from Area Supervisor in the managed restaurant hierarchy. 'Reducing bureaucracy requires more than removing jobs and becoming more lean. It requires an attitude shift on the part of people in the middle to become more empowered to do what is best for themselves and for the business' (Block, 1987, p. 1). They require less direction over their actions and are more likely to act within operational guidelines and run the business towards their own objectives. That said, there is a difference between a hands-off encouragement of autonomy and empowerment of franchisees, and limited contact and neglect. Stanworth's study (1999) revealed that most franchisees reported that it was they who mostly initiated contact and that less than 10 per cent of franchisees were visited once per fortnight or more. Indeed, when questioned as to the degree of on-going contact he had with his franchisees, one French restaurant franchisor is quoted as saying nonchalantly, 'it is their business not mine – I leave them in the corner to marinate!'. In fact, such neglect was one factor leading to the downfall of this particular franchise system.

The measure of degree of empowerment as experienced by franchisees is similar to that experienced by empowered subordinates. The question that attempts to establish 'what can you do' is essential in defining the objective nature of differences in working practice between franchised and managed units. Here changes to the boundaries of authority are interesting, because they can help in establishing the degree to which franchisees are taking on decision making tasks which are the domain of more senior managers in the managed structure. For franchisees, there is a genuine change in the decisions that they can make. They have more latitude to spend money on new equipment, staffing or advertising without reference to a senior colleague, as would be the case in the managed units. On the other hand, particularly in tightly branded businesses, the franchisee is not usually able to make changes to the product list or operating systems. They are allowed to manage their unit without direct instruction from senior managers but would be expected to operate 'within brand'. They have what Freidmann (1977) called, 'responsible autonomy' in that they are allowed autonomy to operate within set boundaries. Clearly the scope of the boundaries varies between organizations and generally franchisees have more autonomy than would typically be the case in managed units, but there are limits within which they have to operate. Stanworth suggests that franchisors had responsibility for the overall brand offer (pricing, product mix, quality auditing), whilst the franchisees were responsible for the more tactical decisions (opening hours, staffing, book-keeping, meeting service quality standards, local advertising and such like). Table 5.4 summarizes the findings of questions put to both franchisees and franchisors about the limits of authority. Interestingly, although there is broad agreement between the responses of franchisees and franchisors, there were sizeable minorities who held contrary views.

Franchisees need to be convinced that their role and authority are meaningful and that they have some degree of control over the things that they regard as important. Franchisees, like other empowered individuals, soon recognize the inconsistencies if they are told that they are independent, but senior managers in the franchisor organization retain all the important decisions, or 'steam in' with instructions and a directive style when problems arise. The responses to the questions in Table 5.4 show that there is a degree of ambiguity and perceptual differences between the two

Operational elements	Question	Franchisor's view (% agree)	Franchisee's fee (% agree)
Additions/deletions to the product/ service	Mainly or totally the decision of the franchisor	93.3	55.3
Responsibility for pricing	Mainly or totally the decision of the franchisor	80.0	62.8
Hours of operation	Mainly or totally the decision of the franchisee	64.6	76.1
Employment of staff/ staff wage levels	Mainly or totally the decision of the franchisee	60.0/93.3	93.5/86.4
Bookkeeping	Mainly or totally the decision of the franchisee	73.3	85.1
Quality of service to the customer	Mainly or totally the decision of the franchisee	44.7	74.4
Local advertising	Mainly or totally the decision of the franchisee	33.3	91.6

Source: Stanworth (1999)

Table 5.4 Views on the operational elements of franchised outlets

parties. These ambiguities can be the source of friction and frustration, and managers within the franchisor organization need to understand the franchisee's position. An understanding of the motivational dimension of empowerment can assist these managers in seeing the tensions inherent in the franchisee's position.

Conger and Kanungo (1988, p. 471) attempt to provide some explanations of the empowerment process which can be helpful for understanding the franchisee and those contextual factors which are likely to influence the development of feelings of powerlessness and feelings of empowerment in organizational life. First they draw a distinction between concepts of empowerment which are **relational** and those which are **motivational**. Relational constructs stress the power relationships between individuals at different levels in the hierarchy. They state that this focus has led to the development of approaches to the relationship between organization members which equate, even out or redistribute power between levels in the hierarchy. Techniques that involve more participation and involvement can be seen to apply to the franchise relationship because of the nominal independence of franchisor and franchisee. The key problem is that the focus on the independence of the franchisee does not address the experience of being a franchisee. Hence, franchising can be used as an operational rhetoric to cover quite different degrees of involvement, forms, levels, ranges of issues to be addressed and power to influence decisions. As was discussed earlier, the experience of being a franchisee can be quite different in different organizations, and these experiences are not always empowering.

Empowerment as a motivational construct relies more on an understanding of empowerment through individuals' internal needs for power and control (McClelland, 1975) and feelings of personal efficacy (Bandura, 1986). Under this model, individuals perceive themselves as having power when they are able to control events or situations and deal effectively with the environments and situations which they encounter. Conversely, individuals are likely to feel powerless in situations which they cannot influence or where they do not have the time, resources or skills to be effective. From a motivational perspective, power is intrinsic, based on a need for self-determination, and managers should adopt techniques that strengthen the franchisee's needs for self-determination and personal efficacy. Sparrowe (1994) adds that to be effective in generating feelings of empowerment, the empowered have to both value that which they have been empowered to do, and feel that their empowerment encompasses meaningful actions.

Under this motivational construct of empowerment, franchisees are enabled through the development of the franchisee's sense of personal efficacy. Implicitly this means that the franchisee's perceptions of their ability to cope in situations, where they value success and can exercise a range of judgements and skills that they value, become paramount. Effective management needs to be aware that heightened motivation to complete organizational tasks and aspire to greater organizational goals will be achieved through the development of a 'strong sense of personal efficacy' (Conger and Kanungo, 1988, p. 474). Using the motivational construct, they define empowerment as:

> a process of enhancing feelings of self-efficacy among
> organizational members through the identification of
> conditions that foster powerlessness and through their

removal by both formal organizational practices and informal techniques of providing efficacy information.

For Conger and Kanungo, relational models of empowerment may or may not provide necessary conditions for the empowerment of franchisees. Thus a redistribution of power over organizational resources, with more participative forms of empowerment through franchising units, may provide an environment in which individuals develop a sense of personal efficacy; however, they are not guarantees of feelings of personal efficacy in themselves.

This focus on the motivational concept of empowerment does allow a consideration of the possibility of individuals developing a sense of personal efficacy even in situations where there has been no alteration to relational power. Organizations can develop this sense of personal efficacy in franchisees if there is an organizational commitment to identifying those policies and practices which create barriers to its development, and changes are made so as to overcome the barriers and individuals are encouraged to track their development.

Conger and Kanungo provide a model for understanding how personal efficacy might be developed at an individual level. Whilst recognizing the significance of content theorists in suggesting that discomfort with disempowerment may stem from inner need states, for example, the need for power (McClelland, 1975) and the need for self actualization (Maslow, 1954), they look to process theory for explanations of how variations in the strengths of these needs might occur. Lawler's (1973) expectancy theory and Bandura's (1977, 1986) self efficacy theory provide for suggesting the feelings of empowerment will develop through franchisees' evaluations of the situations in which they find themselves. Put simply, this assumes a two-stage process of empowerment to result in changes in franchisee behaviour. First the franchisee has to believe that their efforts will result in an improvement in their performance, and second, that their improved performance will produce valued outcomes.

Thomas and Velthouse (1990) also suggest that individual expectancies are likely to be key to the development of feelings of empowerment. They suggest a four-dimensional model based on a cognitive assessment of their own **competence** to operate effectively in the situation, the **impact** which they as individuals can make to effective performance, the **meaningfulness** which they attach to the tasks that they undertake, and the **choice** which they can exercise. In other words, the state of empowerment is likely to be a consequence of the individual's assessment of their ability to be effective, that they can make a difference in a task which they perceive as worthwhile, and that they have some degree of freedom to act as they see fit in the situation.

Franchising involves both the objective facts of what a person is empowered to do and the subjective feelings which the individual experiences as a result. Operational systems introduced by franchisor management will, therefore, be tested against the experience and the sense of personal efficacy created. The boundaries set for the empowered (van Oudtshoorn and Thomas, 1993), the organizational processes in which the franchisees work and the management of those processes become crucial factors in the development of personal efficacy and the empowerment of franchisees.

Individual differences between franchisees are also factors that need to be considered. Orientations to work, personal needs and past experience are likely to be important factors in the way an individual interprets and responds to a particular system (Alpander, 1991). Personal experience and previous status may shape the approach to an initiative. Thus one individual may see the empowering experiences of franchising as a positive development allowing greater scope for personal growth, whilst others might view the same initiative as an increased burden, demanding an unacceptable increase in emotional contribution to their work. Stanworth (1999) reports that franchisor organizations tend to recruit franchisees who are both former paid employees and those who have some past experience of self employment. This combination of people from different backgrounds impacts on their responses to the experiences of being a franchisee.

There are therefore likely to be a number of problems in assuming that franchising units will produce a motivating state of empowerment in all franchisees. Each franchise will be judged in so far as it delivers responsibilities and authority which are worth having to an individual who has the competence to be effective and value the outcome of their efforts. Individuals will approach franchising with different personal experiences and different affiliations to work. These will all influence the way that individuals achieve the state of empowerment which will then, in turn, drive franchisee performance.

In these circumstances franchisors need carefully to consider the selection and recruitment of franchisees (see Chapter 6), as well as the training and support systems which help them to develop a shared understanding of the franchisor's system and the skills needed to be effective in the role. Overly bureaucratic and autocratic systems may well extend the franchisor's control and management of standardized hospitality products and services required of a national brand, but taken too far these systems may be counter-productive because they create feelings of disempowerment and demotivation amongst franchisees.

Most organizations that go through the process of franchising report that some individuals find it difficult to work under these arrangements. In some cases, the approach requires different skills that are not available to all franchisees. In other cases, the change in role cuts across the role expectations with which they have been socialized. Thus managers from franchisor organizations, say like McDonald's, who convert to franchisee may find their changed role difficult, because they are suddenly having to operate with less direction than they have been used to receiving (see Chapter 11). In other cases, the entrepreneurial individual may find the brand and operational system restrictions within which they have to operate too limiting. For example, an early and clearly formative experience of franchising McDonald's in the USA resulted in the franchisee introducing new menu items which were not appropriate to McDonald's. The result was an acrimonious separation, which influenced future franchisee arrangements with the company.

Barriers to empowering franchisees

As was discussed above, the generally tight definition of the brand offer to customers and the need to control the standardized service offer to the market limit the ability of franchisees to exercise judgements. This is further exacerbated by the need to take advantage of economies of scale in purchasing, advertising and promotion, and finance, which create situations where the organization's control procedures limit the freedom of franchisees. The franchisee's responsibilities and freedom of action usually restrict the franchisee's actions to a narrow range of operational decisions. This may represent an improvement from past experiences where even operational decisions were tightly managed and junior managers were subjected to command and control management. However, it may also present barriers to the franchisee which in effect mean that initiatives which claim to be empowering and entrepreneurial allow little scope for the franchisee to make any significant impact with this new found 'power'.

The impact on the management hierarchy and management progression is another issue which organizations that have introduced franchising report can cause problems. This is an aspect of adopting a franchising strategy that is frequently neglected. One of the consequences of removing one or more tiers of management and flattening the structure is that there are fewer management jobs to which junior managers can aspire. Not surprisingly, this can have a counter-productive impact on the commitment and motivation of the managers whose improved commitment is one of the objectives of the franchise arrangement. As an organization moves to franchise more of its units there can be growing concern amongst those managers who are unlikely to take on a franchise in the near future. In part these managers' concerns are about material rewards, promotion and status, but in part, they are also about expectations and past practice. Rapidly expanding branded service businesses have, in many cases, grown in such a way as to provide managers with rapid promotion prospects. Managers have learnt to live in an organization culture where colleagues were promoted quickly and most senior executives have grown with the company. Managers in these organizations come to expect rapid promotion. A flatter structure, with more franchised units, changes that and there are some shocks to manager expectations which can represent negative effects of empowerment within company-managed units.

The issue of who benefits from franchising is something that impacts on the effectiveness of all concerned. For franchisees, the perceived gain from their own enterprise and 'empowering' them is no less important. If franchisees perceive empowerment to mean that they are now under more financial pressure with little or no support from the franchisor organization, they are unlikely to develop the positive feelings upon which rest the supposed benefits of being a franchisee. Similarly, if compensation does not appear sufficient for the extra pressure and responsibilities, the supposed empowerment of being a franchisee will seem somewhat hollow. Even allowing for the possible developmental benefits of individuals taking on more responsibilities, the issue of perceived rewards is an important one because each franchisee is concerned with the personal outcomes from the working relationships. At root, the question of 'what's in it for me?' has to produce a positive response if the experience of being a franchisee is to be beneficial to both the individual and the organization. Chapter 6 considers the transaction costs economics of this relationship in more detail.

Summary

Franchising of units is a strategy followed by many service organizations. The benefits for the franchisor organization are that franchising units allow the management of multi-unit businesses in a way that both reduces costs and complexity, and delivers more responsive unit management through empowered and entrepreneurial franchisees. Internationally, McDonald's is an example of an organization that operates a large proportion of its units through franchisees. In most countries in which the company operates, over 70 per cent of the units are franchised. In the USA, the company claims that returns from these businesses out-perform those from company-managed units.

That said, franchising as an organizational strategy is not without risks. First there are tensions inherent in running a branded business that standardizes the offer to customers through consistent and planned operating systems. To some extent the tensions arise from customers who want both the certainty of knowing what the branded service will deliver, but who also want to be treated as individuals. Certainly from the franchising perspective the franchisee has to be an independent entrepreneur prepared to work within the boundaries set by the brand operating system. Secondly, franchising out units can represent a reduction in direct control by the franchisor organization. The maintenance of consistent standards across all the brand's units are now not directly in the hands of managers, and the organization has to rely on franchisees. Without effective operating systems and quality auditing processes, franchised units may soon experience inconsistencies in service quality (see Chapter 7). The now defunct Pierre Victoire restaurant company reveals the problems that can arise from too much local freedom for the franchisees. Similarly, the differences in the UK operation of McDonald's show that a concern for consistent quality may require the company to manage a higher proportion of its units.

Though rarely explicitly discussed in these terms, franchising represents an attempt to empower franchisees. Like initiatives to empower managers and employees, empowerment represents a management strategy, which aims to tap the energies, enthusiasm and commitment of the empowered. In this case, the supposed independence of the business, the direct personal reward to the franchisee and the sense of 'running their own ship' are elements in encouraging the franchisee to feel empowered. That said, franchised businesses are not truly independent. The entrepreneur does not have complete independence to operate the unit as they see fit. The brand's operating system, standards and offer to customers require consistency across all units. Franchisees have to be prepared to manage the tension between apparent independence and control by the franchisor organization. As with other initiatives, which claim to be empowering, individuals are empowered with boundaries and limits set by others. The extent to which individuals feel empowered is fundamental to the success of the approach. Both the objective nature of the boundaries set, and the subjective response to these boundaries will determine each individual's response to the experience. In other words, the boundaries set within which franchisees have to operate may be more or less empowering, and individuals will vary in their response to these limits placed upon them.

Debate topics

- Franchising represents an attempt to flatten the organizational structure and manage business through empowered franchisees to the sole benefit of the franchisor.

- Theoretically there are no potential limits and barriers to creating feelings of empowerment in franchisees.

- In voluntarily selecting franchising as a means of business entry, individuals are explicitly expressing a desire to be empowered.

Selected readings

Goffee, R. and Scase, R. (1995) *Corporate Realities: the Dynamics of Small and Large Organizations*. Routledge.

Lashley, C. (1997) *Empowering Service Excellence: Beyond the Quick Fix*. Cassell.

McClelland, D.C. (1975) *Power: the Inner Experience*. Irvington Press.

References

Alpander, G. (1991) Developing managers' abilities to empower employees. *The Journal of Management*, **10**, 13–24.

Bandura, A. (1977) Self-efficacy: towards a unifying theory of behavioural change. *Psychological Review*, **84**, 191–215.

Bandura, A. (1986) *Social Foundations of Thought and Action: Social-Cognitive View*. Prentice-Hall.

Barry, T. (1993) Empowerment: the US experience. *Empowerment in Organizations*, **1** (1), 16–26.

Beaver, G. and Lashley, C. (1998) Competitive advantage and management development in small hospitality firms: the need for an imaginative approach. *Journal of Vacation Marketing*, **4** (2), 145–60.

Block, P. (1987) *The Empowered Manager.* Jossey–Bass.

Braverman, H. (1974) *Labor and Monopoly Capital.* Monthly Review Press.

Conger, J. and Kanungo, R. (1988) The empowerment process: integrating theory and practice. *Academy of Management Review,* **13**, 471–82.

Ferlie, A. and Pettigrew, A. (1998) Managing through networks. In Mabey, C., Salaman, G. and Story, J. (eds) *Strategic Human Resource Management.* Sage.

Freidman, A. (1977) *Industry and Labour.* Macmillan.

Goffee, R. and Scase, R. (1995) *Corporate Realities: the Dynamics of Small and Large Organizations.* Routledge.

Johnson, P. (1993) Empowerment in the global economy. *Empowerment in Organizations,* **1** (1), 27–35.

Lashley, C. (1997) *Empowering Service Excellence: Beyond the Quick Fix.* Cassell.

Lawler, E. (1973) *Motivation in Work Organizations.* Brooks/Cole.

Levitt, T. (1972) Production line approaches to service. *Harvard Business Review,* September–October, 41–52.

Levitt, T. (1976) The industrialization of service. *Harvard Business Review,* October, 63–74.

Lockwood, A. (1996) Empowerment: the key to service quality – an operations perspective. *Conference Papers – Fifth Annual Hospitality Research Conference.* Nottingham Trent University, Nottingham.

Mabey, C., Salaman, G. and Story, J. (1998) *Strategic Human Resource Management.* Sage.

Maslow, A. (1954) *Motivation and Personality.* Harper.

McClelland, D. (1975) *Power: the Inner Experience.* Irvington Press.

Mitchell, D. (1979) *Control Without Bureaucracy.* McGraw–Hill.

NatWest (1997) European Franchise Survey. NatWest Retail Banking Services.

Ritzer, G. (1995) *The McDonaldization Thesis.* Sage.

Sparrowe, R. (1994) Empowerment in the hospitality industry: an exploration of antecedents and outcomes. *Hospitality Research Journal,* **17** (3), 43–56.

Stanworth, J. (1999) National Westminster Bank/BFA Survey, British Franchise Association.

Taylor, R. (1947) *Scientific Management.* Harper & Row.

Thomas, K. and Velthouse, B. (1990) Cognitive elements of empowerment: an interpretative model of intrinsic task motivation. *Academy of Management Review,* **15**, 666–81.

van Oudtshoorn, M. and Thomas, L. (1993) A management synopsis of empowerment. *Empowerment in Organizations,* **1** (1), 1–14.

CHAPTER 6

Financial fundamentals

Alison Morrison and Angus Macmillan

Key points

- Franchising is frequently presented as a low-cost approach to business development. However, that is not necessarily the most astute perspective to adopt in the creation and development of a sustainable and successful franchise system.

- For franchisors three key financial aspects are associated with the creation and development of a franchise system: franchisor fee structure; the piloting of the business concept; and franchisee recruitment costs.

- The dominant source of funding for both franchisors and franchisees is that of the major clearing banks. They generally adopt a positive stance towards lending to support ethical franchise systems, and perceive there to be a reduced risk element for franchisees in comparison to that associated with independent small business start-up.

- It is important to recognize that as a business expansion strategy franchising possesses many positive attributes. However, it is not without an element of failure, a feature that is often suppressed in the popular media.

Introduction

The generally accepted financial theory underpinning franchising as one form of expansionist strategy is that it facilitates the development of a network of outlets selling products and services in a relatively short period of time. At first glance, it would appear that this could be achieved without the need for large-scale capital investment on the part of the parent company. Franchisees are recruited to invest their own personal funds in a franchised outlet. This leads to a further financial plus, as it is frequently proposed that franchisors have the potential to benefit from the profit-driven motivation of franchisees given their financial stakeholding in their business. The fact and/or fallacy of this rhetoric will be explored during this chapter (see also Chapter 3). However, at this stage it is proposed that there must be some financial credence in the strategy given the significant growth in franchising across Europe. It is now the home of almost 170,000 franchised units, operating under some 4,000 franchise systems with a total turnover of 95.56 billion ECU. This represents a growth of 2.1 per cent over 1997 (NatWest, 1998a). In Chapter 2, from a financial perspective, Fulop attributes its popularity to the support accorded franchising, by the government and major clearing banks, as a reduced risk means of business entry.

This chapter explores the fundamental financing issues associated with franchising, from both the perspectives of franchisees and franchisors. First, is a detailed analysis of the costs and considerations associated with the creation and development of a franchise system, including franchisee recruitment. Second, the focus turns to the franchisee and the range of financial issues that prospective franchisees should be advised to consider. Third, is an exploration of the area of obtaining funds for both franchisors and franchisees. Finally, financial performance is addressed.

Creation and development of a franchise system

The strategy of business expansion via the creation and development of a franchise system has been referred to above as obviating the need for large-scale capital investment on the part of the franchisor. This is primarily due to the fact that franchisees carry some of the investment burden (Price, 1997). However, it has been observed that the promise of low-cost expansion can frequently serve to blind would-be franchisors to the typically high costs of franchise system piloting and the even more expensive task of franchise system development through to 'break-even' point. The process is heavily 'front-loaded' in the sense that a business system has to be tried-and-tested, and a management team, and fieldwork support system, put in position. This all takes place well ahead of any substantial income flow to the franchisor, maturing in the form of franchisee fees. Indeed, for most franchise systems, break-even point is estimated to take four to five years to attain and to require the establishment of around thirty to forty outlets (Costello, 1999). Franchisors who embark on national expansion too early, and according to Macmillan (1996) the vast majority (89 per cent) do, need to take into account the costs of managing and supporting a dispersed network of franchisees. Furthermore, Macmillan (1996) states that few companies embarking on creating a franchise system have a full grasp of the intricacies involved. Too many enter franchising for anticipated short-term gain, lured by the expectation of quick profits and revenues from the sale of franchises, without due regard to the long-term consequences for their franchisees.

So it would appear that the creation and development of a franchise system should certainly not be regarded as a low-cost strategy for business expansion. It requires substantial 'front-loaded' investment, sufficient working capital to provide cover until break-even point, and thereafter continuous funding of management and support for the network to fuel its prosperity. All this leads Costello (1999) to caution that new franchisors should be prepared to commit a substantial amount of time and money to establishing a network of franchisees before realizing any income. A range of costs will be incurred which may include those presented in Table 6.1.

Table 6.2 gives some further indication of the order and nature of initial costs that will be involved in the creation of a franchise system. Clearly, these costs will vary widely depending on some key factors, which include:

- the type and industry sector of business;
- the degree of conversion required from the existing concept in order to make it 'franchisable';
- the availability of the time, resources and skills within the company which is directed at franchising;
- the proposed approaches to franchising, e.g. single, multiple or master franchisees.

Three key financial aspects of creating and developing a franchise include establishing the source and amount of franchisor fee structure, the piloting of the business concept to enable system

Pilot operation	Before franchising a business the concept should be piloted. This will prove to prospective franchisees that the business can be replicated by way of franchising
Franchise support staff	The future network of franchisees will require continuous support from the head office. This will probably mean an increase in staff numbers and management capabilities in order to support this central function
Legal costs	A legal contract will be required to be drawn up by a solicitor with franchising expertise
Marketing	Publicizing the new franchise system will involve time, effort and expense. For example, it may be necessary to consider investing in national, regional or local advertising, participating in franchise exhibitions, and conducting roadshows
Recruitment of franchisees	Costs incurred for production of prospectuses, advertising, attendance at exhibitions and the time spent on the selection process
Franchise package development	This is the cost of developing the package for the franchisees. The package will provide them with all the systems, procedures and other support they need to operate successfully. The costs cover training, sales literature and operation manuals

Source: Royal Bank of Scotland (1998)

Table 6.1 Costs associated with business expansion strategy through franchising

	Cost
Professional fees, accountant, consultant, solicitor, agreements/trademarks, etc.	£20,000
Training and operations manuals, research, compiling, printing	£15,000
Corporate identity, logos and prospectus (design and printing)	£10,000
Advertising for initial franchisees, interviewing costs, training (continuing at approximately £2,000 per franchisee per year)	£5,000
TOTAL	£50,000

Source: Costello (1999, pp. 74)

Table 6.2 Initial costs of franchise system creation

Hospitality, Leisure & Tourism Series

development, and franchisee recruitment. Each of these is now discussed.

Franchisor fee structure

According to Acheson (1999, p. 80), 'The important maxim of franchising is simple – both parties should get rich, but not at the expense of each other.' He justifies this approach in that the selection of a franchisee should ideally commence a long-term relationship between franchisor and franchisee. As such, the franchisor must not view the franchise fee structure as a short-term solution to any cash flow difficulties, which the company may have in the early stages of launching a franchise system. Furthermore, Horne (1999) argues for complete transparency over the risk and/or reward prospects, and the payment structure of the business. This will help to minimize any discontentment some franchisees may experience later on once the system becomes established.

The setting of the franchise fees (for examples, see Chapter 8) represents one of the biggest challenges at the planning stage of a new franchise system. In the final analysis, the franchise should be constructed to ensure that the franchisor receives an acceptable return on their capital employed, and the franchisee equally should be able to obtain a return on their investment, comparable with opportunities elsewhere in the marketplace. This was not the case in the example given by Pender (Chapter 10) relative to Exchange Travel. Macmillan (1996) found that franchise fees are frequently set and monitored in an *ad hoc* fashion, largely driven by what franchisors 'can get away with', or in relation to what the competition are charging. It is also standard practice in the UK for each franchisor to have uniform franchise fees, which do not vary by territory or location. The fees are not open to negotiation.

So, in a spirit of fairness, transparency and careful calculation it has been recommended that the franchisor could ethically derive income from the following eight principal sources:

- **Initial franchise fee:** This is paid when a franchisee starts up in business. In essence the initial fee should take into account the cost of constructing the franchise concept, both initially and on a continuing basis. The amount should be apportioned among the number of franchisees which it is anticipated will be recruited over a start-up period of say three to five years. In general, most franchisors tend to set their initial franchise fee at the £5,000–£10,000 level. Wimpy, Britain's oldest-established franchise, sets the benchmark at £7,500 (whilst the total initial capital outlay may be up to £200,000). However, there are now several well-established UK franchises with a higher initial fee, for example, Mongolian Barbeque.

- **Management service fee**: The majority of franchisors derive their income from the management service fee; this is particularly relevant within the hotel sector (see Chapter 8). Based on the experience of company-owned pilot operations, the franchisor sets a percentage. This is usually taken as a percentage of the franchisee's gross sales, and generally fall within a range of 4–10 per cent. The level of fee, to be competitive in comparison with those of other franchisors already operating in the same market, will also be taken into consideration.

- **Fixed management service fee**: A franchisor may wish to impose a fixed level of management services fees. This is where that fee is pitched at a set level, regardless of the sales turnover or the level of maturity of the business. This may be problematic in two main ways. First, the franchisee could struggle to meet the fixed fee in the early days of business trading when turnover is relatively low. Second, the franchisor may be in a position where they are unable to benefit from the increased business as the franchise develops.

- **Mark-up on goods supplied**: In some cases, particularly where trademarked goods are involved, the franchise agreement compels the franchisee to buy goods from the franchisor, or a nominate supplier of the franchisor. For example, this is the type of relationship that underpins tenanted and leased pubs (see Chapter 9). Where there is a mark-up on goods supplied, the franchisor is, in fact, receiving their franchise service fee by taking a larger gross profit on the goods. This may amount to 2–10 per cent of sales.

- **Advertising fee**: A further percentage of the franchisee's gross sales is often taken as a fixed levy to cover national advertising. This may range from 1–5 per cent. Banks recommend to the franchisor that this money be placed in a separate fund for the exclusive benefit of the franchise network.

- **Administration fee for leasing of premises**: Where the head lease is taken by the franchisor and a sub-lease is granted to the franchisee, it is common to add a small fee to the rentals collected from the franchisee to cover administration costs.

- **Renewal fees**: These fees occur once the initial term of the franchise agreement has come to an end. Basically, it is a fee charged to rejoin the network. They are often calculated as a percentage of the gross profit of the proceeding year's trading figures. This could result in a substantial financial gain for the franchisor. Therefore it is essential that any renewal clause in the franchise contract sets out clearly and exactly how any fee is to be calculated.

- **Other sources of income**: In theory, the franchisor does have the opportunity of deriving further income from other sources, including the items in the start-up package which might include the lease of premises and/or equipment, and the sale of equipment. In most cases, these items or services will be passed on at cost with the addition of modest handling charges or administrative costs, which are perfectly legitimate.

From the above, it can be observed that the initial and management services fees represent the major sources of income for franchisors. Relative to the challenge of setting these at an optimum, Sen (1993) suggests the following summary of ideas to be of use in building a framework for structuring fees based on US franchisors' experience:

- initial fees should be related to the total investment required for the outlet;

- an increase in the strength of the franchised brand name should lead to higher management services fees;

- management services fees should decrease when a higher degree of downstream managerial responsibility is required;

- initial fees should increase with the length of the contract period;

- both initial and continuing service fees should decrease if the franchisor imposes mandatory purchase requirements on the franchisee for the supply of goods etc.;

- provision of more initial services, in particular the length of training and financial assistance should lead to higher initial fees;

- provision of more continuous services by the franchisor should increase management services fees;

- a higher level of environmental risk faced by the franchisee should lower initial fees and increase management services fees.

The above would suggest that the franchisor fee structure must not be regarded as static, but be under continuous review in reflection of the dynamics of the business environment being experienced. Furthermore, it is apparent that both the initial franchise fees and the on-going fees charged by a franchisor are important in structuring the franchise opportunity, as they can communicate a lot about the ethics, attitude and standing of the company (Stanworth *et al.*, 1998).

Pilot stage

It is generally accepted that new franchises principally come from two sources:

- existing companies, which wish to expand;
- individuals, partnerships or companies with a new business concept which, when proven, will be capable of being franchised.

For both of these sources the main initial task of the business concept creator, the franchisor, is to develop a tried-and-tested formula to prove that it can be transformed into a successful business. That is, to question is it franchisable? According to the NatWest (1998b), the best businesses to franchise are those with a good trading record, strong branding and marketing pro- grammes, and an established business system which can be encapsulated in an operations manual and easily passed on in a short time to newcomers. It is the responsibility of the potential franchisor to invest their own money to provide that proof, primarily through a pilot operation.

For an existing company, it may need to open a new outlet or outlets to re-prove the system. Alternatively, it may designate an existing company-owned outlet for this purpose. Conversely, a new company will need to start from scratch. In both cases, it is recommended that the pilot operation is a typical outlet as to size, market area, cost etc. and one that can be cloned effectively in due course when the franchise is ready to be launched. Therefore, it is difficult to give an indication as to the costs of a pilot operation. It will depend on how much expenditure is necessary to maximize the performance of the outlet to make it capable of being franchised.

In financial terms, the pilot operation must show that a typical outlet is capable of providing a return on the investment within a reasonable term, approximately two to four years, depending upon the basis of the calculation. If such a financial performance cannot be achieved, the business opportunity will be unlikely to attract investors and will not be competitive with comparable market opportunities. The franchisor, from their experience with the pilot operation, should be able to give reasonably accurate projections to potential franchisees of the profit and loss profile of the business. In addition, an indication of a possible growth pattern, based on the business becoming established in its particular locality, should be able to be communicated.

In summary, successful completion of the pilot stage should result in:

- a proven business concept;

- established term of return on investment;

- a full set of financial projections;

- business growth patterns.

Franchisee recruitment

Once the franchise system has been piloted and is ready for development, it is time to look towards recruiting franchisees. Macmillan (1996) found that too few franchisors fully understand the nature and extent of the costs associated with franchise recruitment. Furthermore, a significant percentage (44 per cent) of experienced franchisors indicated that they could not put a figure on the direct and indirect costs. Macmillan argues that financial expediency demands franchisors understand the costs associated with franchisee recruitment and set the initial franchise fee at an appropriate level to cover costs, including appropriate overhead allocation costs and not just direct marketing costs. He observes that too many companies ignore executive time and other overheads when reaching their calculation.

According to Lloyds Bank/IFRC (Stanworth et al., 1998), depending on which communication strategy is adopted, a combination of low enquiry-to-franchisee appointment ratios and associated marketing costs, produce recruitment costs falling typically in the range £3,000 to £10,000 per franchisee. The cost is a reflection of appreciable numbers of applicant rejections. Indeed, in Chapter 11, Lashley records that only 12.5 per cent of all applicants to McDonald's are invited to attend an interview, and only 3 per cent of these will become franchisees. Most of the more professional franchise companies convert no more than 4 per cent of initial enquiries from franchise prospectuses into sales. Even this is judged by some to be, if anything, on the high side, with 2 per cent being a better target figure.

In general, it is apparent that the manner in which recruitment costs are approached varies significantly. Many companies still enter franchising overly dependent on the initial franchise fee, either to make a significant profit or maintain the cash flow needed to keep the company in business. In these circumstances, decisions may be taken to recruit franchisees based on short-term financial imperatives rather than investing in the long-term financial viability of the franchise system.

Franchisee financial considerations

Prior to formal recruitment into the franchise system, potential franchisees are urged by the professionals to consider carefully a wide range of financial aspects. For example, in their franchisee guidance information, Barclays Bank (1999) lists the following questions for consideration, which reflects some of the areas discussed in the previous section.

- How is the franchisor remunerated?

- What is the franchise fee, the training and setting-up costs, and the volume of working capital required for day-to-day operations?

- What are the ongoing fees, and are they in the form of management services fees, or a mark-up on goods?

- What is needed in addition to the standard equipment package and can it be financed by hire purchase, leasing or contract hire?

- Are contributions to training costs and advertising and promotion levies required, and if so, the amount?

- How does the franchisor arrive at the financial projections? Are they based, for example, on the average performance of company outlets, individual franchisee performance or other criteria?

- What happens if projections are not met?

- How long does it takes to obtain a full return on the franchisee's investment?

- What is the sum of the total investment required?

Most franchisees experience a set of start-up costs when going into business. According to 85 per cent of franchisors, some sort of costs will be experienced by new franchisees. Table 6.3 shows that nearly all franchisors (96 per cent) charge an initial franchise fee, and other significant start-up costs centre on equipment, stock and working capital (NatWest/BFA, 1998).

Hospitality, Leisure & Tourism Series

Initial cost	1995 (%)	1996 (%)	1997 (%)
Equipment	59	70	66
Franchisee fee	89	94	96
Stock	50	55	43
Working capital	74	77	79

Source: The NatWest/BFA Franchise Survey (1998, pp. 28)

Table 6.3 Percentage of franchisees experiencing start-up costs

The overall level of start-up costs has varied little in the past years. In 1994 the average initial outlay was £44,900, falling to £43,700 in 1995 and £40,200 in 1996. The NatWest/BFA (1998) survey indicates an increase of the average initial outlay by 6.5 per cent to £42,800. In the same way that average franchisee sales turnover is a somewhat academic figure, so too is the initial

Initial franchise fee	This is a one-off to 'buy in' to the business
Training fees	These are sometimes included in the franchise fee, but generally they are itemized separately
Premises	Occasionally the franchisor may take the head lease and grant franchisees a sub-lease. There will sometimes be a premium and/or advance rent to pay
Shopfitting	The franchisor may have arranged for a specific firm to fit premises out in a standard format. However, the franchisee will be expected to pay
Vehicles	Franchisees may choose to purchase any vehicle outright, but are more likely to take out a lease or hire purchase agreement
Initial stock	May be purchased from the franchisor
Equipment	May be purchased from the franchisor, although franchisees may be able to hire or lease it
Working capital	The money required covering initial wages and salaries and other business expenses
Promotional costs	The cost of local advertising, mail shots etc. to assist in the launch of the business. These may be covered by the franchisor and included in the franchise fee

Source: Midland Bank (1998)

Table 6.4 Starting-up stage costs for a franchise

outlay figure. Much is dependent on the type of business that is being started up. For example, a typical property based franchisee will need to invest over £50,000, whilst a home or mobile business will require just £34,100 on average. There are also wide disparities by industry sector (see Chapters 7, 8, 9 and 10). For example, on average franchisors in hotel and catering claim £70,700 is required. Conversely, those in building or vehicle services will typically only need a third of this amount.

Factor	Baskin 31 Robbins Ice Cream	Dunkin' Donuts	Dix-Neuf Brasserie and Bar	Mongolian Barbeque	Sargent Peppers
Total investment cost (excl. working capital)	£75,000	£250,000	£100,000	£150,000	£120,000
Working capital	£30,000	£100,000	£10,000	£25,000	£15,000
Ready cash requirement	£50,000	£100,000	£50,000	£75,000	£60,000
Initial franchise fee	£5,000	£25,000	£15,000	£10,000	£10,000
On-going management services fees	No	5%	5%	4.5%	5%
Advertising levy	N/A	5%	N/A	1%	2%
Fixed fee	No	No	£230 per month	No	No
Mark up on goods	Yes	No	No	No	No
Typical outlet, projected turnover	Year 1 £100,000	Year 1 £300,000	Year 1 £464,500	Year 1 £325,000	Year 1 £500,00
	Year 2 £125,000	Year 2 £400,000	Year 2 £502,000	Year 2 £400,000	Year 2 £550,000
	Year 3 £150,000	Year 3 £500,000	Year 3 £553,000	Year 3 £450,000	Year 3 £600,00
Typical outlet, projected profit	Year 1 £25,000	Year 1 £75,000	Year 1 £74,320	Year 1 £56,000	Year 1 £85,000
	Year 2 £30,000	Year 2 £100,000	Year 2 £100,000	Year 2 £76,000	Year 2 £99,000
	Year 3 £35,000	Year 3 £150,000	Year 3 £110,00	Year 3 £90,000	Year 3 £120,00
Typical outlet, return on investment	Year 3	Year 3	Year 2	Year 3	Year 2

Source: Franchise World (1999)

Table 6.5 Catering: franchise profile comparison

Once a franchisee's business is established there will typically also be a series of recurring costs. Specifically, these include management service fee, contribution to advertising, and mark-up on goods supplied. Associated fees and costs at start-up stage are summarized in Table 6.4.

Table 6.5 presents a franchise profile comparison for the catering sector. It encompasses the range of financial considerations which potential franchisees should ascertain prior to formal recruitment. This includes initial investment and franchise fee along with recurring charges and financial projections.

Table 6.5 clearly illustrates the similarities and disparities associated with these five franchise companies, even within the same industry sector. The cause of the disparities may be due to a number of factors, including: business type; franchising approach; strength of the brand; and/or the degree of system support provided.

Obtaining funds

It is highly likely that both the franchisors and the franchisees will require to obtain funds from sources external to their own savings in order to progress their respective business ventures. This is now discussed from the respective perspectives following an overview of the positioning of the major clearing banks.

Major clearing banks

The major clearing banks are often willing to lend finance to potential investors with collateral at low rate of interest, because they perceive that franchising is low risk in comparison to starting up an independent small business (Stern, 1999). This attitude serves to reduce some of the financial barriers to entry and, consequently, the banks are supportive of ethical franchising in the UK. Most of them, such as the Royal Bank of Scotland, and Lloyds TSB have dedicated central franchise sections. These are responsible for guiding their branch offices and lending departments on the credit stance for each respective franchise system. They also have a business development role to play in building relationships with the leading franchisors in order to obtain referral business. In respect to the involvement of the clearing banks in franchising, Price (1997) takes a realistic, maybe slightly cynical, perspective. He suggests that their key motivation for entering the franchise 'advice' market is because it offers the banks a new route to broaden their business loan services. The following illustration provides an example of the range and extent of involvement in franchising undertaken by the NatWest Bank (Illustration 6.1).

Illustration 6.1 About the NatWest's franchise section

- A support service consisting of a national network of 93 area managers based at its business centres throughout the UK.

- An advisory team established for more than 15 years.

- Franchise lending through the section is in excess of £400 million.

- More than 400 seminar presentations made on franchising to institutes, including the Confederation of British Industry, Institute of Directors, Business in the Community, Institute of Marketing and Royal Society of Arts.

- It has produced an informative video and an audiocassette together with brochures to provide a better understanding of franchising and to look at essential questions that need consideration.

- Sponsorship of the annual NatWest/BFA Franchise Survey, currently in its 15th year.

- Sponsorship of the first survey of franchising covering the whole of Europe (1998).

Source: NatWest (1999)

Franchisor funding

Development of a franchise system most likely will require funding from funds external to those possessed by the franchisor. There are two principal avenues, which could be considered.

First is clearing bank finance. The case with franchising is that a bank is being asked to finance a business concept as opposed to the actual acquisition of assets. It will, therefore, look critically at the level of security cover and the viability of the projects, which form the basis of a business plan. With respect to a company with a profitable mainstream business, which is already generating profits from a core business, it has an advantage. Thus, loan facilities over a set period should be available, together with a measure of working capital as is necessary. In the case of a completely new franchise venture, financial support is not so easy to obtain and the banks will take a more cautious attitude to both the size of the fund contribution and the security cover required. Furthermore, Silvester *et al.* (1997) found that franchise systems that were able to attract bank finance at the start-up stage differed quite considerably from their unsuccessful counterparts. In particular, they appeared to take a longer-term view of their development, were more likely to join the BFA and use other external sources of advice. In addition, they were also more conservative in their expectations of franchise industry growth and had a better understanding of what motivated franchisees. In summary, for franchisors looking to finance the creation and development of a franchise system, the banks associated with franchising will normally:

- provide funding up to 60 per cent of development costs;
- offer loans for periods of up to ten years;
- provide asset finance to help establish the system;
- consider giving equity support.

A second source of funding is that of equity finance. There may be a case for looking for some element of equity finance if the franchisors are not able to raise the finance needed, or to provide a sufficient proportion of the risk capital themselves. For example, in 1999 the Dublin based O'Brien's Irish Sandwich Bars attracted an additional £1 million in funding. ICC Venture Capital, the largest venture capital firm in Ireland, made the investment in return for a 20 per cent stake in the company. The money will be used to fund O'Brien's expansion in its native Ireland and internationally. O'Brien's managing director said that ICC's participation would add credibility to the company and give it the ability to develop at a faster rate. The investment director of ICC described O'Brien's as a well-managed, entrepreneurial Irish company with a strong record of achievement and potential for worldwide growth.

Wherever the source of funding derives for the development of the franchise system, as has been emphasized earlier in this chapter, it would be a grave business mistake to underestimate the volume of 'front-loaded' funding required. This is a crucial point in its life – or death! A franchise concept may have worldwide potential but without sufficient financial resources it could easily become a local has-been.

Franchisee funding

Based on knowledge developed through thoroughly researching the associated franchisee financial considerations identified in the previous sections of this chapter, potential franchisees should be able to identify the total costs associated with the franchise package and how much of this can be met from personal financial resources. Founded on these details, the extent of borrowing to cover start-up, working capital, and recurring costs can be calculated. The need to borrow depends largely on the scale of the operation being started, personal funds and assets, and tends to be a reflection of the sector that the new franchisee chooses to enter.

Source of loans	All borrowing franchisees (%)
Bank	76
Building Society	8
Relatives/family	9
Franchisor	3
Finance house	1
Other	3
Value of loan	
Up to £10,000	28
£10,001 to £50,000	58
£50,001 plus	14

Source: NatWest/BFA Franchise Survey (1998, p. 31)

Table 6.6 Loan amounts and sources

Across all industry sectors, the NatWest/BFA (1998) survey found that just over half of franchisees (52 per cent) needed to borrow money when they started their franchise. This figure is down from 58 per cent in 1996 and 60 per cent in 1995. Of those who did, the average amount borrowed was £29,900, the same figure as reported for 1996. Table 6.6 shows that 76 per cent of franchisees that borrowed money did so from a bank. By contrast, just 8 per cent borrowed from a building society, slightly fewer than those who borrowed from one of their relatives. Twenty-eight per cent of borrowers claim that the value of their loan was no more than £10,000. The majority (58 per cent) borrowed between £10,001 and £50,000.

The high percentage of borrowing from the major clearing banks (Table 6.6) reflects their positive stance towards applications for franchise, as mentioned earlier in the chapter. Put simply, the concept of business format franchising offers new franchisees the opportunity to join an established, proven franchise network. This insinuates a lower degree of risk involvement than a new market entry of an unproven business concept as embodied in small business start-up (see Chapter 3 for alternative arguments). For example, traditionally, banks will fund small business propositions on a 50:50 gearing basis. By contrast, for an established franchise concept, many banks will consider financing up to around 70 per cent of the total start-up costs for a new franchise.

However, until such time as a new franchise network is well established and proven, banks will generally take a cautious line,

Factor	Comment
Business plan	Prospective franchisees will be expected by the banks to develop a detailed business plan. This will contain market research findings and details of finance requirements and security available
Buying an established outlet	Purchasing an existing, established franchise outlet may have advantages in terms of an established market position, and a track record of trading to present to the bank manager in order to facilitate the leverage funds
Finance schemes	For certain long-established franchise concepts, some of the major banks have arranged special finance schemes for their franchisees. These offer a standard range of terms to franchisees of that particular concept (see Tables 6.8 and 6.9)
Insurance	In most cases, the bank will require the franchisee to take out 'keyman' type insurance cover, and, depending on the circumstances, probably also cover for stock, property, vehicles, etc
Interest rates	Insofar as interest rates are concerned, each franchisee's finance proposal will be judged on its own merits. However, generally a franchisee proposition for a successful, established franchise concept should attract a finer interest rate margin than would an equivalent independent business start-up
Loans and overdrafts	Funding will normally be provided by way of either a term-loan or an overdraft, or most frequently a mixture of the two. The term-loan will cover that part of the project cost which relates to the capital start-up costs of the business. The loan will normally be over a period not exceeding the term of the franchise agreement, which the franchisor is granting. Overdrafts are normally available for working capital purposes
On-going relationship with the bank	Once the finance is agreed, the bank will expect regular management information on the progress of the new franchise business. The bank in return will also probably have a business banking charter, which will set out the basis of the relationship between the bank and customer
Security	Banks normally require security over the finance that they provide. Typically, for many franchisees, this security might be represented by the free equity in their home. However, other forms of security such as shares, collateral deposits or guarantees may also be acceptable

Source: Rose (1999, pp. 16–20)

Table 6.7 Franchise funding: the banks' perspective

Hospitality, Leisure & Tourism Series

perhaps by initially financing new franchisees at a 50 per cent level. Thereafter, they may increase the percentage lend to 70 per cent, once the new franchise concept has established its own successful track record. Interestingly, some franchisors will insist on their new franchisees contributing at least 50 per cent of start-up costs despite 70 per cent bank funding being on offer, as they wish to avoid over-borrowing by the franchisees at the outset. Table 6.7 summarizes the key franchise funding factors from the perspective of the banks.

In exceptional cases the banks will provide formal finance schemes for franchises with attractive lending packages built in (see Table 6.8). This is particularly the case with quick-service restaurants and limited service hotel chains where companies like McDonald's and Holiday Inn lead the way (Rose, 1999). Again, this emphasizes that across all the sectors it is easier to obtain finance from the banks for the purchase of a franchise business with good cash flow cover and a demonstrable ability to repay debt than it is for a new start-up.

Interest rates	Base rate +2 – 4%
Arrangement fee	1% maximum £200 + VAT
Repayment period (maximum)	5–7 years
Capital repayment holiday	Up to 12 months
Free banking	Up to 12 months

Source: The Royal Bank of Scotland

Table 6.8 Example of a bank's franchise finance scheme

The rationale for a bank's lending stance to franchisees in any franchise system is based upon a number of factors including cash generation and assets in the business but also franchising issues. These include:

- the cash flow and profit forecasts provided by the franchisor appears to be feasible;
- the level of income will be sufficient to support the outlet and repay the borrowing;
- the franchisor's figures allow for taxation, depreciation etc.;
- the figures for projected income provide an acceptable standard of living as well as covering business commitments; and

- there is a margin that enables the ability to borrow more, or fall back on own financial resources, if sales and/or profit projections are not met.
- training support and back-up from the franchisor;
- financial strength of the franchisor;
- quality of management and strength of brand; and
- operating systems and purchasing and marketing benefits to franchisees.

Franchise loan	It can be used to finance the purchase or expansion of a franchised business. Minimum loan is £10,000, there is no maximum
Fixed or variable interest rates	A fixed rate guards against an increase in base rate, and makes it easier to manage the cash flow. A variable rate allows benefits from any fall in base rate. Interest rates can be fixed for a period of up to ten years on loans over £25,000, but it depends on the length of the franchise agreement
LIBOR linked lending and base rate caps	For loans over £100,000 franchisees can choose to pay interest fixed to the London Inter-bank Offered Rate (LIBOR). For borrowing higher than £250,000, base rate caps are available to help protect against any future base rate fluctuations
Frequency of payment	Franchisees can choose when to make repayments with the options of monthly, quarterly, half-yearly or yearly payments
Capital repayment holiday	This is available for a maximum of two years, on loans over £25,000. During this time franchisees will pay only the interest, which will reduce the amount of the early payments
Pension-linked repayments	By linking the franchise loan to a pension plan, franchisees can receive tax relief on contributions
Option to defer monthly repayments	For loans between £25,000 and £250,000 this option lets franchisees defer up to two monthly repayments per year at no extra cost
Protecting repayments	The banks advise that it is sensible to take out some form of life assurance so that if the worst happens the franchise loan will be repaid, without having to sell assets or liquidate the business
Security required, costs and fees	Security is normally required for the lending and an estimate of the banks' security costs will generally be provided to potential franchisees at the outset. The only cost that is usually incurred is a reduced arrangement fee of 1 per cent of the amount borrowed

Source: Midland Bank (1998)

Table 6.9 A bank's franchise financial arrangements

Table 6.9 presents the financial arrangements offered to potential franchisees by the Midland Bank.

In summary, for a potential franchisee intending to purchase a franchise, the banks associated with franchising will normally:

- provide attractive funding packages for leading franchise concepts, particularly in the quick-service restaurant and hotel sectors;

- consider lending up to 70 per cent of the start-up costs for well established franchises;

- consider partially unsecured lending, including the use of the Government's Loan Guarantee Scheme for eligible concepts;

- offer competitive rates of interest and other banking benefits as an enticement.

Finally, from Table 6.6, it can be seen that another source of funding assistance for franchisees may be the franchisor themselves. The NatWest/BFA survey (1998) found that 60 per cent of franchisors assist their franchisees in raising their initial investment. Of those that do, nearly all (91 per cent) help arrange the finance needed to start up. However, only 9 per cent actually supply finance. McDonald's provides an example of one franchise system that assists franchisees in the financial routes into their company (see Chapter 11).

Financial performance

In theory, the majority of business concepts lend themselves to franchising. However, there are some for which franchising would be difficult and some where it would not be practical. In particular, businesses with small gross profit margins usually make poor candidates, unless the franchisee has the opportunity quickly to build up a substantial turnover. Thus, there has to be sufficient profit margins in the business to make it worthwhile for both the franchisor and franchisee. In the case of Exchange Travel (see Chapter 10), the profit margins were so low as to defy the logic of being part of a franchise system. Without a mutually acceptable financial profit performance the relationship will have little chance of survival. Furthermore, this has to be achieved within the constraints of a competitive marketplace.

Thus, the financial performance of the franchise system is intrinsically linked, individually and collectively, to the capabilities and behaviours of the franchisor and franchisees. Of significance to this linkage is a study which was carried out to determine whether or not entrepreneurs' decisions to enter into a franchise contract, rather than choose the alternative of independent business ownership, is consistent with wealth-maximization (Williams, 1998). It was found that franchisees generate below average profits and independent business owners generate above average profits. One interpretation of this finding is that the self-selection process that generates the pool of franchisees is such that franchisees are entrepreneurs drawn from the lower tail of the skill distribution of entrepreneurs, and independent business owners are drawn from the upper tail. In short, franchisees possess fewer, or lower quality entrepreneurial skills, than independent business owners. This supports the arguments presented in Chapter 4, whereby Morrison asserts that franchisees are in fact intrapreneurs, lacking in some of the entrepreneurial spirit need to 'go it alone'. Lashley and Lincoln also pick up on this theme in Chapter 9, describing franchisees as 'halfway house' entrepreneurs. Clearly, this has significant implications for degree to which the financial performance of the franchise system can be optimized. Furthermore, Price (1997), refers to Kaufmann and Lafontaine (1994), who use McDonald's as a case study. This points out that the company's desire for a particular type of individual to operate its franchises, namely owner–operators whose livelihood will be tied to the success of their outlet(s), increases the likelihood that franchisees will face liquidity constraints, and thereby increases the dependence on the franchisor.

However, despite the potentially negative aspects relative to the business acumen of franchisees and the degree to which dependence is healthy or unhealthy, the strategy of franchising has obvious positive elements that relate to financial performance. In particular, these include:

- **Risk sharing**: the profit-sharing provision of the franchise contract facilitates risk sharing between the franchisor and franchisee. By accepting part of their compensation in the form of a management fee (calculated as a percentage of sales), franchisors bear a portion of the variation in the cash flows of individual franchise units, thereby reducing the risk borne by franchisees.

- **Market entry:** franchising may also reduce the risk associated with demand uncertainty that entrepreneurs face. When entering a new product market, independent entrepreneurs face both product-specific and location-specific demand uncertainty. For a given product or service and economic market, a branded franchised product may face less product-specific uncertainty than an unbranded product, as is clearly illustrated in Chapter 10 relative to scheduled airlines.

- **Financial forecasts:** because franchisors make demand projections each time they open a new outlet, the forecast error of franchisors should be smaller than the forecast error of franchisees on average if there are learning economies in forecasting activities.

These positive elements are borne out by the NatWest/BFA (1998) survey. It found that franchising remains a highly profitable way to run a business. Nearly all franchisees (92 per cent) surveyed claim to be profitable, just 2 per cent down on the peak of 94 per cent reported in 1997. In line with the 1996 findings, 36 per cent of franchisees have a business that they regard as 'marginally profitable'. Interestingly, those holding a franchise for five or more years are nearly all profitable. This was claimed by 99 per cent of well-established franchisees. A number of reasons were given by franchisees for their positive profit performance. Rather than the application of any sophisticated management techniques, the most commonly quoted reasons were hard work, effort and commitment. Other profitable franchisees also point to having a sound, quality product or service. Good marketing and advertising are also highlighted (Table 6.10).

Reason	Good (%)	Marginal (%)	Negative (%)
Hard work/effort/commitment	38	15	0
Good product/service	18	9	0
Location/area	11	16	5
Profitable business	19	4	0
Good marketing/advertising	19	2	0
Good support/marketing support from franchisor	13	3	0
Good staff	11	1	0
Lack of sales/business	0	6	37
Cost of initial set-up	0	13	8

Source: NatWest/BFA Franchise Survey (1998, p. 35)

Table 6.10 Reasons for positive profit performance

Hospitality, Leisure & Tourism Series

Nunn *et al.* (1998) found that the main barriers relative to a positive financial performance of **franchisees** were:

- recruitment of quality staff who the franchisees would want to retain on a longer term basis;

- time and paperwork demands associated with VAT compliance;

- changing business climate;

- the franchisor–franchisee relationship.

From the perspective of **franchisors**, a survey (Nunn *et al.* 1998) enquired into the greatest threats to franchise system survival during the first two years of franchising. The most frequently cited threats were: shortage of funds for system development; difficulties with franchisee recruitment; and difficulties in building the support system. Consequently, the authors of the survey suggest that there appear to be two critical messages for would-be franchisors:

- they must be prepared to research, and understand, franchising thoroughly;

- an ability to access extra 'contingency' finance, for example, when system development progresses more slowly than first expect, can be of paramount importance.

Price (1997) introduces the little discussed topic of franchise failure in relation to financial performance. He says that it would appear that franchises have been promoted, and possibly sanctioned by the clearing banks, as a relatively risk-free entry method to potential entrants of business management. However, Price points out that there are problems with this message. In view of the lack of non-corroborated franchise failure data, there appears to be a suggestion that the link between franchising and low levels of failure is a highly speculative one, but also one that illustrates a popular line of thought. Indeed, Price states that 'the very thought of the "tried and tested" business format being vulnerable to failure is an anathema to many of the franchise fraternity' (p. 385).

Consequently, there appears to be some question concerning the accuracy and appropriateness of views propounding low rates of failure (see Chapter 3). Ball, in Chapter 7, explores this within the confines of the catering sector. It is generally accepted that failure by small and larger franchisors alike ensues as a result of under-estimating the financial and managerial costs of the project as well as lack of ability. The reasons for franchise failures due to franchising related factors, as opposed to 'generic' factors, have been seen by academics as falling essentially into five key categories (Stanworth *et al.*, 1998):

- Business fraud, such as the use of celebrities to attract franchisees to ill-founded franchise schemes in the USA during the 1960s and 1970s.

- Intra-system competition, involving franchise outlets being located too close together and cannibalizing each other's sales whilst maximizing the franchisor's sales-based royalties. Also company-owned outlets might be sited close to franchisee-owned outlets.

- Insufficient support of franchisees, encompassing advertising support, pre-opening programmes and on-going management assistance.

- Poor franchisee screening, possibly fuelled by a drive to maximize front-end fees, resulting in a mismatch between franchisee's attributes and criteria for success.

- Persistent conflict between franchisor and franchisee.

An example of the type and complexity of failure factors, of a purely financial nature, that can combine to cause the demise of a franchise system was provided by the Pierre Victoire restaurant chain in 1998 (see Chapter 7). Specific financial failure factors relating to this company included:

- company growth undertaken at too rapid a rate with insufficient capitalization;

- investment cost and subsequent failure of a pilot concept outwith the UK;

- pressure placed upon the company by major venture capital investors to put the company up for sale in order to realize a return on their investment;

- decision to buy back twelve franchised restaurants in London and refurbish them increased the company's overdraft by 160 per cent in the space of a year and left the assets overstated in the balance sheet, since the costs were not written off;

- two aborted attempts at floatation on the Alternative Investment Market, which would have raised much needed finance;

- the expense of supporting the founding entrepreneur's ostentatious life-style.

Hospitality, Leisure & Tourism Series

A positive franchise system financial performance requires that the business concept is sufficiently robust in order to sustain, or exceed, reward expectations from the perspectives of both the franchisor and franchisee. Furthermore, it is strongly dependent upon the effectiveness of the relationship between the two parties. This requires a match in terms of personal and business characteristics in order that the challenges and opportunities can be effectively addressed in order to avoid failure, which is an aspect of franchising as in any other type of business venture.

Summary

Franchising is generally accepted as one means of expanding a business system with relatively low-levels of capital investment on the part of the franchisor. Furthermore, it is propounded that the profit-driven motivations of franchisees will enhance the wealth-creation capabilities of the system as a whole. What has become blatant in this chapter is that to underestimate the degree of capital investment in the creation and development of a franchise system is to make a grave mistake.

Three key financial aspects have been identified as being associated with the creation and development of a franchise system. First is the franchisor fee structure that requires to be calculated in a business-like, and not an *ad hoc*, manner, and presented in a way that transparently communicates reward and risk prospects to franchisees. Significantly, it communicates to the business world much about the ethics, attitude and standing of the franchise company. Second is the need to invest in the piloting of the business concept in order to prove both its franchisability and viability. The successful completion of the pilot stage should result in: a proven business concept; established term of return on investment; a full set of financial projections; and business growth patterns. The third financial aspect is that of the costs associated with franchisee recruitment. It has been proposed that financial expediency demands that franchisors understand these costs, and that they be accurately reflected in the initial franchise fee.

The major source of funding for franchising is that of the major clearing banks. They generally adopt a positive stance towards lending, support and development of franchise systems. Relative to the franchisor sourcing funds, the banks are being requested to finance a business concept as opposed to the more tangible acquisition of assets. This leads them to be more stringent in scrutinizing aspects such as the professionalism of the management team, the degree to which they are receptive to external professional advice, and their understanding relative to the long-term nature of franchise system development. Another source of franchisor funding is that of the venture capitalists. Investment by such institutions can assist in the 'fast-tracking' of a franchise system and add an element of credibility within the business environment.

With respect to financial performance, franchise systems survive on mutually acceptable financial profit performance from the dual perspective of the franchisor and franchisee. They are intrinsically linked. In theory, financial performance should be enhanced due to elements of franchising, such as shared risk, market entry with proven branded products or services, and business decisions based on mature financial forecasts.

Finally, the topic of franchise failure was discussed. There is evidence that franchising is just as fallible as other approaches to business development. Indeed, many 'generic' components of business failure are associated with that of franchise failure. These include: unethical practices; insufficient support systems; flawed recruitment of personnel; insufficient capitalization; and general mismanagement. The linchpin in franchise success or failure is the relationship between the franchisor and franchisees.

Debate topics

- The financial advantages of selecting franchising as a strategy to expand a business outweigh the disadvantages.

- There is less financial risk for a franchisor deriving their income from mark-up on goods supplied as opposed to drawing an on-going management fee.

- The risk attached to an individual starting up an independent small business is greater in comparison to the purchase of a franchise.

Selected readings

Nunn, M., Stanworth, J., Purdy, D., Thomas, J. and Hatcliffe, M. (1998) *Franchisee Success: Perceptions and Barriers*. Lloyds Bank Plc/International Franchise Research Centre.

Price, S. (1997). *The Franchise Paradox*. Cassell.

Williams, D. (1998) Why do entrepreneurs become franchisees? An empirical analysis of organizational choice. *Journal of Business Venturing*, 14, 103–24.

References

Acheson, D. (1999) The big balancing act – fixing initial and on-going fees. In *Franchise World Directory*, 15th edn, Franchise World, pp. 80–4.

Barclays Bank (1999) *Running a Franchise*. Barclays Bank.

Costello, D. (1999) Financial aspects of launching a franchise. In *Franchise World Directory*, 15th edn, Franchise World, pp. 71–6.

Franchise World (1999) *Franchise World Directory*, 15th edn. Franchise World.

Horne, J. (1999) The elements that go in to make up the franchise package. In *Franchise World Directory*, 15th edn, Franchise World, pp. 21–4.

Kaufmann, P. and Lafontaine, F. (1994) Costs of control: the source of economic rents for McDonald's franchisees. *Journal of Law and* Economics, 38, 417–53.

Lloyds Bank/IFRC (1998) *Franchise World Directory 1998: Listing Supplement*. Franchise World.

Macmillan, A. (1996) *Aspects of Franchise Recruitment*. The Royal Bank of Scotland/International Franchise Research Centre. Special Studies Series No. 8. University of Westminster Press.

Midland Bank (1998) *Starting a Franchise: Business Banking*. Midland Bank plc.

NatWest (1998a) *European Franchise Survey Supplement*. NatWest Retail Banking Services.

NatWest (1998b) *The NatWest Guide to Franchising Your Business*. NatWest Retail Banking Services.

NatWest/BFA (1998) *Franchise Survey 1998*. Business Development Research Consultants.

Nunn, M., Stanworth, J., Purdy, D., Thomas, J. and Hatcliffe, M. (1998) *Franchisee Success: Perceptions and Barriers*. London: Lloyds Bank Plc/International Franchise Research Centre.

Price, S. (1997) *The Franchise Paradox*. Cassell.

Rose, G. (1999) Finding the finance to buy the franchise. In *Franchise World* Directory, 15th edn, Franchise World, pp. 16–20.

Royal Bank of Scotland (1998) *Franchisees*. Royal Bank of Scotland plc.

Sen, K. (1993) The use of initial fees and royalties in business format franchising. Working Paper. Washington University.

Silvester, T., Stanworth, J., Purdy, D. and Hatcliffe, M. (1997) *Lloyds Bank Plc/IFRC Franchising in Britain Report*. Lloyds Bank Plc/International Franchise Research Centre.

Stanworth, J., Purdy, D. and Hatcliffe, M. (1998) *Franchising Your Business: Getting Started*. Lloyds Bank Plc/International Franchise Research Centre.

Stern, P. (1999) The two partners of franchising. In *Franchise World Directory 1999*, 15th edn, Franchise World, pp. 1–7.

Williams, D. (1998) Why do entrepreneurs become franchisees? An empirical analysis of organizational choice. *Journal of Business Venturing*, 14, 103–24.

PART 2

Franchising at Sub-sector Level

Catering

Stephen Ball

Key points

- The catering industry and in particular the fast food sector have been key areas for business format franchising. It has been a critical growth factor for many fast food chains, but does not always bring success.

- Contradictory evidence exists concerning productivity performance being greater in franchised restaurants than owner-operated restaurants.

- The Ansoff (1987) market options matrix demonstrates that a number of ways have been used by catering franchises for expansion.

- The internationalization of catering franchise concepts can be problematical due to, in particular, a lack of cultural affinity and quality management inconsistencies associated with geographic remoteness from central control.

Introduction

A casual observer of the catering industry might think that development and expansion is inextricably linked to the use of franchising. Whilst this is true in fast food, and in particular in fast food chains, it is far less the case for the non-fast food element of the catering industry. Franchising has played a role in non-fast food restaurants but it has been far less significant.

To many, fast food is the home of franchising. It certainly has made a key contribution to the popularization of the concept with its simple menus, quick product finishing and service times, standardized production methods and service delivery systems, and heavily branded chains. These factors have made it easier for the fast food concept to be rolled out across the world and has attracted entrepreneurial financing through franchising. This in turn has enabled businesses with sound fast food concepts to achieve rapid distribution independent of having to raise extra capital funds. Pizzas, hamburgers, sandwiches, pasta, fried chicken, fish and chips: minimal cooking, maximal speed, are prime for franchising. Fast food giants such as McDonald's, KFC, Dunkin' Donuts, Burger King and Subway, household names worldwide, have all developed their chains through franchising.

However, despite the notoriety of the chains, over 70 per cent of take-away businesses are run as independents in the UK with each often operating only one establishment (Ball, 1996d). In such circumstances franchising effectively has no role to play. For non-fast food restaurants, chaining and groups are even less prominent features and hence franchising is less of a proposition. The dominance of independents in the restaurant sector is noted by Jones (1996, pp. 122), who states that:

> restaurants tend to be owned and operated by individuals and individualists. There is no neat formula for opening and operating a successful establishment.

This contrasts with modern fast food concepts. Despite this, there are some well-known corporate-owned non-fast food restaurant chains that have used franchising to expand their concepts, including TGI Friday's and Harry Ramsden's. While food may be produced and served less quickly and be relatively highly priced compared to fast food products, they are standardized and themed restaurant branded concepts. These factors, along with the desire for geographic expansion, often on an international scale, have facilitated franchising.

This chapter reviews the size, significance and growth of the catering franchise sector in the UK, analyses franchising as a method of involvement, and the various routes for the expansion of catering franchises. Much is said in the populist literature about the success rate of franchises and franchisees compared to independent start-ups (see Chapter 3). The success and failure of catering franchisees compared to conventional businesses and also productivity levels within franchised fast food restaurants will be examined. Finally, the rationale for the internationalization of catering franchises and some of the associated factors will be considered.

Size, significance and growth

Much franchising activity in the UK occurs in the catering market, which has about a quarter of all franchises. Table 7.1 shows that there were over 1,700 franchisee-owned catering establishments in 1991; an increase of nearly 500 compared to two years earlier. In catering franchise systems, 76 per cent of all establishments were franchisee-owned in 1991.

Business format franchising is the most common arrangement and has been utilized by many leading catering businesses in the UK to grow their businesses. McDonald's, Wimpy, Harry Ramsden's and a number of other well-known names developed through franchising. Fast food has been a particular target and franchising has been synonymous with the growth of fast food.

Total number of establishments within franchised businesses	1989	1991
Company owned	229	548
Franchised owned	1297	1735
% of franchisee-owned to total establishments	85	76

Volume of sales within franchised businesses	1990
Company-owned sales (£000)	154,280
Franchisee-owned sales (£000)	636,880
% of franchisee-owned sales to total establishments	80

Source: Based on data from Power, M. in Horwath International and Stoy Hayward Franchising Services (1991)

Table 7.1 Business format restaurant franchising in UK

The growth of both fast food and franchising has been influenced by a variety of economic, demographic and social factors, as was identified by Fulop in Chapter 2 for franchising in general. (Khan, 1992, p. 10) adds to this:

> The ageing of the baby boom generation, the increase of women entering the workforce, the growing number of active retirees, and the continued increase in the existence of two-income families are creating a demand for services, which franchising is the most logical way to supply. Changing attitudes toward convenience, techno-logical advances, mass advertising methods, emergence of electronic devices for home or business, and emphasis on quality are all encouraging the development of franchise businesses.

Fast food concepts lend themselves to franchising. This is primarily as a result of the simplicity and often limited nature of their menus (enabling food and drink preparation and service to be uncomplicated and equipment requirements to be limited), the brief contact with customers and the non-requirement for a catering background for a franchise.

Franchising is said to have been introduced to the restaurant sector in the 1930s by Howard Johnson to expand his North American operation to over 100 restaurants by the 1940s (Rudnick, 1984). Elsewhere the earliest practice of restaurant franchising has been attributed to A&W Root Beer restaurants (Parsa, 1996). Price (1997) refers to Bain's Deli, having its first franchise in 1910, and A&W Root Beer restaurants, commencing franchising in 1925. Regardless of who was first and when this actually occurred, the proliferation of catering franchising effectively began in the USA in the 1950s.

The McDonald brothers opened their first carhop unit in 1940 and in the early 1950s began to sell franchises. In 1955 Ray Kroc, a kitchen equipment salesman, was granted exclusive rights to McDonald's hamburger franchises in the USA. This was effectively the start of this leading restaurant franchise. Six years later the brothers sold him the worldwide proprietary rights to the McDonald's idea. In 1954 Colonel Harland Sanders, a franchising pioneer, was convinced to franchise his spiced chicken product in the USA under the brand name Kentucky Fried Chicken (KFC). It was 1954 which also saw the origins of the Burger King franchise system, called at that time Insta Burger King. Wimpy opened their first franchised outlet in the UK in Ramsgate in 1957.

Unlike the USA, where fast food and franchising became dominant forces, in the UK there were, with the exception of KFC in 1965, few new entrants to the market until the mid 1970s with the arrival of McDonald's and Burger King. Since then catering franchising activity has increased in the UK. In Britain the restaurant sector contributes an average of 18 per cent of sales to the total franchise sector, whereas in the USA by comparison this is 11 per cent (Price, 1992). Table 7.1 shows the expansion of franchised restaurants between 1989 and 1991. Much of this growth has been in the fast food industry, which has long been in the forefront in franchising. Similar patterns of development for restaurant franchising have been identified in Australia (Hing, 1996) and Canada (Reiter, 1996). Franchising enables the relatively low risk expansion of an established product/service, and fast food franchises are especially popular. An analysis of *Franchise Magazine* readers' preferences indicated fast food to be the third most sought-after franchise type (Franchise Development Services Limited, 1998–9).

The attraction of fast food franchising to potential franchisees as opposed to the opening and running of an independent fast food business may be associated with franchised outlets becoming viable and achieving positive cash flow more quickly than independents. This is primarily due to their market recognition and the elimination of unnecessary start-up costs, and with their better survival rate as a result of a proven business concept and accelerated profitability (Mendelsohn, 1990). These factors may contribute to the faster growth of a franchised concept than an independent business.

Another fact that contributes to the popularity of franchising is that it proves a method of developing fast food businesses and has enabled them to achieve a wider distribution of their products. As the fast food sector has grown in the UK, the chains, especially those operating franchise systems, have benefited. This is illustrated by recognizing that the largest fast food companies are involved with franchising (Acheson and Wicking, 1992). Table 7.2 includes examples of UK fast food franchise outlets. Six of the top ten international franchisors in 1999 are in the catering industry, according to Entrepreneur International, with McDonald's in the top position.

Acheson and Price (1992) claim that most American fast food franchisors regard the UK as the 'gateway' to Europe, with there being more American franchise units in the UK than the rest of Europe combined. This 'gateway' status is also recognized by Taylor in relation to hotels in Chapter 8. When it comes to location, London and the South East are the most popular destinations in the UK, with the number of franchisee-owned

Name of franchise	Description	Year established in UK	Started franchising
Dunkin' Donuts (UK)	Fast food takeaway	1945	1945
Baskin Robbins	Retail outlet ·	1945	1974
Burger King	Quick service restaurant	1954	1986
Henry J Beans	Full service restaurant	1977	1985
Delifrance	Full service restaurant/ coffee shop	1991	1991
Dix-Neuf Brasserie & Bar	Full service restaurant and bar	1992	1994
Dixie Fried Chicken	Fast food takeaway	1986	1986
Fatty Arbuckles American Diner	Full service restaurant	1983	1991
Harry Ramsden's	Full service restaurant and takeaway	1928	1990
Juicy Lucy	Quick service restaurant	1994	1995
KFC	Quick service restaurant	1965	1965
McDonald's Restaurants Ltd	Quick service restaurant	1974	1986
Mister Donut	Fast food takeaway	1955	1988
Mongolian Barbeque Ltd	Full service restaurant	1988	1992
O'Brien's Irish Sandwich Bars	Fast food takeaway	1988	1994
Perfect Lunches Ltd	Mobile catering	1993	1995
Perfect Pizza	Fast food takeaway and delivery	1978	1982
Pierre Victoire/ Chez Jules	Full service restaurant	1988	1992
Pizza Express	Full service restaurant	1965	1970
South Beach Café	Full service restaurant	1996	1997
Spud U Like	Full service restaurant and takeaway	1982	1982
Tennessee Secret	Retail outlet	1989	1990
Wimpy Fast Food Restaurants	Fast food takeaway	1954	1954
Wimpy International Ltd	Quick service restaurant	1954	1957

Source: Franchise Development Services Limited (1998–99)

Table 7.2 Examples of UK fast food franchise outlets

outlets by far the greatest in London and the South East compared to any other region of the UK (Power, M. in Horwath International and Stoy Hayward Franchising Services, 1991).

A recent catering franchise phenomenon has been co-branding of hotel groups via franchise agreements with national chains. For example, Stakis (now merged with Hilton) with Henry J. Bean, Radisson with TGI Friday, Choice Hotels' partnership with Pizza Hut and McDonald's within some Cendant (known as Hospitality Franchise System until 1997) hotels. Likewise, franchise agreements between brands, or between a brand and a company, have enabled fast food concepts to move to non-traditional sites such as transport termini, hospitals, educational establishments and employee workplaces. For example, Compass Group has adopted the Pizza Hut, Taco Bell and McDonald's brands within UK catering contracts in an attempt to woo customers who use these outlets on the High Street and in other locations. Similarly Granada and other motorway service area operators have built branded fast food outlets such as Burger King, McDonald's and KFC outlets on motorway service sites.

Methods of involvement

There are a number of business relationships or methods of involvement in the fast food industry. Table 7.3, from Emerson (1990), indicates how certain companies have chosen to direct their operations, whilst Figure 7.1 clarifies the operational choices for a catering franchisor and franchisee.

Company	Company-owned	Franchise	Lease to franchisee	Joint venture	Sell product or equipment to franchisee
Arby's	•	•			
Burger King	•	•	•		•
Domino's	•	•			
Dunkin' Donuts	•	•			•
KFC	•	•		•	
McDonald's	•	•	•	•	
Pizza Hut	•	•		•	•
Taco Bell	•	•			
Wendy's	•	•			

Source: Emerson (1990)

Table 7.3 Methods of franchise involvement in the fast food sector

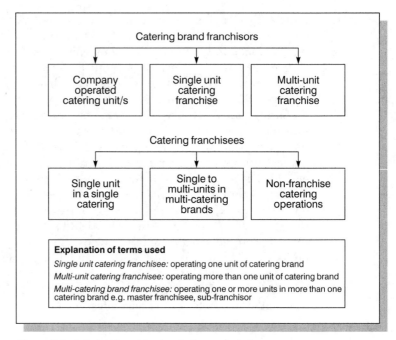

Figure 7.1 Catering franchise typologies and choices

Franchising has been a particularly successful method of business and geographical expansion for fast food and for franchisors and the independent franchisees, not only in the UK but also internationally. Companies usually consider franchising or other methods of joint development when they are not capable of expanding as they wish through internal means and when they want to add value to the organization. The barriers to internal expansion may be associated with a lack of capital, difficulties of acquiring, controlling or motivating a large dispersed labour force, lack of market knowledge or a need for direct control of stock (Acheson and Wicking, 1992; Ball, 1996a).

Catering brands/chains have used various ways to develop through franchising. This can be demonstrated by reference to a simple market/product matrix (sometimes termed the Ansoff (1987) matrix). These ways or options, which are presented in Figure 7.2, are: market penetration in the existing market; market development using existing products; product development for the existing market; and new markets and/or diversification.

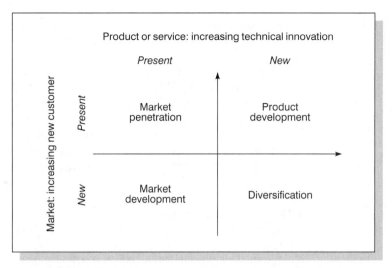

Figure 7.2 Market/product options matrix for catering franchise development

- **Market penetration**: many fast food operators have attracted customers from directly competing products by penetrating national and international markets through franchising. Direct attacks on competitors are usually achieved through improvements in product and service quality along with promotional activity. Burger King's 'Breaking the Rules' campaign of the early 1990s was a direct attempt to penetrate McDonald's stronghold on the UK. It encouraged franchisees and managers to provide 'what customers want'.

- **Market development**: this has also been a popular route to development for franchise chains. When, for example, KFC franchised many of its outlets in 1976, franchisees opened for longer periods than managers in the company-owned and operated outlets. As a result they obtained greater revenues.

- **Product development:** as the UK fast food market has matured this strategy has been observed increasingly. This is particularly as customers have become susceptible to menu fatigue and as operators have sought sales growth. It includes additions to the product mix and the creation of new delivery systems such as drive-throughs and home delivery, which combines product and market development to attract new customers. Franchisees expect the franchisor to provide product or concept innovation (Acheson, 1995), or have sometimes been responsible for these innovations or developments themselves (Price, 1997). It is rumoured that the Big Mac and the Egg McMuffin were both suggestions of McDonald's franchisees. Khan (1992, p. 95) notes the importance of product development and innovation in catering franchising:

> Franchising is fundamentally based on innovation and uniqueness in products and services provided. In order to be competitive, a franchisor should always be involved in innovative addition to the products and services offered by the system. This can be in the form of additions to the menu, refinement of equipment, new methods of preparation, or a revised method of service.

- **Diversification:** franchise catering organizations have also developed by diversification into related markets through integration, and unrelated markets. Examples of these can be found in Acheson and Wicking (1992, p. 164) and Ball (1992, p. 69). Horizontal integration is synonymous with franchising and occurs when a prospective franchisor develops a retail based concept and replicates this for cloning by others (franchisees). If the franchisor develops and improves operating and delivery systems within any of its company-owned units then in time these improvements will probably be transferred to franchisees. When J. Lyons developed Wimpy in the UK it created a franchise subsidiary which made use of the distribution and food manufacturing resources within the company. This is an example of vertical integration. McDonald's involvement with the sale of clothing could be taken as an example of diversification into an unrelated market. There are risks associated with this option as an organization may have limited knowledge of the key factors for success in unrelated markets.

Franchisor organizations have been considered to be convert franchisors, rapid grower franchisors or mature franchisors according to when they commenced franchising and how long they have been following this strategy. In the UK McDonald's at first spread slowly (see Chapters 1 and 11). By the end of 1984 there were 165 restaurants. It did not begin franchising until 1986, twelve years after entering the UK, and can thus be considered a convert franchisor. Since 1986, and partly as a result of franchising, growth increased rapidly. In 1994 it had over 500 outlets, 16 per cent of which were franchised. By the end of 1996, when it would have over 600 outlets, 33 per cent were expected to be franchised (Key Note, 1994). Today McDonald's has approximately 900 outlets in the UK, a figure that changes upwards almost daily, and serves around 2.5 million customers a day.

Brand	No. of company outlets	No. of franchised outlets
Arby's	208	2144
Burger King	817	4761
Domino's Pizza	1223	3670
Dunkin' Donuts	16	1748
KFC	1571	5782
McDonald's	2600	7110
Pizza Hut	2984	3461

Source: Price (1993)

Table 7.4 Number of company and franchised owned fast food outlets worldwide

McDonald's worldwide, however, like Burger King, can be regarded as a mature franchisor as it has been franchising a relatively long time. The extent of franchising by some fast food chains in the international market can be seen in Table 7.4. In contrast, some newer companies have grown extremely rapidly through franchising, which has been taken up immediately on inception. Perfect Pizza is an example of a rapid grower franchisor in the UK.

Most fast food restaurant franchisees in the UK are individuals owning a single unit. Some individuals do have several units, which are run by managers. Some large franchises are owned by companies (Ball *et al.*, 1988). These companies may be:

- catering companies themselves, such Allied Restaurants who used to operate a number of Wimpy counter service restaurants until the Burger King acquisition of Wimpy International in 1989;

- companies with other business interests, such as Gowrings group which in 1999 derived three-quarters of its sales from its motor business but 60 per cent of its profit from its 31 Burger King restaurants (Anon, 1999).

Franchisee buy-ins and franchisor/management buy-backs

A number of contingencies such as size, environment and technology are likely to affect the number of company-owned and operated versus franchisee-owned and operated outlets in a catering franchise system. Also of significance is the decision when to franchise or to withdraw, partially or totally, from franchising. The stage in the system's life cycle is another possible factor (see Chapter 4). At the introductory stage when a potential franchise company is trying to develop interest in a new catering product and attempting to develop a quality standard, it will usually commence operation with a company-owned and operated outlet core. As it pursues expansion the need for sharing investment costs and risk leads it possibly towards the adoption of franchising. With time and increased competition, pressures on costs and prices often ensue and quality becomes more difficult to control, and thus standardization becomes threatened. In such circumstances the buy-back of franchisee outlets could occur.

Ozanne and Hunt (1971) noticed from their studies that some franchisors illustrated a tendency to buy back their franchised operations and revert to being a wholly owned chain when critical mass was achieved. Pizza Express operated over 70 units in the UK in 1993 and has since bought back all but three of its UK franchised outlets. The company's average profit on franchises was 4 to 5 per cent, but 20 per cent on owned premises, so the decision to buy back was virtually a foregone conclusion. Petit Delice and Pret à Manger made early exits from franchising to build up company-owned chains as the high prospects for the concept became increasingly apparent to their owners (Anon, 1998).

Catering franchise businesses have been subject to other forms of corporate reorganization. The attraction of a sizeable chain was also apparent when Grand Metropolitan Plc took over Wimpy in 1989, and subsequently rebranded the larger counter service units to Burger King, which it had bought a year or so earlier. However, the company decided to sell the traditional table-service concept and associated units because these no longer fitted with its strategic plan. Wimpy International acquired these in a management buy-out. They now have 270 franchised outlets and only eight company operated units.

One of the first ever franchisee buy-ins in the UK occurred in October 1998, when a consortium of twelve franchisees of the budget French-style bistro restaurant chain Pierre Victoire bought the core parts of the franchisor's business for £4 million. The consortium acquired the name and operates thirty-six of the better-performing restaurants, which represents about a third of the original group. Pierre Victoire seemed to be a thriving and fast-developing concept under its founder Pierre Levicky. The business was founded in Edinburgh in 1988 and began franchising in 1992. Its comparatively low investment and simple menu attracted franchisees and within eight years of establishment there were 100 restaurants and three new concepts (Chez Jules,

Pierre Lapin and Beppe Vittorio). However, it became apparent that the company had expanded too quickly and franchisee performance was not reaching expectations. Eventually the receivers were called in. The failure was attributed to imprudent and inadequate management, too rapid growth and shabby restaurants in unsuitable sites (Anon, 1998).

Success, failure and expectations

It has often been claimed that franchise businesses are more successful than conventional businesses. For instance, promotional literature for *Franchising Research: An International Journal* (see Price, 1997, p. 456) states that:

> The success rate for franchise operations is far higher than that of other small businesses mainly due to the support offered by the franchisor. The shared knowledge available, the economies of scale to be gained from the relationship with the franchisor, the established image and identity of the franchisor and the benefits from the franchisor's marketing efforts.

Stokes (1995) states that it has been suggested that the readiness of banks to lend money to franchisees is evidence that success is more likely. However, the true picture is equivocal, with franchisees and those propounding franchise opportunities contributing to a distorted picture. Franchisee failures are often unreported by franchisors, 'unethical' franchises are excluded from failure data and ownership changes of franchised outlets disguise failure figures (Hoy, 1994). Certain franchise promoters, academics, banks and the franchise press have all been accused by Price (1997) of presenting information of dubious accuracy to encourage business. The real and main dilemmas lie in two key areas. First, is the problem of distinguishing industry-specific figures on franchise failure, such as for the catering industry, when official franchising statistics comprise businesses from a wide variety of business activities (Standard Industry Classification codes). Second, is the problem of quantifying failure when there are issues associated with defining failure and then measuring rates of 'failure'. These are matters further explained and discussed by Storey (1994) with regard to small businesses generally and Price (Chapter 3) with regard to franchise businesses in particular.

Accepting the definitional and methodological issues and that it is not possible to separate out catering from the broader industry grouping of hotels and catering, Table 7.5 suggests that

	1989	1993
Total hotel and catering bankruptcies and insolvencies	1,090	3,349
Total UK bankruptcies and insolvencies	18,597	51,724
Hotel and catering bankruptcies and insolvencies as a percentage of all UK	5.9%	4.5%
Total number of UK franchise failures	1,577	1,760

Note: Figures refer to England and Wales only

Source: Department of Trade/Business Monitor PA1003/BFA

Table 7.5 Bankruptcies and insolvencies in UK industry and hotels and catering in 1989 and 1993

in 1989 there were fewer bankruptcies and insolvencies in hotel and catering than in franchising. In 1993 the converse was the case. Price (1997) summarizes and explores various explanations of franchisee and franchisor failure, and concludes that no known empirical evidence exists that suggests that these explanations differ significantly for restaurant franchisees and franchisors.

Franchising has undoubtedly been one of the keys to the success of many fast food chains (Lee, 1987; Acheson and Wicking, 1992; Khan, 1992), although not all chains have found franchising successful. Popeye's Famous Fried Chicken, Subway and Arby's are all US franchised concepts which, although they succeeded elsewhere, failed in the UK after a short time following their initial entry. Lum's, Minnie Pearl's Fried Chicken and General Foods' Burger Chef are all examples of chains that expanded so fast through franchising in the United States that, in the case of the first two, inconsistent quality and too many disparate (or competing) locations led to the chain's downfall (Lee, 1987). Burger Chef was drastically pruned and eventually sold off to Hardees. The failure effectively to control quality of product and service in its large and rapidly expanding and far-flung estate contributed to its problems. Hartley (1992, p. 258), in analysing Burger Chef's mistakes, says that:

> Unless operating standards and procedures are imposed – and enforced – the results are likely to be lack of uniformity of performance, great unevenness of quality and service and a lack of co-ordination and continuity among the different units – instead of a tight ship, a very loose and undisciplined one will be the natural consequence.

Similar difficulties of controlling the food product quality from franchised outlets have also been apparent in the UK. The changes of Kentucky Fried Chicken ownership in 1986 were quickly accompanied by a plan to improve restaurant standards and control, one of the consequences of which was that a number of franchisees lost their franchises. Some of these formed new competitor franchise companies, for example, Dixie Fried Chicken and Kansas Fried Chicken. However, their growth was held back by their lack of resources.

Differing expectations?

A franchised restaurant can be considered as an exchange system comprising varied expectations and satisfactions of the persons involved, sometimes referred to as stakeholders. These stakeholders, franchisor, franchisees, operatives, customers etc. make varied contributions to the restaurant's operation and expect something back in return. Some of these expectations may be conflicting while others are complimentary. Take the roles of the franchisor and the franchisee (which are considered in various publications, including Housden, 1984; Acheson and Wicking, 1992; and Mendelsohn, 1992, for example). The franchisor offers a proven business format along with various advantages of size, such as, bulk purchasing power, national marketing and advertising, personnel and training expertise and ongoing product development, whereas the franchisee, usually being small, provides most of the necessary capital and localized knowledge. One of the main attractions of franchising to catering chains is that it provides the capability of rapid geographical expansion in a limited time period without major capital outlay and risk taking. Franchisors also normally collect an initial franchise fee and continuing royalties from the franchise.

Franchisors normally seek to maximize control and expect standardization of operations (see Chapters 4 and 5). The presence of the control is very real due to the existence of the franchise agreement. Franchisees are aware of the franchisor's expectations when they become franchisees but still expect some independence, even if it is restricted.

Ozanne and Hunt (1971, p. 33) concluded in their study of franchising that:

> franchisees believe they are independent since they perceive themselves to have primary responsibility for six out of seven key operating areas, such as determining hours of operation, bookkeeping, pricing, advertising, standards of cleanliness and numbers of employees.

Such independence, Ball (1996b) states, may be acceptable to the franchisor but if abused could result in franchisor/franchisee conflict, particularly if standards are being compromised. Pollard and Voss (1985) vividly detail an example of this related to Wimpy International. They tell of the conflict in 1980 between Wimpy International and one of its franchisees. The issue was that a particular franchisee had four restaurants, which were failing to meet Wimpy's standards of quality and that the franchisee refused to amend this. The dilemma and one of the factors hindering the solution to the problem was that the restaurants were extremely profitable (both to the franchisee and to Wimpy). Ultimately the contract was terminated, as Wimpy had to place the maintenance of standards, uniformity of operations, and the brand along with long-term success before short-term profitability. Thus, a clash of interests and/or expectations could be damaging not only to the integrity of the franchise system, but to the financial health and well-being of the franchisor and franchisee. Early awareness of each other's expectations, perhaps even before the franchise agreement is signed, could prevent or reduce such conflict.

Productivity levels

One of the key institutional features of the fast food sector, and in particular in what Ball (1992, 1996c) refers to as modern fast food operations, is that many chain operations possess a dual distribution organization. Within such chains some restaurant outlets are completely owned and operated by the parent company, while others are owned and allowed to operate as clones of the parent chain by other people (the franchisees); either as single units or as multi-units (see Figure 7.1). To the external observer these clones are identical to the parent company-owned and operated outlets, having the same name, logo, system and operating procedures and generally the same product offering.

It was suggested earlier in this chapter that the abuse by franchisees of any independence, which they enjoy, may have adverse consequences on the franchisor/franchisee relationship and be dysfunctional to the franchise system as a whole. If this is so then it could be hypothesized that franchising a system could have detrimental effects upon the maintenance of standards of performance, consistency of quality, productivity and the maintenance of a desired uniform image of a fast food chain generally. This is a particular concern if tight controls are not implemented throughout the chain (see Chapter 5).

Other factors may also hinder long-term productivity development. Doutt (1976), for instance, in discussing the influence of innovation on fast food business performance, argues that the evidence concerning innovation is heavily weighted against franchise systems (see Chapter 4). He refers to the slowness of some franchised systems, when compared to independent operators, to introduce certain ideas such as self-service even though on market entry they were innovative. Certainly standardization, which usually accompanies the franchising of systems, whilst being potentially beneficial to productivity in the short term, could be stifling. Furthermore, in the longer term, it may inhibit innovation or the ability to adapt to change simply because of the desire to retain the status quo. This is due to the benefits to consumers of obtaining a reliable, known product and to the provider of adhering to known practices.

When comparing the productivity levels of company-owned and operated units with franchised units in the same chain it might be expected that those in the former type would be higher. This could be expected because the parent company would choose the most desirable, highly trafficked sites for its own units and would exert the maximum degrees of control over its own units. Research findings related to the productivity levels of the different ownership types of fast food outlets appear contradictory. Doutt's investigation into productivity in fast food restaurants in the US found that ownership type was not a significant influence on productivity of labour. Leibenstein (1979), however, discovered that owner-managed units had costs that were about 10 per cent lower than those run by company-hired managers. The difference in costs was explained by Leibenstein as 'X-efficiency', which suggests that motivation is greater for owner (franchisee) managers and hence their costs would be lower. Franchisees have strong incentives to minimize costs as they receive the residual profit generated by the enterprise (Krueger, 1991). The effect of these incentives on the performance of franchisees is implied in a statement of Fred Turner, a previous President and CEO of McDonald's (Love, 1986, p. 292–3): 'Running a McDonald's is a 363 days-a-year business and an owner–operator, with his personal interests and incentives, can inherently do a better job than a chain manager.' This debate is illustrative of the agency theory discussed in Chapter 1.

Table 7.6 shows that on average employment in each company-owned unit was over double that in each franchisee-owned unit within UK franchises, while sales were only about 25 per cent higher. Based on this, productivity would appear to be twice as high in franchise restaurants compared to their

Productivity factor	Company-owned unit	Franchisee-owned unit
Average sales (£000)	532,000	417,000
Employment	8,425	12,575
Average number of employees	23.9	9.2
Labour productivity (average £ sales/ average number of employees)	22,259	45,326

Source: Based on data from Power, M. in Horwath International and Stoy Hayward Franchising Services (1991)

Table 7.6 Labour productivity in UK franchisee-owned and company-owned and operated restaurants in franchises in 1990

company counterparts. While this might provide a pointer to a productivity difference, accepting this as a true assessment of productivity levels would be short-sighted given that at the very least no account is taken of the number of hours employees work in franchise and company-owned restaurant types.

Differences in research methodology negate confirmation that a contradiction does exist between Doutt's and Leibenstein's findings. Nevertheless, it does seem likely that factors associated with the ownership and management of franchised and company-generated units belonging to a fast food chain will affect their respective performance. A similar conclusion was reached in research undertaken by Ball (1993), which examined productivity awareness, perceptions and practices within the Wimpy fast food chain in the UK. No significant difference was found when responses of restaurant staff (managers and operatives) in the company division of Wimpy to questions about their explanations of productivity were compared with those of their counterparts in the franchised division. This suggests that ownership type did not influence productivity perceptions and that any productivity differences between the two restaurant types would be due to other factors. When Ball (1993) compared the respondents in franchised and company-owned units relative to productivity measurement, evaluation and improvement, few differences were revealed. Those that were noteworthy related to measurement and evaluation and pointed to a greater emphasis by company respondents upon the qualitative aspects of operations and worker activities, whereas financial measurement seemed more prevalent in franchised restaurants.

Internationalization

A franchised system generally has standardized systems of operation, standardized menus and products and may even attempt to standardize its employees. This facilitates internationalization. When a restaurant brand/company enters into a franchising agreement with a foreign franchisee, it expects that franchisee to run its restaurants in exactly the same manner in which they operate elsewhere and to produce identical products. An organization that can provide a customer with a standardized product around the world could gain from worldwide familiarity. McDonald's has certainly gained, with in excess of 23,000 restaurants operated in over 111 countries by the company and its franchisees in 1998, making it the biggest single provider of food. Khan (1993) discusses some of the reasons for international expansion in restaurant franchises. These reasons include:

- the enormous market size and potential demand;
- the attraction in other countries of highly regarded products and services provided by such franchises as McDonald's, KFC and Hardees which in some countries have a symbolic status;
- a whole host of economic and demographic trends;
- increased travel and tourism;
- favourable political climates;
- technological advancements, for example related to information technology;
- favourable conditions for foreign investment;
- the movement towards the universality of business management methods.

Obstacles to international restaurant franchising include factors associated with the political environment; for instance, McDonald's franchise restaurants in Belgrade came under physical attack in protest against the NATO air strikes in early 1999. Cultural food habits, languages and traditions can be problematic. Certain foods are unacceptable in some countries while even the trading name of a franchise operation may cause offence in certain instances. Other impediments include the availability of the right standard and quantity of raw materials, employees and equipment. The identification and recruitment of suitable franchisees is a particular challenge. McDonald's has attempted to attract candidates by:

- reducing the set-up costs of restaurants;
- being sensitive to the independent and creative entrepreneurial disposition of potential franchisees;

- providing good marketing support and thorough training; and
- showing a willingness to adopt franchisees' advice on local food preferences.

An advantage of international restaurant franchising is that the franchisor does not have to bear the development costs and risks of opening up a foreign market on its own, for the franchisee typically assumes those risks and costs. Hence franchising can enable a restaurant brand/company to gain an international presence quickly and at low cost. Rowe (1996) provides some catering franchise case studies, which demonstrates the benefit of franchising to overseas expansion. This benefit, he says, derives because franchising is based on the provision of consistent customer service and strong brand recognition. It allows the franchisor to regularly test and develop the system in order to meet changing customer expectations. Most international catering franchising has occurred in the fast food market. Major international theme restaurant franchises include Hard Rock Cafes, and My Kinda Town Restaurants, which had twenty-three franchised restaurants out of a total of thirty-nine in 1997 (Marketpower, 1997).

In contrast to the advantages, the involvement of franchisees, which in practice could amount to a large number just for one brand, and the geographical distance of the franchisor from its foreign franchisees, create potential disadvantages. One downside of international franchising to a restaurant brand/company may be its inability effectively to co-ordinate its international strategy, whilst another relates to the difficulties of controlling quality. One way of reducing any potential quality problem, according to Hill and Jones (1998), is for a company to set up a wholly owned or joint venture subsidiary in each country or foreign region into which it is expanding. By doing this, as McDonald's, KFC and others have done, the rights and responsibilities for franchisees are then transferred to the subsidiary. Other steps taken by catering franchisors have included effective training programmes, and the strict application of quality guidelines throughout all units in an international franchise. Thus while there are significant international opportunities, the process of internationalizing a restaurant franchise concept is challenging and not all franchises prove successful at it.

Summary

Franchising has been a major factor in the growth of many conspicuous fast food concepts, and some other restaurant concepts. It has been an increasingly popular method of developing businesses. The attraction of franchising can in part be explained by business success rates, which for franchises is quoted as high as 98 per cent, whilst the failure rate of conventional methods of starting a business is quoted as high as 90 per cent. Fast food franchising has enabled geographical expansion and growth of what in many locations is regarded as a maturing market. However, whilst franchising offers the advantages of developing a concept rapidly, with little investment, and obtaining a healthy return in royalties and advertising awareness, it does present challenges in maintaining control over the concept's brand identity and product quality. Bernstein and Paul (1994, p. 161) claim in the USA context that:

> Most [restaurant] chains prefer not to franchise unless they have to – which is often necessary to penetrate markets. It is difficult for franchisees . . . to stay focused on the concept and to consider the welfare of the entire franchise system. They often get caught up in their own market and their own restaurant, worry about their own problems, and try to get other franchisees involved in their own problem. Eventually the franchisee can lose focus, and when a series of franchisees do this, it can cause the whole chain to lose focus.

Where standards become compromised, perhaps as franchisees abuse any independence they possess, then franchisor/franchisee conflict can result, which, if unresolved, has on occasions led to court battles. Similar battles, particularly in the USA, have occurred for other reasons, such as the alleged lack of advertising support from the franchisor, and from the geographical encroachment of other franchises in the same franchise system. Because of these problems other options to franchising may be increasingly selected for catering growth.

Another conclusion drawn from this chapter is that restaurant businesses may experience a franchise life cycle. After initial set-up and consolidation with a company-owned and operated outlet core, franchising is often chosen for rapid expansion at low cost and risk to the franchisor. With success, the franchisor could be able to fund further development from its own reserves. It may then buy back franchised outlets. This process could be fuelled by difficulties of controlling product quality across the franchisee estate. The buy-back is just one of a number of catering business franchise reorganization forms.

Fast food chains have a compelling need to be productive in their restaurants to ensure increased profitability and growth.

If productivity levels of company-owned and operated outlets were compared with franchised units in the same chain it might be expected that those in the former type would be higher. Research findings related to the productivity levels of the different ownership types of fast food outlets are inconclusive. It does seem likely, however, that factors associated with the ownership and management of franchised and company-generated units belonging to a fast food chain will affect their respective performance.

Franchising is becoming an increasingly popular and important vehicle for international expansion of catering chains, especially those in the fast food industry. All the indications are that international catering franchising will continue to play a significant role in the new millennium. To be successful, however, franchises must have regard for a series of factors associated with franchising. The political and economic climate of other countries are particularly important considerations. Furthermore, the application of sound business and financial management practice remains imperative.

Debate topics

- The systems and processes associated with the fast food sector lend themselves to business format franchising to a greater degree than those implemented in fine-dining concept restaurants.

- Franchised fast food outlets are more likely to succeed than an independently owned small business.

- All catering companies should adopt franchising as an effective internationalization strategy.

Selected readings

Ball, S. (1996) Perceptions and interpretations of productivity within fast food chains – a case study of Wimpy International. In *Productivity Management in Hospitality and Tourism* (Johns, N., ed.), Cassell.

Hing, N. (1996) An empirical analysis of the benefits and limitations for restaurant franchisees. *International Journal of Hospitality Management*, **15** (2), 177–87.

Rowe, I. (1996). *Globalisation of the Catering Industry.* FT Management Report, Pearson Professional Limited.

References

Acheson, D. (1995) The big balancing act – fixing the initial and ongoing fees. In *Franchise World Directory*, 11th edn. Franchise World Publications.

Acheson, D. and Price, S. (1992) Chain reaction. *Business Franchise*. October/November, pp. 25–9.

Acheson, D. and Wicking, N. (1992) Fast food franchising and finance. In *Fast Food Operations and Their Management* (Ball, S., ed.), Stanley Thornes, pp. 147–68.

Anon. (1998) Victoire! for franchisees. *Franchise World*, November/December, No. 108, pp. 5–11.

Anon. (1999) Gowrings puts 21 Burger Kings on menu. *Daily Telegraph*, 22 February, p. 29.

Ansoff, H. (1987) *Corporate Strategy*. Penguin.

Ball, S. (1992) Understanding fast food operations. In *Fast Food Operations and Their Management* (Ball, S., ed.), Stanley Thornes.

Ball, S. (1993) Productivity and Productivity Management within Fast Food Chains – A Case Study of Wimpy International. Unpublished MPhil dissertation, University of Huddersfield.

Ball, S. (1996a) Location Factors and Trends in the Takeaway and Fast Food Industries. Discussion Paper No. 16, Leeds Metropolitan University.

Ball, S. (1996b) Perceptions and interpretations of productivity within fast food chains – a case study of Wimpy International. In *Productivity Management in Hospitality and Tourism* (Johns, N., ed.), Cassell, pp. 166–93.

Ball, S. (1996c) Fast food. In *Introduction to Hospitality Operations* (Jones, P., ed.), Cassell, pp. 172–89.

Ball, S. (1996d) Whither the small independent take-away? *International Journal of Contemporary Hospitality Management*, **8** (5), pp. 25–9.

Ball, S., West, A. and Black, A. (1988) *Britain's Fast Food Industry 1988*. Jordan and Sons (Surveys) Ltd.

Bernstein, C. and Paul, R. (1994) *Winning the Chain Restaurant Game*. Wiley and Sons.

Doutt, J. (1976) Productivity in Fast Food Retailing. Unpublished PhD thesis, University of California.

Emerson, R. (1990) *The New Economics of Fast Food*. Van Nostrand Reinhold.

Franchise Development Services Limited (1998–9) *The United Kingdom Franchise Directory*, 14th edn. Franchise Development Services Limited.

Hartley, R. (1992) *Management Mistakes*. John Wiley.

Hill, C. and Jones, G. (1998) *Strategic Management: An Integrated Approach*. Houghton Mifflin.

Hing, N. (1996) An empirical analysis of the benefits and limitations for restaurant franchisees. *International Journal of Hospitality Management*, **15** (2), 177–87.

Horwath International and Stoy Hayward Franchising Services (1991) *Franchising in the Economy 1991*. International Franchise Association Educational Foundation Inc., Horwath International and Stoy Hayward Franchising Services.

Housden, J. (1984) *Franchising and Other Business Relationships in Hotel and Catering Services*. Heinemann.

Hoy, F. (1994) The dark side of franchising or appreciating flaws in an imperfect world. *International Small Business Journal*, **12** (2), 26–38.

Jones, P. (1996) Restaurants. In *Introduction to Hospitality Operations* (Jones, P., ed.), Cassell, pp. 122–37.

Key Note (1994) *Fast Food and Home Delivery Outlets*. Keynote Publications.

Khan, M. (1992) *Restaurant Franchising*. Van Nostrand Reinhold.

Khan, M. (1993) International restaurant franchises. In *The International Hospitality Industry* (Jones, P. and Pizam, A., eds), Pitman, pp. 104–16.

Krueger, A. (1991) Ownership, agency and wages: an examination of franchising in the fast food industry. *Quarterly Journal of Economics*, February, pp. 75–101.

Lee, D. (1987) Why some succeed where others fail. *Cornell Hotel and Restaurant Administration Quarterly*, November, pp. 33–7.

Leibenstein, H. (1979) X-efficiency from concept to theory. *Challenge*, September–October, pp. 13–23.

Love, J. (1986) *McDonald's: Behind the Arches*. Bantam Books.

Lynch, R. (1997) *Corporate Strategy*. Pitman.

Marketpower (1997) *Themed Restaurants*. Marketpower Ltd.

Mendelsohn, M. (1992) *The Guide to Franchising*. Cassell.

Ozanne, U. and Hunt, S. (1971) *The Economic Effects of Franchising*. Government Printing Office.

Parsa, H. (1996) Franchisor–franchisee relationships in quick-service-restaurant systems. *Cornell Hotel and Restaurant Administration Quarterly*, June, pp. 42–9.

Pollard, C. Voss, C. (1985) Case study: Wimpy International (A) and (B). In *Operations Management in Service Industries and the Public Sector* (Voss, C., Armistead, C., Johnston, R. and Morris, B., eds), John Wiley, pp. 65–80, 196–213.

Price, S. (1992) *The British Fast Food Industry*, Volume 3. Hotel and Catering Research Centre, University of Huddersfield and Stoy Hayward Franchising Services.

Price, S. (1993) *The UK Fast Food Industry 1993*. Cassell.

Price, S. (1997) *The Franchise Paradox*. Cassell.

Reiter, E. (1996) *Making Fast Food: From the Frying Pan Into the Fryer.* McGill-Queen's University Press.

Roh, Y. and Andrew, W. (1997) Sub-franchising. *Cornell Hotel and Restaurant Administration Quarterly,* December, pp. 39–45.

Rowe, I. (1996) *Globalisation of the Catering Industry.* FT Management Report, Pearson Professional Limited.

Rudnick, L. (1984) An introduction to franchising. In *International Franchising – An Overview* (Mendelsohn, M., ed.), Elsevier Science Publishers, pp. 1–47.

Stokes, D. (1995) *Small Business Management: An Active-Learning Approach.* DP Publications.

Storey, D. (1994) *Understanding the Small Business Sector.* Routledge.

CHAPTER 8

Hotels

Stephen Taylor

Key points

- Hotel franchising is particularly attractive as a means of supporting international expansion where equity based strategies are frequently perceived as a high-risk foreign market entry mode.

- One distinctive feature of hotel franchises is the frequency with which these might be allied to a management contract arrangement.

- Entry costs to franchising can be high, particularly for an older, less well maintained property, but franchisees must also consider the continuing fees they will be required to pay under a given franchise arrangement.

- Research findings suggest that the modal form of involvement selected by hotel groups is directly related to the type of financial capital available in a given country or region.

Introduction

The focus of this chapter is franchising in the hotel sector with a particular emphasis upon the international context. This enables hotel franchising to be examined in a more balanced way in the light of the considerable diversity across regional markets as to the prevalence of this mode of organization. The chapter commences with an examination of the mechanics of hotel franchising in terms of the nature and level of fees charged by franchisors and how these fees are typically calculated. The next section locates franchising within the wider discussion of hotel firm modal choice decision making. Initially, an overview is given of the extent of hotel franchising across the three global regions of America, Europe and Asia before moving on to attempt to understand why the observed pattern has emerged. Here, within the context of the international hotel chain, the factors which influence the decision to chose between the use of franchising, management contracts and full or partial ownership is examined. The chapter concludes with a brief examination of the use of franchising by three international hotel chains.

An anatomy of hotel franchising

Modern, business format hotel franchising has its origins in America, where, in 1954, Holiday Inn launched its franchising system. However, the earliest example of any form of franchising in the hotel industry probably occurred in 1907, when Cesar Ritz granted permission for his name to be attached to hotels in New York, Boston, Montreal, Lisbon and Barcelona. Hotel organizations with established brand names and market reputations use franchising as a relatively low risk method to expand their chain system. It is particularly attractive as a means of supporting international expansion where equity based strategies are frequently perceived as a high risk foreign market entry mode.

One distinctive feature of hotel franchises is the frequency with which these might be allied to a management contract arrangement. Indeed, the first hotel management contract granted by the Puerto Rican government to Conrad Hilton in 1948 also involved the property trading as the Caribe Hilton and thus it is also the first management contract/business format franchise arrangement. Here the owner contracts with the franchisor or a third party management firm to undertake the day-to-day operation of the franchised property. It is important to be aware of this situation as frequently those arrangements which are reported as management contracts also involve a franchise arrangement.

As with any form of business format franchising, a hotel franchise involves an agreement between a hotel company (franchisor) and a hotel owner (franchisee) that enables the latter party to gain access to the use of the former's brand name and associated support services in return for payment of the prescribed fees. Agreements will normally be for a period of ten to twenty years, with the franchise duration often directly linked to the life of any mortgage applying to the hotel property. Typically, a franchise agreement will involve a one-off, up-front payment plus ongoing fees, discussed below (see also Chapter 6).

Later in this chapter we examine the international diffusion of franchising as a modal form of organization within the hotel industry and the high incidence of arrangements reported as management contracts, which suggests that the prevalence of franchising is likely to be under-reported. This situation arises because researchers typically have used single categorizations for reporting hotel governance arrangements. Prior to exploring the prevalence of hotel franchising we first examine the nature of the typical hotel franchise agreement.

Fundamentally, the existence of business format franchising (and indeed, management contracting) is a recognition that capital intensive assets and knowledge-based assets can be separated (Contractor and Kundu, 1998). The franchisee undertakes the necessary investment in the capital assets (i.e. the hotel building, plant, furnishing and fittings) and then enters into a franchise agreement to access the value-adding services of the franchisor. These take the form of a brand name and reputation which facilitate the market positioning of the property, plus additional services such as operating procedures and controls, marketing, and referral and reservation systems. In this way the franchise enables the hotel owner to enhance the return from the investment made in the capital assets. The selection of the correct franchise for a given property is an important task for, as Rushmore and Henriksen (1999) note, after payroll costs, franchise fees are typically the largest operating expense for many hotels.

Initial fees

The basic structure of a hotel franchise arrangement normally involves an initial minimum fee with an additional sum for every room over a designated number, which is paid on submission of the franchise application. For example, a firm might be required to pay £20,000 as a minimum fee, with an additional £100 for every room over 100. Thus a hotel with 200 rooms would involve an initial franchise fee of £40,000 (see Table 8.1 for initial fees in

Chain	Initial cost	Royalty cost	Reservation cost	Marketing cost	Misc. cost	Frequent traveller cost	Total ten-year cost	Total cost as a % of total rooms revenue
Economy-rate hotels								
AmericInn	30,000	766,172	0	306,469	0	74,606	1,177,247	5.7
Motel 6	25,000	612,938	229,852	229,852	133,790	0	1,231,431	6.0
Ramada Ltd	36,000	612,938	344,778	344,778	132,399	0	1,470,892	7.6
Mid-rate hotels								
Best Western	44,000	51,290	269,342	500,050	0	0	864,682	1.8
Holiday Inn Express	100,000	2,451,752	889,845	735,525	395,764	55,290	4,628,177	7.4
Sleep Inn	60,000	1,961,401	858,113	1,029,736	397,673	196,140	4,503,063	7.2
First-class hotels								
Crown Plaza	150,000	5,056,738	1,748,501	1,625,021	689,497	407,539	9,677,296	7.6
Hilton	55,000	5,056,738	2,021,691	1,011,348	1,070,417	415,662	9,630,855	7.5
Marriott	90,000	7,888,511	670,662	1,011,348	1,333,680	517,810	11,512,011	9.4

Source: —to come—

Table 8.1 Sample initial hotel franchise fees ($US)

a sample of US hotels). This initial payment is used by the franchisor to administer the application and to undertake a feasibility study of the property and its market as well as the provision of support during the pre-opening (if a new build) or conversion (if an existing hotel) phases. In cases where the franchisor decides not to proceed and grant a franchise contract the fee is usually returned minus a deduction (typically, 5–10 per cent) for the cost of the application review process (Rushmore and Henriksen, 1999).

Prospective franchisees face additional costs, over and above the initial application fee, if their application is successful. This will include items such as signage, perhaps even towels with the franchisor's logo, plus any refurbishment or upgrading specified by the franchisor as a condition of acceptance. This latter category can include anything from new carpets through to more extensive refurbishment and renovation. Consequently, this, and not the initial joining fee, might represent the single largest cost for a prospective franchisee wishing to enter a particular franchise system. One compensation, however, is that this investment is directly into the assets of the hotel owner and not a payment to the franchisor. Overall, entry costs to franchising can be high, particularly for an older, less well maintained property, but the initial fees are only half of the story, franchisees must also consider the continuing fees they will be required to pay under a given franchise arrangement.

Continuing fees

Once a property has been accepted under a franchise agreement the hotel owner will be required to make further payments when the affiliation becomes active. These payments will typically always include a royalty payment, a contribution towards marketing costs and reservation fees. If the franchisor operates a frequent traveller/guest loyalty scheme then there will probably be a charge for this and any other miscellaneous services provided. While the continuing fees represent the franchisor's main source of profits, many of the fee elements are set at a level that is intended simply to cover the costs of the services provided.

The royalty fee acts as a compensation payment for the use of the franchisor's brand name, logos, goodwill and so on. The majority of the franchisor's profits is likely to be obtained from this source. Fees for marketing cover chainwide advertising and other marketing activities. This includes the costs of producing a chain directory and any marketing programmes developed to target specific market segments (e.g. leisure breaks, over-55s, business travellers and so on). Normally, marketing fees go directly on marketing expenditure and do not act as a source of profit for the franchisor. Where a chain reservation system is provided, the franchisee will be required to pay a fee for each booking this generates for the property. Reservation fees will be set to cover the franchisor's administration costs incurred in operating this facility. There might be a small profit margin factored into the reservation fees, although the main objective is to ensure cost recovery.

Under the category of miscellaneous fees are payments required for additional activities the franchisor undertakes to provide for franchisees. This can include training programmes, payment of travel agent commissions and fees for the use of global distribution systems (GDS). Once again, these are unlikely to be a profit source for the franchisor. Additionally, with the increasing diffusion of technology across hotel franchise systems, hotel owners are responsible for covering the costs of any hardware and software specified by the franchisor. While much of these costs can be more appropriately considered to be part of the initial start-up fees, there will be ongoing maintenance and upgrading costs that the hotel owners will be required to meet during the life of the franchise agreement. Where the franchisor provides any additional services to an individual franchisee in the form of management consultancy or other types of support, these will attract additional fees, but will not normally be specified in the standard franchise agreement.

How are continuing fees calculated?

Hotel franchisors have a number of options as to how they calculate the continuing fees levied upon franchisees. In the case of royalty fees the most common approach is to use a percentage amount of accommodation revenue. In HVS International's 1999 survey of hotel franchise fees (Rushmore and Henriksen, 1999) this percentage was reported to vary between 2 per cent and 6.5 per cent. In the case of marketing and training fees, HVS reported that these ranged between 1 per cent and 3.75 per cent of rooms revenue. Alternatively, some franchisors may levy a fixed amount for these services calculated as a monthly monetary amount per available room. Similarly, reservation fees can be based on a percentage of accommodation revenue or as a monthly amount per available room. A further variation sometimes used for reservation fees is where the franchisor charges a fixed monetary amount for each reservation generated for a property by the central reservation system. In some instances franchisors may use a combination of these methods for calculating reservation fees.

With the increasing prevalence (and the costs of their administration) of frequent traveller programmes franchisors will normally expect operators to pay a fair share of the associated operating costs. This could be based on a percentage of total guest spend or just accommodation spend or a fixed monetary amount per room night. A property's participation in a frequent traveller scheme (almost certain to be mandatory) may require an initial, one off, payment of a fixed amount per room. Once again, some franchisors set fees for participation using a combination of all these methods. Indeed, franchisors may operate a method for calculating any of its fees which specifies a minimum monetary amount and a percentage amount with the applicable fee being the higher of the two figures. Clearly, for individual properties each approach can offer both advantages and disadvantages. Where fees are calculated as a percentage of accommodation revenue those properties deriving significant amounts of their revenue from food and beverage sales will benefit. Fixed monetary amount based fees are attractive to high volume properties, but less so to those experiencing a lower volume of business.

Modal choice in the international hotel industry

Having reviewed the mechanics of hotel franchising, we now turn our attention to exploring those underlying factors which influence the decision to use franchising as a method of strategic development. The international hotel firm has a choice as to the organizational mode(s) it can use to support its growth and development. In addition to franchising, this includes another form of non-equity alliance – the management contract (which is often used in combination with a franchise arrangement). Both represent an alternative to equity based arrangements such as full ownership (i.e. full equity) and partial ownership arrangements (i.e. joint ventures). The selection process as to which modal form provides the optimum choice requires consideration of both firm- and country-specific factors (Contractor and Kundu, 1998). Of particular interest here are those factors which are conducive to supporting a franchising strategy. Initially, we review the diffusion of each of the modal forms in the international hotel industry before proceeding to examine the underlying reasons for the observed pattern.

What is the extent of franchising in the global hotel industry?

Contractor and Kundu's (1998) large scale survey of international hotel groups reported that 37 per cent of foreign properties (i.e.

those outside a hotel group's domestic market) were operated under a management contract; 34.6 per cent involved partial or full equity involvement; and the remaining 28.4 per cent were franchised. They did note, however, there were some important regional variations. Thus in North America, franchising was the dominant mode of organization and equity involvement was uncommon, whereas in Asia, they reported that this relationship was inverted, with equity ownership modes being the most common. This is a significant finding that appears to contradict the findings (reported below) of the research undertaken by Slattery (1996). That research covered the first half of the 1990s, and revealed some interesting data on quoted hotel chain development across the American, European and Asian regions. Even within the European region considerable diversity was found in relation to the preferred modal forms of organization. For example, while in the UK, full equity ownership (measured in terms of hotel rooms) at 80.4 per cent was the dominant modal form, in Western Europe as a whole it represented only 31.9 per cent of rooms, while in Eastern Europe it accounted for a mere 4.9 per cent of hotel rooms. In the case of franchising in the European quoted hotel sector, it was reported to account for 4.1 per cent of UK rooms, 23.3 per cent of Western European rooms and 55.9 per cent of Eastern European rooms.

When we look further afield to America and Asia, Slattery's (1996) findings as to the most common forms of modal choice are highly revealing. In America, franchising accounted for 70.8 per cent of hotel rooms, but only 14.9 per cent in Asia. In the latter region, management contracts were the dominant modal form, representing 74.8 per cent of hotel rooms, but in America, the use of management contracts was limited to 20.5 per cent of quoted group rooms. Overall, across all the regions, leasing was the least popular modal choice of organization, but even here, considerable variation is apparent, with its use ranging from 12.9 per cent of hotel rooms in Western Europe through to a mere 0.6 per cent in Asia. As one might suspect, the revealed patterns of development are not accidental and an understanding of the influencing factors is important if one is to begin to develop an appreciation of the use of franchising as a mode of organization in the hotel industry. A useful starting point is the issue of the nature of capital availability across the key regions for international hotel development.

Influence of capital availability

In Chapter 1 it was highlighted that one of the theories of franchising involved resource scarcity. The main resource typically cited is that of financial capital. Slattery (1996) suggested that the modal form of involvement selected by hotel groups is directly related to the type of financial capital available in a given country or region. He differentiated between two principal sources of capital: first, '**hotel-chain capital**' which hotel groups raise from the stock market (i.e. share equity) and through bank debt; the second type, '**hotel capital**' sourced from (i) direct equity investment by financial institutions; (ii) property development companies; (iii) local governments; (iv) local hotel entrepreneurs; and finally, (v) private individuals and syndicates. Slattery suggested that 'hotel-chain capital' will favour direct ownership and leasing, while 'hotel capital' favours the non-equity modal forms of management contracts and franchising. As such, this prediction would appear to be directly compatible with the resource scarcity thesis of franchising in that one would anticipate that franchising (and indeed management contracts) will be prevalent in those countries and regions where hotel-chain capital is not available for investment. In this situation finance will be required to be raised from one of the 'hotel capital' sources listed above.

The data presented by Slattery (1996) would appear to support this scenario. For example, in the UK, only 10 per cent of rooms were funded by 'hotel capital' which accounts for the low utilization of non-equity modal forms of franchising and management contracts. In America, the low availability of 'hotel-chain capital' was evident in that only 6 per cent of rooms were funded by this source. Thus the dominance of non-equity modal forms, in particular franchising, is linked to the heavy dependence (94 per cent) upon 'hotel capital' sources. However, the situation is not as straightforward as these figures might suggest, as the cases of Eastern Europe and Asia make clear. In the former, while 'hotel capital' funds 94 per cent of quoted rooms and in Asia it funds 90 per cent – and thus both situations favour non-equity modes – the actual modal forms which dominate each region are different. In the Eastern Europe market, franchising accounts for 55.9 per cent and management contracts 38.2 per cent of rooms. However, in Asia, the management contract is the dominant modal form, accounting for 74.8 per cent of rooms, while franchising accounts for only 14.9 per cent. While these findings suggests that an apparent absence of 'hotel-chain capital' promotes the use of non-equity modal forms of organization, it does not explain either why this capital scarcity occurs (or indeed the true nature of this apparent scarcity) and which conditions favour franchising over management contracts (and vice versa).

Other key influences upon modal choice

At this juncture a key question is, in addition to capital availability, what influences international hotel groups to favour one particular modal form of organization over another as a means of development? In particular, with relation to the focus of this chapter, what are the circumstances which will lead hotel groups to prefer the use of franchising over other modal forms? Drawing upon the general literature on firm internationalization, it is possible to identify two distinct sets of factors which influence modal choice: (1) those which are firm-specific; and (2) those which are country- or market-specific.

Firm-specific factors

When considering the firm-specific factors that influence modal choice across international markets, Contractor and Kundu (1998) suggested it is possible to discern two groups of factors. The first of these is **objective factors** (or structural factors), which includes firm size, its level of international experience and degree of internationalization. The second group is termed **subjective factors,** and these concern a firm's top management's perceptions and attitudes (Perlmutter, 1969) towards factors such as global scale, branding, central reservation systems, training, management control and quality. Some research has suggested that it is this latter category of subjective factors that is typically more significant than the objective factors as influences upon the decision to internationalize franchise operations (Kedia *et al.*, 1995).

Objective factors

- **Firm size:** Previous research has suggested that larger firms will tend to favour equity modes of involvement (Gomes-Casseres, 1989), while smaller firms possibly lacking in the necessary resources and international experience will tend to favour non-equity modes of involvement (Erramilli and Rao, 1993). The implication being that direct control is the favoured strategy where resources permit. However, there is some research which challenges the applicability of the received view as to the influence of firm size, particularly in the context of the service sector. Gatignon and Anderson (1988) have suggested in some service industries such as hotels, the effective scale required to be a global player is so large that hotel firms are compelled to have recourse to strategic partnerships in the form of joint ventures, franchising and management contracts. Additionally, it is suggested that in the hotel industry these alliances have the potential to deliver the desired benefits to be gained from size just as effectively as direct ownership. The findings of Contractor and Kundu (1998) would tend to support Gatignon and Anderson (1988), in that the large international hotel chains in their sample appeared to utilize non-equity modal forms such as franchising and management contracts rather than control oriented equity forms.

- **International experience:** It is generally held that the more international experience a firm gains and its degree of globalization (as measured by the ratio of a hotel firm's overseas rooms to its home country rooms) then the less likely they are to resort to host country partnerships of any form (Johanson and Vahlne, 1977; Erramilli and Rao, 1993). This traditional view was supported by Chang's (1995) examination of Japanese firms whereby it was found that a sequential process was utilized that led to increasing levels of foreign market commitment congruent with increasing international exposure. Thus firms initially serviced markets by exporting or licensing and gradually moved towards an equity involvement in overseas markets. Contractor and Kundu's (1998) findings suggested that hotel firms' behaviour supports this traditional view, with non-equity modes (franchising and management contracts) being preferred by the less experienced, less globalized international hotels groups.

Subjective factors

- **Firm perceptions:** This second group of firm-specific factors concerns the so-called subjective factors which reflect the beliefs and views of the firm's senior management who are responsible for strategic decision making. This involves the **perceived importance** a hotel firm's senior management place upon: (i) global scale for effective hotel operations; (ii) control over unit management and quality; (iii) firm size for effective global operations; (iv) the role of central reservation systems (CRS); and (v) the role of branding.

Where a hotel firm's managers perceive global scale as being strategically important the extant literature draws two quite different conclusions as to the mode of operation likely to be favoured. On the one hand there is the view that obtaining global economies of scale (where this is believed to be important) necessitates high levels of control and ownership of modes of operation (Yip, 1989). Alternatively, if one takes the view that achieving globalization necessitates that firms form partnerships in host countries to achieve the desired scale of operations then this will tend to favour franchising and management contracts. Central to this approach is the accessing of scale effects through what are referred to as 'economies of information' (Galbraith and Kay, 1986). In the case of international hotel operations, scale could be viewed as resting mainly upon electronic distribution systems, unit design and its associated operating processes and standards. In all of these elements, the desired scale effects can be obtained without resorting to direct ownership or high levels of day-to-day control.

In some instances, senior management may perceive that quality concerns are such that these can only be accommodated through direct ownership. In this instance, one would expect the firm's portfolio of properties to be heavily skewed towards direct ownership with a limited and very reluctant use of non-equity modes of operation in the form of franchising and management contracts. Similarly, where senior management consider size *per se* is important then equity based arrangements are likely to be preferred for the purposes of greater operational control and the appropriation of a greater level of operating profits. The research by Contractor and Kundu (1998) lent support to both of these propositions.

With respect to the perceived importance of global reservation systems (GRS) and hotel brands, these codified assets will always tend to remain under the full control of a hotel company regardless of the modal choice selected (Dunning and McQueen, 1981; Viceriat, 1993). This is due to the fact that these represent the major knowledge capital of the firm and thus embody a significant proportion of its added economic value. Recognition of the nature of these codified assets by senior management should be supportive of a hotel firm's ability to engage in non-equity based arrangements such as franchising and management contracts as their control is a powerful barrier against opportunism by contractual partners. At the same time the addition of new franchises or management contracts represents a significant increase in revenue compared to the incremental costs of allowing access to these two key assets. Accordingly, where managers recognize the value of the GRS and hotel brand(s) which they control, then this will tend to increase the firm's propensity to grant franchises and to use management contracts. The findings of Contractor and Kundu (1998) also supported this outcome.

Country-specific factors

In addition to firm-specific factors, we need to recognize that the external environment will also influence a hotel firm's behaviour. In this instance we are explicitly concerned with the conditions that pertain to the specific foreign market under consideration. These will affect the nature of the commitment a hotel group is willing and able to make in respect of how it perceives a given country in relation to a number of key variables:

- country political and economic risk;

- level of economic development;

- cultural distance.

- **Political and economic risk and level of economic development:** Here we are concerned with the stability of a country's government and (often related to this first factor) its economy, both in terms of risk and its level of development. Where these are considered to be unstable then the hotel firm's perceived level of risk associated with that country is likely to be higher. A number of researchers (Agarwal and Ramaswami, 1992; Kim and Hwang, 1992; Madhok, 1994) have suggested that where a high level of country and political risk is perceived then firms will tend to favour those entry modes with a lower level of resource commitment, such as franchising and management contracts. Where a high degree of uncertainty is associated with these two variables (e.g. a high level of currency volatility), then this will tend to favour the use of franchise agreements (Shane, 1996). Related to this is the extent to which a hotel firm is confident of market demand as this is driven by the economic conditions in a given country.

    Where 'demand uncertainty' is high, it is suggested that this will make firms less amenable to equity based arrangements for market entry or expansion (Kim and Hwang, 1992; Erramilli and Rao, 1993). A further factor which favours non-equity based arrangement in high risk environments is that these offer a high degree of control while mitigating against any threat of fixed assets (i.e. the hotel and its contents) being appropriated due to political change (Dunning and McQueen, 1991). The research undertaken by Contractor and Kundu (1998) provided some interesting findings which generally support the above discussion. They suggest that franchising and management contracts will be preferred in those countries with high incomes, while equity based arrangements are preferred where country income levels are lower. This situation arises because the costs of transferring knowledge assets, maintaining quality standards and protecting intellectual property rights are considerably higher than in developed economies. However, Contractor and Kundu (1998) reported that where political and economic risk is perceived to be high then non-equity based arrangements such as franchising and management contracts will be favoured. An additional consideration in this choice is that royalty fees are considerably more certain in this type of environment than returns on equity since the former are paid regardless of whether the property achieves a profit or not.

At first glance, the above findings by Contractor and Kundu (1998) may appear somewhat contradictory in respect of country risk and income levels. However, as these researchers point out, if one uses a two-dimensional classification matrix (see Figure 8.1) then it is possible to discern four possible groupings into which countries fall: (1) low per capita income/ low risk (equity based modes preferred); (2) high income/low risk countries; (3) low income/high risk countries (both of which were found to favour non-equity based modes); and finally (4) high income/high risk countries, which is in reality a highly unlikely combination. With regard to category (1) countries, the argument is that non-equity modes of involvement are likely to provide very small levels of income compared to equity based involvement. In addition, equity based arrangements provide hotel firms with access to growing returns as country income levels increase. In category (2) countries, royalty returns will be sufficiently high to provide an attractive revenue stream combined with significant system-wide growth potential. With category (3) countries, the high risk levels mitigate against hotel companies entering through equity based arrangements when the low potential returns are considered. Regarding category (4) countries, this, as stated above, is an unlikely combination, but we could argue that where it did arise that depending on the hotel company's level of risk adversity either equity or non-equity based modes might be preferred.

- **Cultural distance:** When a hotel company is considering a foreign market entry the extent to which it is culturally different (that is 'distant') from the company's home country is an important consideration. The international business literature strongly supports the view that the greater the cultural distance then the greater the reliance will be on non-equity based modes such as franchising and management contracts (Kogut and Singh, 1988; Erramilli and Rao, 1993). The reasons advance for this outcome are quite straightforward. Where a

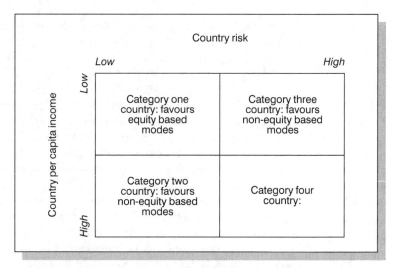

Figure 8.1 Impact of country risk and per capita income on favoured operating market entry modes (based on Contractor and Kundu, 1998)

hotel company perceives the proposed market is much less culturally familiar to them, they will tend to perceive a greater need for local market knowledge and support. A key concern here is that the greater the cultural distance, the greater the information costs imposed on the hotel company (Fladmoe-Lindquist and Jacque, 1995). While Contractor and Kundu's (1998) own findings found little support for the proposition regarding cultural distance, they cited Madhok's (1997) observation that what might be happening is that the cultural distance is sometimes so great that local partners are incapable of absorbing the necessary knowledge because of the cultural distance. In other words, the knowledge assets to be transferred are too culturally bounded or embedded to be transferred.

Summarizing the key influences on the decision to franchise

Summarizing the discussion above on modal choice, we can make the following observations on when hotel firms are likely to franchise international operations. First, the type of capital available would appear to have a direct effect on whether franchising is likely to be used. Where the major source of capital is what Slattery (1996) termed 'hotel-capital' (see above), then this will favour franchising and management contracts. Second, drawing upon the international business literature and its application to international hotel chains, we identified a number of influences upon the decision to franchise. These were sub-divided into firm-specific factors and country- or market-specific factors. Within firm-specific factors a further division was made between 'objective' and 'subjective'. Under the former, it was suggested that size is a consideration, with smaller hotel firms likely to favour franchising as a development strategy due to resource constraints. Similarly, it was suggested that those hotel firms with less international experience are more likely to resort to franchising.

Under subjective, firm-specific factors the focus was upon the perceptions of a hotel firm's senior decision makers. Where these managers believe scale of operations, control of quality, the size of their own organization to be important, then they are less likely to use franchising as a growth strategy. Where managers fully recognize the importance and nature of codified assets in the form of GRS and brands, then this is likely to be supportive of a franchising strategy due to the control that can be exerted through the ownership of these assets.

When examining country-specific factors, it was suggested that hotel firms will favour franchising in those countries where low political risk is combined with high per capita income levels and also those countries where low income levels are combined with high levels of political risk. With regard to the concept of 'cultural distance', franchising is likely to be preferred where this is quite great, but there are indications that if this distance becomes too great then franchising might not be a feasible strategy.

Hotel franchising in action

Having discussed hotel franchising in somewhat general terms above, this chapter concludes by examining: some of the current practices of a selected range of hotel franchisors, and; future franchising trends across the key market regions globally. The companies discussed have been selected in order to provide a range of examples of how international hotel chains use franchising as a development strategy.

Groupe Accor

With its origins in France in 1967, Groupe Accor is the largest of the European hotel groups who have made extensive use of franchising. A relatively late adopter of franchising in 1980, by the mid–1990s Accor was operating a portfolio of nearly 2,600 hotels and more than 288,000 rooms across 65 countries, using a mixture of equity based arrangements in addition to management contracts and franchises (Hotels, 1998). In the 1990s Accor prioritized the Mercure brand for franchise development, with a targeted total of 1000 franchised hotels worldwide by the year 2000 (McGuffie, 1996). Interestingly, in a recent interview, Sven Boinet, responsible for much of Accor's hotel development, stated that:

> In Asia, as in Europe franchising doesn't work because there is no existing management capabilities within the country. To develop a franchising strategy, you have to have existing companies or management capabilities so you can run the hotels, accept the brand, accept the reservation system and know how to use it (quoted in Hotels, 1998a, p. 64).

However, Accor has found that franchising works well in the United States because the necessary management capabilities do exist. Consequently, Accor is likely to prefer equity based arrangements in future developments in Asia and Europe, reserving the use of franchising mainly for expansion in the United States. Here it has developed a very selective franchising strategy using the 800 property Motel 6 chain it acquired in the mid–1990s (Dela Cruz, 1998a)..

Cendant Corporation

This organization, until 1997 known as HFS Inc, is somewhat unusual in the hotel industry, in that with its eight brand (Wingate Inns; Ramada; Villager Lodge; Days Inns; Super 8 Motels; Travelodge; Howard Johnson; and Knights Inn) hotel portfolio of 5,300 units, with in excess of 500,000 rooms, it relies entirely upon franchising. This organization believes that to own or manage properties would involve competition with its own customers, the franchisees (Lodging Hospitality, 1997).

Cendant are thus an example of a pure franchisor who use no other modal form of involvement. While heavily dependent on the North American market, it is currently expanding overseas, most notably with its new Wingate brands, with eight properties planned for the Philippines.

Unlike many franchisors, Cendant does not believe that it is essential to operate some properties itself to establish quality standards and brand reputation in new markets (Dela Cruz, 1998b). This is a view contrary to that held by many other hotel groups who believe that some 'strategic' ownership is required to support a successful franchise development strategy. In the European region Cendant has decided to expand its franchising through granting a series of master franchises to local partners. The European strategy is designed to concentrate on what it sees as key gateways and strategic destinations. It is for this reason that it has selected the island of Malta as one of its platforms for its European franchising. Though the company admits it would have preferred to commence its European operations in the UK, Germany or France, it points out that Malta receives over a million tourists a year, representing more than four times the size of its indigenous population. Additionally, it has brands in Israel and through a subsidiary company specializing in timeshares, an infrastructure that will support its franchising in certain European countries (Dela Cruz, 1998b).

Choice Hotels International (CHI)

Originating in the United States as long ago as 1934, CHI claims to have been the originator of hotel product segmentation. This is based on the fact that it was the first hotel group to develop a comprehensive tiered product range from the economy segment (Friendship Inns, Econolodge, Rodeway Inns, Sleep Inns), through to the mid-market segment (Comfort Inns and Suites, Quality Inns and Hotels), and up to the luxury segment (Clarion Brand: Hotels and Resorts; Clarion Carriage House Inns and Clarion Suites). According to company derived information, as of 1999 it had a hotel system containing in excess of 4,300 hotels across thirty-three countries. Overseas expansion has historically mainly been based upon the granting of master franchises. In 1998 CHI was named the number one US lodging franchise company by Entrepreneur Magazine. It is recognized as being the leading franchise organization for new constructions, and in 1997 it added over 250 newly constructed properties to its system.

CHI owns a majority stake in the London-based Friendly Hotels, to which it granted in 1998 the master franchise for the European region (Dela Cruz, 1998b). Friendly Hotels have 212 franchised and 71 owned hotels across Europe. Indications are that it is taking a very tough approach to maintaining standards as it axed 21 sub-standard franchisees in 1998/1999. Most of the problems here related to franchisees being unable to meet the company's expectations regarding renovation and refurbishment programmes (Golding, 1999). It is unclear what the future growth plans are in the next five years or so; given the relatively low penetration of the CHI brand portfolio in Europe, however, considerable expansion is likely if suitable franchisees can be located.

Future trends in hotel franchising

Attempting to forecast the nature of hotel franchising activity in the future is no easy task. The wide diversity of hotel chain approaches and practices in respect of modal choice, combined with a complex and constantly evolving business environment, suggests that convergence on a uniform pattern globally is far from certain. If we take the United States as representing the most mature hotel market, one might be tempted to speculate that other regions will eventually approximate this particular industry's structure, with franchising being the dominant mode of operation. However, such a prognosis is probably unlikely given the widely different environmental conditions and development pathways found across the three key global regions.

Overall, it is likely that franchising will experience some growth in Europe and in Asia, but it is perhaps highly unlikely that franchising will become the dominant organizational mode in these international hotel markets given the historical conditions pertaining to both these regions. Indeed, who knows, perhaps the Oxenfeldt and Kelly (1969) conjecture discussed in Chapter 1 could eventually be proved correct, and at some future date the American hotel groups might reverse current practice by acquiring existing franchises in a shift towards corporate ownership?

Summary

This chapter has focused on business format franchising in the hotel industry. Commencing with an overview of the mechanics of franchising, the chapter then moved towards a discussion of franchising within the wider context of the international hotel industry. It was emphasized that the issue of franchising needs to be seen in the context of modal choice. Franchising represents but one option for hotel companies who wish to pursue a growth strategy. Other options include management contracts (often allied to a franchise), full ownership and, finally, some type of partial ownership in the form of a joint venture.

The majority of the chapter was concerned with an exploration of the factors that influence hotel organizations to select franchising or one of the other modal options. It was demonstrated that capital availability, firm-specific and country-specific factors all can influence modal choice. Based upon existing research, it was possible to draw some broad generalizations as to where and when franchising might be the preferred development strategy for a hotel chain. Finally, the chapter presented three examples of actual hotel company franchisors and offered some tentative speculation as to future trends for the global diffusion of hotel franchising.

Debate topics

- Management contracts represents a franchise arrangement by another name.
- Capital availability, firm-specific and country-specific factors are the only influences on modal choice.
- Cendant Corporation's strategy can be described as 'pure franchising'.

Selected readings

Contractor, F. and Kundu, S. (1998) Modal choice in a world of alliances: analyzing organizational forms in the international hotel sector. *Journal of International Business Studies*, **29** (2), pp. 325–57.

Rushmore, S. and Henriksen, K. (1999) *1999 Hotel Franchise Fees Analysis Guide*. HVS International.

Slattery, P. (1996) International development of hotel chains. In *The International Hospitality Business* (Kotas, R., Teare, R., Logie, J., Jayawardena, C. and Bowen, J., eds), Cassell, pp. 30–5.

References

Agarwal, S. and Ramaswami, S. (1992) Choice of foreign market entry mode: impact of ownership, location and internalization factors. *Journal of International Business Studies*, **23** (2), 128–51.

Chang, S-J. (1995) International expansion strategy of Japanese firms: capability building through sequential entry. *Academy of Management Journal*, **38** (2), 383–407.

Contractor, F. and Kundu, S. (1998) Modal choice in a world of alliances: analyzing organizational forms in the international hotel sector. *Journal of International Business Studies*, **29** (2), 325–57.

Dela Cruz, T. (1998a) Chains to watch, *Hotels*, May, pp. 54–60.

Dela Cruz, T. (1998b) Speed to market, *Hotels*, February, pp. 40–8.

Dunning, J. and McQueen, M. (1981) The eclectic theory of international production: a case study of the international hotel industry. *Managerial and Decision Economics*, **2** (4), 197–210.

Erramilli, M. and Rao, C. (1993) Service firms' international entry mode choice: a modified transaction-cost analysis approach. *Journal of Marketing*, **57** (1), 19–38.

Fladmoe-Lindquist, K. and Jacque, L. (1995) Control modes in international service operations: the propensity to franchise. *Management Science*, **41** (7), 1238–1249.

Galbraith, C. and Kay, N. (1986) Towards a theory of multinational enterprise. *Journal of Economic Behavior and Organization*, **7** (1), 3–19.

Gatignon, H. and Anderson, E. (1988) The multinational corporation's degree of control over foreign subsidiaries: an empirical test of a transaction cost explanation. *Journal of Law, Economics and Organization*, **4** (2), 305–36.

Golding, C. (1999) Friendly kicks out 'substandard' hotels. *Caterer & Hotelkeeper*, 15 April, p. 14.

Gomes-Casseres, B. (1989) Ownership structures of foreign subsidiaries. *Journal of Economic Behavior and Organization*, **11** (1), 1–25.

Johanson, J. and Vahlne, J.E. (1977) The internationalization process of the firm – a model of knowledge development and increasing market commitments. *Journal of International Business Studies*, **8** (2), 23–32.

Kedia, B., Ackerman, D. and Justis, R. (1995) Changing barriers to the internationalization of franchising operations: perceptions of domestic and international franchisors. *International Executive*, **37** (4), 329–48.

Kim, W. and Hwang, P. (1992) Global strategy and multinationals' entry mode choice. *Journal of International Business Studies*, **23** (1), 29–53.

Kogut, B. and Singh, H. (1988) The effect of national culture on the choice of entry mode. *Journal of International Business Studies*, **19** (4), 411–32.

Lodging Hospitality (1997) Inside HFS. *Lodging Hospitality*, April, pp. 24–30.

McGuffie, J. (1996) Accommodation: franchising hotels in Europe. *EIU Travel and Tourism Analyst*, No. 1, 36–52.

Madhok, A. (1994) Mode of foreign market entry: towards a more comprehensive perspective of firm behaviour. Paper presented at the Annual AIB Conference, Boston, MA.

Madhok, A. (1997) Cost, value and foreign market entry mode: the transaction and the firm. *Strategic Management Journal*, **18** (1), 39–61.

Oxenfeldt, A. and Kelly, A. (1969) Will successful franchise systems ultimately become wholly-owned chains? *Journal of Retailing*, **44** (49), 69–83.

Perlmutter, H. (1969) The tortuous evolution of the multinational corporation. *Columbia Journal of World Business*, **4**, January–February, pp. 9–18.

Rushmore, S. and Henriksen, K. (1999) *1999 Hotel Franchise Fees Analysis Guide*. HVS International.

Shane, S.A. (1996) Explaining why franchise companies expand overseas. *Journal of Business Venturing*, **11** (2), 73–88.

Slattery, P. (1996) International development of hotel chains. In *The International Hospitality Business* (Kotas, R., Teare, R., Logie, J., Jayawardena, C. and Bowen, J., eds), Cassell, pp. 30–5.

Viceriat, P. (1993) Hotel chains. In *Market Services and European Integration: the Challenges for the 1990s* (Buigues, P., Ilzkovitz, F., Lebrun, J-F. and Sapir, A., eds), Commission of the European Communities, No. 36580.

Yip, G. (1989) Global strategy . . . In a world of nations? *Sloan Management Review*, Fall, pp. 29–41.

Licensed retail

Conrad Lashley
and Guy Lincoln

Key points

- There is a long tradition of a form of franchising through the tied pub tenancy in the licensed trade in the United Kingdom.

- In recent years the industry has undergone rapid change, in part due to the restructuring brought in after the Monopoly and Mergers Commission Report (1989), and in part due to changes in the marketplace.

- As the industry has been restructured, licensed retailers have increasingly introduced pub leasing as a way of overcoming some of the shortcomings of the traditional tenancy.

- The need to manage tensions, between profit maximization and risk minimization, is largely responsible for variations in the control of the pub estate, and the adoption of a mix of management by company, lease and/or tenancy.

Introduction

The licensing laws which have prevailed in the United Kingdom for the major part of the twentieth century have given the British pub and bar sector a unique character and created ownership structures which are highly concentrated when compared with international competitors. In few other countries have brewers had a distributive incentive for owning the outlets through which beer, spirits and alcoholic drinks in general were sold to the public. National and local curbs on the sale of alcohol restricted the number of both 'on' and 'off' licences and thereby the channels of distribution through which brewery output could be sold. Brewers, therefore, needed to own pubs, bars and 'off-licences', as a means of both securing distribution for their products and restricting the market of competitors. The result was that these brewery-owned retail properties were restricted to selling only the products of the company that owned them. This is an arrangement which has come to be known as the 'tie', and is a unique and key feature of the UK licensed trade.

Throughout the decades after 1945 the industry underwent considerable concentration, as regional breweries and their estates of licensed properties either merged or were taken over by larger national companies to create a shrinking number of firms controlling more of the licences. By the late 1980s six major brewers controlled over 75 per cent of all the beer sales in the United Kingdom (Williams and Lincoln, 1996). Operating arrangements for licensed premises varied according to the location and success of the unit. Although the estate varied, a dominant pattern of ownership and control emerged during this period. The successful, typically urban pubs and bars were usually directly managed and controlled by the brewery. More marginal and peripheral properties, in suburban or rural settings, tended to be owned and tied to the brewery but operated by a tenant. In this respect the tenant can be described as a nominally independent businessperson who was supplied by, and paid rent to, the brewer. In many cases, brewers were prepared to take less than economic rents for these properties in exchange for the guaranteed outlet for their product (Williams and Lincoln, 1996). Indeed, this very fact was cited as a key factor in the 1998 EU ruling on the tie. This ruling allowed the tied system to continue in the UK despite the fact that it was in clear breach of EU regulations. There were also a smaller number of 'free houses' that existed. These free houses were owned independently from the breweries and were 'free' to be supplied by any brewery willing to supply them. In practice, these tended to be some of the most marginal and risky properties in rural settings. In many ways these properties are 'free houses' in both senses, and this helps them to be 'viable' as businesses (Price *et al.*, 1999). Even in these cases, breweries would try to 'tie' the pub to the brewery's products through soft-loans or preferential bonus schemes.

It is our view that even in these early arrangements, tenancies represent a form of franchising agreement, a view endorsed by Slade (1998) and Taylor (see Chapter 1). Furthermore, recent changes within pubs, and in both the trading and legislative environments, have had the effect of increasing pressures to franchise in a number of forms including:

- changes in drinking habits and loyalties, and uses of licensed premises;

- liberalization of drinking laws;

- the effects of measures to increase competitiveness in the industry.

This has meant that pubs owned and operated by the majority of larger firms have seen a dramatic increase in size and turnover as well as a focus on branding and blueprinting of operating concepts. Consequently, unit managers need to be more astute and skilled in an array of retailing and business management skills. In addition, the emergence of retailer organizations concerned to introduce business formats that empower the local operator has expanded interest in leasehold and more formal franchise relationships as well as the traditional tenancy.

This chapter specifically refers to licensed retailing as involving public houses and bars that retail alcoholic beverages on the premises, the companies who operate multiple units of these properties and the organizations that brew and wholesale beer. The chapter does not include consideration of franchising restaurants, hotels, clubs or other business that do not sell alcoholic beverages as a primary business function, nor does it consider the retailing of alcoholic beverages for consumption 'off' the premises. Using this definition, it is estimated that there are 76,091 pub outlets in the UK (Mintel, 1998a) and over 140,000 licensed outlets in total (Williams and Lincoln, 1996).

Recent background

By the late 1980s the major brewers dominated an increasingly concentrated brewing industry. The number of brewers supplying more than one outlet (that is, excluding micro breweries) had shrunk from 362 companies in 1950 to 141 in 1988, and a handful of firms supplied three out of every four pints of beer drunk in Britain. Furthermore, the major brewers controlled over 53 per cent of pubs, mostly the larger more profitable properties. Against this background the then Conservative government enacted legislation which might be typified as an example of ideology over self-interest. The major brewers had always provided significant financial support to the Conservative party, yet the 'Beer Orders' resulting from a Monopoly and Mergers Commission (MMC) Report in 1989 set about breaking up a 'complex monopoly' (Williams and Lincoln, 1996), much against the advice of the major companies. This led to a significant and concerted campaign resulting in a watering down of the original recommendations. The key provision in these regulations were:

- brewers owning over 2000 licensed premises had to make half the number owned over 2000 free of the exclusive tie to the brewer;

- brewers were required to allow the tied pubs to stock one 'guest' beer from another brewer;

- all pubs were free of any tie for the supply of non-beer products, including soft drinks, wines and spirits, etc.

Although there is considerable doubt whether the subsequent structure of the industry has increased choice and reduced uncompetitive pricing for customers (Slade, 1998), the effects of the 'Beer Orders' have been profound. The intention of the free market ideology was that the industry would subsequently be ordered round smaller brewers and more independent publicans. Mintel (1998a) estimate that there was a 6 per cent reduction in pub outlets between 1993 and 1998 – some 5,000 fewer properties. Similarly, there are now fewer brewers because several national and regional brewers have sold off their brewing interests to concentrate on retailing activities. Greenall Whitely, Boddingtons, Devenish and Grand Metropolitan are all examples. In the latter case, Grand Metropolitan did a 'pubs for breweries' swap with Courage. Courage subsequently set up Inntrapreneur Estates with Grand Metropolitan's leased pubs. As a consequence of this and other acquisitions, there are now only four major brewing companies in the UK. There was considerable speculation that this will reduce to two though it has not happened yet (Williams, 1996), despite the Office of Fair Trading turning down the proposed Bass/Carlsberg Tetley merger in 1998. The immediate impact of the 'Beer Orders' on pub ownership by the major brewers can be seen in Table 9.1. Since these changes were charted, however, Allied Lyons and Grand Metropolitan have

	1989 (pre-MMC rules)			November 1992 (post MMC rules)				
	Tenant	Manage	Total	Tenant	Manage	Lease	Total tied	Total owned
Allied-Lyons	4,458	2,400	6,858	1,900	2,700	1,200	4,600	5,800
Bass	4,285	2,469	6,754	-	3,100	1,400	3,100	4,500
Courage	4,620	400	5,020	-	-	-	-	-
Grand Metropolitan	3,200	1,580	4,780	2,300	1,650	4,200	3,950	8,150
Scottish & Newcastle	1,504	850	2,354	1,000	850	-	1,850	1,850
Whitbread	4,600	2,000	6,000	400	1,600	2,300	2,000	4,300

Source: Williams (1996)

Table 9.1 Pub ownership by the UK's biggest brewers, 1989–1992

	Pre MMC 1989	Post MMC 1992	1998
Nationals			
Tenanted/leased	22,000	9,700	4,000
Managed	10,000	9,500	8,500
Regionals			
Tenanted/leased	9,000	10,000	3,000
Managed	3,000	5,000	7,000
Independents			
Single outlets	16,000	15,800	16,000
Multiples			
Managed	–	750	3,500
Tenanted	–	7,250	15,000

Sources: Williams and Lincoln (1996); Martin and Coulson (1998)

Table 9.2 The structure of public house ownership, 1989–1992

ceased to brew altogether, Allied Lyons have divested themselves of all their pubs, the estates of Bass and Whitbread have been reduced and Scottish and Newcastle has more than doubled their pub holding (Price *et al.*, 1999).

The MMC recommendations resulted in different types of companies emerging as owners and operators of pubs. As we have seen, prior to the orders the brewers had been significant owners of pubs. Table 9.2 provides a global picture of public house ownership as a result of the changes precipitated by the Beer Orders.

Subsequently, five types of pub operators or *retailers* emerged as a result of the beer orders:

- national retailer with brewing interests;
- national retailer with no brewing interests (either de-merged or fully independent);
- regional or local retailer with brewing interests;
- regional or local multiple retailer with no brewing interests;
- totally independent operator or freehouses.

There are significant differences between these categories of retailer in terms of the way they operate their outlets and indeed in the type of outlets they own. In particular, there is a tendency for larger brewers and nationals to concentrate on managed

Hospitality, Leisure & Tourism Series

houses and for regional/local brewers and other retailers to concentrate on tenancies/leases. Furthermore, there has been some growth of retail companies focusing on leased/tenanted properties. Certainly these changes have been important factors in shaping the relationships between publican and pub operator. In addition, there have been significant changes in both the marketplace and the nature of pub businesses.

Changing consumer trends

Pub-going and the profile of the typical customer have gone through some dramatic changes over recent years (Lang, 1994). These are having a fundamental effect on the nature of products being offered in the pub, and most importantly for the topic of franchising, on the nature of the management of these businesses. Despite the general growth of other activities, gong to the pub still remains the UK's most popular out-of-home leisure activity (Mintel, 1998a). However, when compared with the immediate post-war period, pub customers are less overwhelmingly male beer drinkers. Typically, pub customers are now likely to include more women, families, youth and older people. They are drinking more soft and low alcohol drinks, wine and coffee. More premium label, premium beers and lagers and packaged drinks are being consumed, and customers are more likely to eat in pubs (Key Note, 1997b).

Increasingly pubs offer leisure facilities and games in the pub and these represent major sources of income. Table 9.3 provides a summary of some of these trends in macro terms. Alcoholic drink continues to be the major source of revenue in the industry,

	1993		1995		1997		% change 1993–97
	£m	%	£m	%	£m	%	
Alcoholic drinks	13,224	63	13,685	62	13,580	59	+3
Catering	3,358	16	3.752	17	4,4143	14	+23
Soft drinks	1,679	8	1,766	8	1,841	8	+10
Other *	2,729	13	2,869	13	3,452	15	+27
Total	20,990	100	22,072	100	23,017	100	+10

*Gaming machines, accommodation, telephones, vending etc.
Source: Mintel (1998)

Table 9.3 UK pubs market size by sector, 1993–1997

Period	Character of a pub	Consumer group	Products	Pub implementations
Up to the late 1960s	Drinking place	Men	• Bitter (mainly casks) • Spirits • Basic food	• Down-market • Basic facilities of the community • Home-grown entertainment • 'Ordinary' to working class men, not to other groups
1990s	Leisure experience	Men Youth Women Families Older people	• Increasing low/non-alcohol products (beers, soft drinks, coffee, spirits) • Increasing food sales • Increasing premium/special products (greater range of packaged products; more premium cask ales; more premium lagers) • Increased leisure facilities	• Signage/brand evolution • Concept types crystallize • Greater consumer recognition • Opportunity to sign and label pubs better • More open retail format • The term 'pub' will become less relevant • 'Pubs' will become more ordinary to society as a whole

Table 9.4 The evolution of the pub

but catering and the revenue from machines and accommodation (a significant part of 'other' in Table 9.3) are growing in both real terms and as a share of total income.

A recent publication by Whitbread Inns summarizes some of the changes in the pub over recent decades. Table 9.4 is a truncated version of the original, which tracked changes over four time periods, and shows just two periods. The top row typifies the pub in the period up to the late 1960s and the bottom row typifies the pub in the 1990s.

The increased emphasis on retailing and identifying market segments to target tightly defined service offers, among other things, has increased the use of branding in the licensed retailing sector. In particular, branding is focused at demographic groupings and pub visit occasions, such as, circuit/pre-club, chatting to friends, special meal out that suggests an array of service attributes, such as service style, ambience, music, food offered, as well as the drinks available. Through the 1990s branding in the licensed retail sector moved away from the beer product to include the total customer experience. Even in units that are not formally branded, the impact of targeting has been profound. Scottish and Newcastle, for example, make a distinction between branding and 'blueprinting'. In the latter case, the pub is aimed at identified customer types, but is not 'presented' as an identified brand with a common name and signage etc. However, unit management is trained to understand the customer occasions relevant to their pub and the **'critical success factors'** in the cloning of customer satisfaction. This approach recognizes the limitations of branding and the application of more sophisticated retailing practices.

The combined impact of these factors has led to dramatic changes in the strategic objectives of businesses and a radical restructuring of the industry sector. Earlier motives to secure distribution outlets and markets for brewed cask beer through the tie have become increasingly less relevant. At the start of the new millennium, the sector is going through a period of turbulent change, with mergers and divestment announced on a regular basis. As a consequence, organization forms are in a period of transition, with several contradictory tensions. The need to establish consistent brands with uniform operating systems creates pressures for highly centralized procedures and controls, yet at the same time successful units require flexibility and responsiveness to local customers and market needs. This relates to the concept of the empowered intrapreneur discussed in Chapters 4 and 5. On another level, the shift away from a preoccupation with outlets for beer sales means that skills needed by the manager are different. The management of fast moving, heavily branded, market focused businesses that have significant income streams from an array of sources require multi-skilled managers who are far removed from the stereotypical husband and wife publican traditionally described as a 'nice couple who keep a good pint'.

In the twenty-first century, unit managers have to be able to understand the food and other income stream operations as well as the alcohol and drinks operation. They need to analyse the markets and customer segments that use the business and the variety of occasions that trigger a trip to the pub. Based on this analysis, they need to be able to promote their pub to precise customer groups and think strategically about how to grow and develop the business over time. In addition, they require to manage and motivate employees, as well as control service quality and standards. They have to run the unit as an independent business whilst at the same time being constrained by brand operating standards and centralized decision making. Bearing in mind some of the comments made by Lashley in Chapter 5, the licensed retail sector has needed to explore alternative organizational forms to meet a variety of situations.

Those firms who continue to have substantial retailing businesses with high volume brands, tend to manage directly the bulk of the larger volume units. In the main these tend to be units with annual sales in excess of £600,000, while some units have annual sales over £2 million. These larger high volume businesses allow the brewer-linked retailers to make profits on both stages in the production and distribution chain, whilst the non-brewery linked licensed retailers can make additional profits through the purchasing benefits which come from high volume sales. With a few exceptions, these branded businesses are still organized round a command and control culture, and there have been few experiments with empowered unit management, or employee empowerment in general. Bass's Harvester Restaurants has been one notable exception (Ashness and Lashley, 1995), though there are currently signs that the brand will in future be managed in a more traditional command and control manner.

In addition to the benefits of increased profits through quasi-vertical integration and bulk purchasing, the branded approach with centrally devised operating standards, and focused customer segments, allows a more identifiable set of skills and competencies to manage and deliver the licensed retail services. These businesses therefore gain from economies due to management skills and development. They are able to defray staff and management training across higher volume sales and can be more focused on the skills and tasks needed by the brand. It would be crude to typify this as management by numbers, but there are some good examples where managers are given clear and simple step-by-step guidance about customers and the reasons why they are visiting the pub or restaurant.

Whilst the high volume branded businesses have generally been very successful and profitable, location limits and property scarcity constrain the role out of brands. In addition, there are beginning to be signs of customer resistance to brands beyond a certain size and the recognition of the brand 'life cycle'. An example of this is Scruffy Murphy's, a pub concept which experienced rapid growth of the brand, measured in the number of pub units, followed by an equally rapid decline of the brand. Furthermore, there are properties which, for one reason or another, are more marginal and do not lend themselves to the brand formula or generation of high volume business. In these cases, franchising units allows scope for a more flexible organization structure that minimizes the capital investment risk, adds a property income stream and increases total purchasing power. At heart though, franchising in licensed retailing aims to tap the creative drive of the individual entrepreneur to build the local business.

Interpretations of franchising

Slade (1998, p. 578) states that: 'One can view pubs owned by chains as well as those operated under long-term leasing as a form of franchising with no up-front fees.' Traditionally this was in the form of the tenancy, a brewery owned but independently operated pub which developed from the 'tie'. These pubs were identified as being part of the owning company by the use of the brewer's name in the signage and merchandising throughout the pub. In these circumstances the brewer's name could often generate a good deal of customer loyalty. For example, in Yorkshire Tetley's has a solid base of core customers who use these pubs because of loyalty to the beer brand on sale. The linking of the pub to the brewery usually had little impact on the operating systems or business format.

The tenancy form of franchising

The traditional pub tenancy has similarities with franchising as follows:

- Restrictions on the supply of products for the pub, with a requirement for the tenant to purchase all alcoholic beverages, and soft drinks through the brewery and often obliged to stock the range determined by the brewery.

- A requirement for the tenant to sell the products at agreed prices.

- Operational support from head office. Usually some or all of the following: an area/regional manager to give business management advice and support; technical support for storage and dispense of products (including free loan of necessary equipment); centrally developed marketing/promotional activity; and financial/accounting support.

- Quality assurance processes used by head office to assess and assist in managing the quality of product delivered to customers, in particular the quality of the brewer's product.

There were, however, some important differences when compared with the more traditional business format franchise. Chiefly, the specified standards applied to the brewer's core product ranges only, usually all or most alcoholic and non-alcoholic drinks. They did not include the range of other, non-drink, products offered. Unlike either the usual franchise agreement or a typical managed licensed retail brand, issues like service standards, cleanliness factors or environment and ambience were hardly ever specified. So the form of contract can be regarded as 'soft' in that it provides for a certain degree of regulation relative to product, and it is 'loose' relative to the enforcement of systems and services.

Without the structure of a rigid business format, the monitoring of unit performance has tended to be limited to sales turnover, ability to pay rents and other bills, and conduct an orderly house within the limits of the law. Service quality monitoring was minimal, if not non-existent, and support for tenants' management development was equally minimal in most companies.

Recent developments in licensed retailing have exposed some flaws in the traditional tenancy arrangement. As we have seen, in the past the pubs were turned over to tenants when the pub was deemed to be marginal to the parent company as a source of revenue and profits (Slade, 1998). In some cases, they were brought back into the managed estate when sales and profits had undergone growth. This was frequently as the result of the tenant's entrepreneurial flare, and some pubs 'yo-yoed' between managed and tenanted arrangements (Williams and Lincoln, 1996), which corresponds to the 'buy-back' approach discussed in Chapter 7. In the vast majority of cases, it suited the brewery to charge lower than market rates for pub rents because it retained the capital asset and ensured a distribution outlet for the beer product. Tenants often invested money into a property, to maintain it, which they had little chance of ever seeing any return on, or even recouping.

Consequently, the tenancy arrangement was criticised because tenants had little incentive to grow the business. They were not able to assign the tenancy and thereby gain from capital investment or improved business value. They could take profits from increased sales and higher volume business activity, but this was not translated into business value. With minimal risk to the brewer and minimal support to the tenant, many tenancies failed to meet their full potential because tenants had limited capital and managerial resources to grow the business. Increasingly, the licensed retail operators have explored leasing arrangements as a way of overcoming the weaknesses of the tenancy. This is a development which was also precipitated by the MMC 'Beer Orders' bringing tenants within the provision of the Landlord and Tenant Act, 1954.

Leasing form of franchising

The leasing agreement is chiefly focused at changing the financial arrangements between the leaseholder and the licensed retail organization. The aim is to encourage a more entrepreneurial relationship in which the leaseholder has a financial incentive to invest in the development of the pub as a business opportunity. Typically, the leaseholder pays a more commercial rent for a property which has some track record as a business.

Like all franchisees, the leaseholder is in part buying access to a business organization that has expertise and a business profile for the venture. As Morrison shows in Chapter 4, the franchisee aims to minimize risk by taking on the franchise arrangement. She describes a typical franchisee as being an intrapreneur rather than entrepreneur because of the restrictions placed on the franchisee by the operating system and the various other requirements to purchase supplies through the franchisor, etc. In many ways similar restrictions exist for the leaseholder in the licensed retail sector. Like tenants, leaseholders have to purchase product through the licensed retail organization, and the range of services and activities, which might be defined in the brand. That said, the operating standards and systems tend to be less restrictive than in some hospitality retail brands.

There are variations in both the levels of restriction placed on the leaseholder and the levels of support given by licensed retail organizations. The branded operations are more likely to require the leaseholder to conform to brand standards, and provide structured management development and training programmes.

Greenall's Pub Partnership charged all franchisees an annual fee based on 2 per cent of turnover, and this financed an active programme of courses to improve the management skills of franchisors. *The Publican* newspaper (1999) lists over 100 small and large licensed retailers who provide some kind of training support for tenants and leaseholders. In many ways the arrangements and relationship between the unit operator and the licensed retail organization have strong similarities. In general, lessees operate with fewer controls from the pub-owning company. The key difference is in the possibilities of the pub as 'volume' business and in the differences in investment arrangements which the lease provides to the leaseholder. Table 9.5 lists some of the key differences between tenancy and leasing arrangements.

Enterprise Inns draw a distinction between forms of operation based on the volume of sales. Where a pub has weekly sales of:

- over £10,000 the pub is managed;

- above £5,000 but below £10,000 the pub is leased;

- below £5,000 per week they recommend that the pub is put out to a tenancy.

This represents a triple prong, product distribution strategy, derived from a combination of agency and resource scarcity theory as discussed by Taylor in Chapter 1. The mixture of forms of control of pub properties can be confirmed in Table 9.6. It lists some major and minor national and regional licensed retailers,

	Tenancy	Lease
Term	5 years maximum	Up to 20 years
Cost	Smaller ingoing rent less than market rate Capital investment shared	Full leasehold purchase Realistic rent Capital investment lessee responsible
Conditions	Non-assignable No minimum barrelage Usually tied for majority of products A number of company imposed constraints	Assignable Minimum barrelage penalties Less wide ranging tie Fewer constraints
Maintenance	Joint responsibility	Lessee responsibility

Table 9.5 Tenancy and lease arrangements in licensed retailing

Licensed retailer	Total number	Managed	Tenanted	Leased
Commer Group	75	75		
Enterprise Inns	2351	96	1570	685
Everards Brewery	153	42	109	2
Greenalls Pubs & Restaurants	794	794		
Inn Partnership	1240		240	1000*
Inntrepreneur Pub Co.	1200		300	900
Phoenix Inns			500	
Scottish & Newcastle Retail	1910	1910		
Scottish & Newcastle Pub Enterprises				880
Tom Cobleigh	108	87	21	
Wolverhampton & Dudley	1890	820	1000	70

*Called franchises

Source: The Publican (1999)

Table 9.6 The estate of a selection of licensed retailers

highlighting arrangements for managed, tenanted and leased properties.

The tenancy/lease option is a way of spreading the risk associated with operating numerous businesses in dispersed properties which becomes difficult to control in a centralized command and control manner. The 'franchise' option through the tenancy/lease maintains a degree of control in the key areas but allows the majority of the 'retail' risk to be taken by the licensee and not the pub owners. This allows the brewer to balance the need to reduce risk against the need to generate income from their pubs. More income would come from managing the pubs themselves but this is considered to be more risky. So the decision on whether a pub is managed or franchised (tenancy/leased) is to a large extent about minimizing risk. As previously mentioned, this has often given rise to the four step **yo-yo principle,** in the following manner:

- Step 1: a pub is operated as tenancy or lease.

- Step 2: it becomes successful.

- Step 3: the brewer takes it back into direct management so the property owners (the licensed retailer) can reap the profit from it.

- Step 4: the pub declines in popularity and is then put back to franchise.

The yo-yo principle occurred more frequently when companies had a greater mix of tenancies and managed pubs in their estates. Larger retailers are now more confident in their retailing ability, have better pubs in their estates and they are concentrating on managing pubs. The majority of other retail companies have smaller/less successful pubs. In addition, the organization structures and/or capabilities of these companies means they are not in a position to operate large managed estates.

If a company has decided against having a predominantly managed estate, then they must decide if it should be tenanted or leased. From a company operating point of view the key elements of this decision centre on an assessment of risk and return. Leases put more of the onus on the lessee and reduce the potential risk (and possible return) for the owning company. Leases also require less capital investment than tenancies from the company. However, these points will depend on the motives for owning the pubs. Some companies (Nomura is an example) own pub properties as a property investment, and they are less concerned with the operation of the pub as a business. If the objective is to maximize property values, therefore, it is better to have tenancies because the company has more direct input into the maintenance of the property and it is easier to take the property back into full company possession for capital sale.

The companies featured in Table 9.6 provide examples of all these different approaches to managing the pub estate.

- The Commer Group is an independent licensed retailer that directly manages all the estate.

- Inn Partnership, recently sold to Nomura, was the former non-tied Greenall's properties. Interestingly, the arrangement was called franchising, though based round leasing arrangements with a limited business format imposed through a brand (see Illustration 9.1).

- Scottish and Newcastle Retail is an example of a major multi-branded brewer holding on to direct management of all its properties, and the non-managed estate is run by a separate division (Scottish and Newcastle Enterprises) through leasing arrangements.

- Wolverhampton and Dudley is an example of a large regional brewer with a mixed estate of directly managed, leased and tenanted pubs.

- Phoenix Inns is an independent licensed retailer with all properties in tenanted control.

Illustration 9.1 Inn Partnership (formally Greenall's Franchise)

Price *et al.*, (1999) describe the company's franchise in the following way: 'Greenall's was the only business format franchise in UK pub sector of any note' (p. 73). Franchisees were required to conform to the Greenall's business format. That is, they had to work to the company's marketing plan, operating procedures and standards, accounting and financial procedures, and other brand requirements such as layout and decor of premises and the uniforms worn by staff.

In return for a one-off franchise fee and a royalty based on sales revenue, the company provide franchisees with training in the operations and business management skills, and support franchisees with advice on staff training, management, advertising and research and development. Franchisees entered into a three-year contract with an option to renew for a further three years.

The Greenall's approach was much closer to the hard brand McDonald's type franchise system (see Chapters 1 and 11). The business format form of franchise: 'gave Greenall's a richer cash flow per unit than was available from tenancies' (Price *et al.*, 1999, p. 73). They compare the Greenall's Franchise arrangement with companies such as Enterprise Inns and Inn Business and show that not only did the company's units compare favourably on income, but they also had a lower vacancy rate. Greenall's franchised estate registered just under 5 per cent vacancies compared to an average of 12–15 per cent in tenanted units.

- Enterprise Inns also manage the majority of properties through tenanted arrangements though some are managed through leasehold and a small number are directly managed.

- Tom Cobleigh's is an example of a national branded business without links to brewing, which directly manages the bulk of the estate, but operates some through tenants.

Franchising arrangements through tenancies have much in common with franchising many other hospitality services. There are requirements to purchase supplies from the licensed retailer, and the licensee has access to skills and support from the larger organization. However, there are few examples of franchising the traditional business format with tightly defined and monitored brand attributes in the manner of McDonald's Restaurants. Licensed retailer organizations vary in their origins and business strategies as follows:

- Retail focused organizations are likely to prefer to directly manage the estate because it maximizes profits, but they are constrained by the variability of the estate.

- Where individual pubs are more marginal, retailers will franchise pubs as a means of reducing risk.

- Organizations that are more interested in pubs as a form of property investment are more likely to franchise the pubs through tenancy agreements because the short-term nature of the arrangements maximizes the property owner's control.

Franchisee profile

From the franchisee's perspective, the requirements to go into tenancy/lease are very similar. The key differences associated with taking a lease as opposed to a tenancy are summarized as:

- the higher initial start-up capital requirement for a lease;

- the lessee needs more on-going financial resources, particularly for property maintenance;

- less rigorous selection procedures of lessees , because 'having enough money' is a key consideration for the brewers;

- the recruitment of tenants has been more formal and more strictly applied because the property owner is more dependent on the tenant, who carries less personal risk.

The aspects that are considered when assessing potential tenants and lessees are financial status, industry experience, personal history and background. In addition, companies are now starting to look for evidence of business management skills and a sound business plan. For example, Whitbread Pub Partnership require all prospective lessees to produce a business plan prior to the selection interview with the company. Sargeant (1995) supports this and points to a number of benefits to both the potential franchisee and the licensed retailer.

The licensed trade tenant has traditionally been thought of stereotypically as the ex-professional footballer/policeman motivated more by lifestyle considerations than pure business goals (Lincoln, 1996). Or perhaps the more risk-averse entrepreneur choosing the easiest option to go into business for themselves. It being a relatively low cost business opportunity which is perceived as simple to operate, while, in addition, offering a domestic family residence above the pub. All in a business of which the potential tenant often has considerable experience. These individuals (or couples) are still prevalent, and the tenancy option continues to offer them good opportunities, providing a steady living with relatively limited risk. Whether it continues to be a stable situation depends on the competitive environment and how many more businesses the industry will lose in the continuing shake-out of the UK's pub stock.

The growth of the leased sector has seen, and is continuing to see, ongoing changes in attracting a more entrepreneurial, business oriented group of applicants. This development comes from the increased attention that the industry is being given as an entrepreneurial opportunity. Often in the past the 'real' entrepreneur would have gone for the freehouse opportunity. There is now an increasing move to look at the possibilities within leasing and the opportunities for developing chains of pubs leased from some of the bigger retail organizations. These entrepreneurs are more aware of the opportunities that now exist and also of the value of branding and the retail management approach being adopted.

The traditional view of the tenancy/leaseholder sector as the 'half way house' for those with a wish for less risk and a willingness to accept the consequent reduced opportunity for reward may be changing. The gap between tenancies and leases can be regarded as small in practical terms but in terms of the franchisee profile is likely to get wider, with tenancies offering the lifestyle option and leases giving a home to those with the entrepreneurial spirit. There can be a tendency for tenancy agreements to stifle the entrepreneurial behaviour of the franchisee. Tenants tend to be older than lessees and when coupled with limited direction and business support available from head office this often leads to the situation where tenants are happy to simply control the business with no thoughts of growth or development. In contrast, leases are closer to the freehouse concept, offering more scope with the consequent risk. This development is also likely to be encouraged by the move to a more retail orientation in these businesses and the recruitment and selection of lessees being taken more seriously than it was in the past.

Finally, many multiple licensed retailers act as franchisees. For example, Whitbread Restaurants and Leisure Division franchise several US based business formats, including TGI Friday and Pizza Hut. In these cases they are larger nationals looking to fill gaps in their portfolio and matching licensed retail skills to the product experience of another organization. As the development of retailing expertise increases in the larger firms, the need to import products will decrease, and this will perhaps increase the opportunities for the smaller firms.

Pertinent management issues

Franchisee selection

The *Publican* (1999) survey of 100 pub companies revealed there were likely to be over 2000 vacancies for managers, tenants and leaseholders over the succeeding twelve-month period. There are difficulties with recruiting suitable tenants and lessees for some companies. Indeed, it would appear that this is a recurring theme relative to franchising in general (see Chapter 6). This is specifically the case where non-managed companies want to operate their pubs in a more structured and retail-oriented way. They need better-qualified and more capable people, who appear to be in short supply. This corresponds to Fulop's finding in Chapter 2, where she points to the need to widen the franchisee recruitment base. It is difficult to match the skills needed in these more entrepreneurial circumstances. The opportunities and rewards being offered by the companies operating large branded and blueprinted estates, where career-minded business people can now see real opportunities, exacerbate these recruitment difficulties. A number of these companies are making concerted efforts to recruit the kind of skilled and capable operators who would be potential tenants. However, there is already evidence that the increased standardization and control of branded outlets may encourage the more entrepreneurial of managers to look to tenancies as an outlet for their flair, much like the McDonald's approach highlighted in Chapters 1 and 11.

Leasing arrangements have had detrimental media coverage in recent years, and this could contribute to the recruitment problem. There are much more rigorous recruitment procedures for 'good' pubs than ordinary ones. Some are advertised through a quarter-page advertisement in trade press. They are seen as important and potentially attractive to franchisees though the main sources of tenants now, as in the past, tends to be through informal networks, word of mouth and speculative enquiries to the operating company.

Financial arrangements

Licensed retail unit rents have been a controversial issue. The European Union recently allowed that the tie was acceptable, though against competition legislation, because of the cheap rents afforded to tenants. The alternatives are to offer cheap rent and the tie, or charge market rent but then loosen the tie. Punch Taverns have had a long running battle with their tenants over attempts to increase rents without recourse to a rent tribunal. In the end, this was a battle which the company lost, establishing that the Landlord and Tenant Act does apply in the licensed retail sector.

The issue of discounts is a major one for both franchisee and franchisor. For a large number of companies, owning and operating tenancies and leases, the discount they receive from the brewers provides the major source of income. The discount is not passed on to their tenants/lessees, who are charged market rate

Hospitality, Leisure & Tourism Series

for their beer. The difference between market price and the discount price, which in 1999 was in some cases up to and over £80 per barrel, being the revenue for the retailing company. In this respect they are effectively acting as wholesalers within the distribution system, negotiating bulk purchase deals, buying in beer and selling on at a profit. In addition, tenants of companies that also brew are tied to that company's products and receive no discount. This results in a bizarre situation which means that beer costs more for internal franchisees than independent retailers. The actual consumer therefore does not receive any benefit from wholesale discounts or any price reductions that may occur. Both the independent managed licensed retailers and the brewery retailers have an interest in tenants/lessees selling more beer at the expense of other products, because the sale of beer generates more income for them. As a result a number of lease agreements have minimum barrelage clauses built in. If lessees purchase below the agreed minimum amount of beer over a given period they are charged penalties reflecting the amount below the limit ordered. This can be seen as a constraint on the retailing decision making within these pubs, which may well inhibit them from competing with pubs that do not operate under such a constraint, i.e. freehouses and managed pubs.

The self-repairing element of leases has been a persistent issue of discussion relative to its fairness to lessees. In most arrangements the leaseholder is responsible for property maintenance, though the property owner may contribute to property development that leads to capital appreciation. In reality this is a fairly regular occurrence. Now that the retailing focused operating companies have significantly improved the quality of their estates, there is a much greater incentive for them to maintain the value of their capital assets. The companies with estates at the bottom end of the market, more often than not the tenanted estates, may still be in the position, as has been the case since the 1970s, of not wishing to invest in pubs that show potential for return in the short to medium term. Often the tenanted pubs are the most marginal properties that the major chains have disposed of and tenants argue that this is also making it more difficult for them to compete. The idea behind the longer term and assignability of leases as opposed to tenancies is that it encourages lessees to invest more capital in the pub and have a keener interest in its success.

Support infrastructure/operational control

The level of control delivered by the tie varies. In some cases the tie is total, in that all products and suppliers must be as specified.

In other cases the tie specifies that certain beer products must be sold. There are financial reasons for the pub owners to maintain the tie at a greater level but some of the more enlightened ones are realizing that increased freedom for tenants/lessees may afford the owners more competitive benefit in the long run.

In terms of organizational culture there tend to be two kinds that apply to tenancy/lease. They reflect the level of control in the tie, and may or may not bear a relationship to the formal agreement between the franchisee and the licensed retail company. They are:

- a collaborative/partnership blueprint where the model is for business development supported by the owning company;

- a more exploitative landlord–tenant model where the owning company look for ways to maximize their income from each pub irrespective of whether it is in that pub's long-term or short-term interests.

The balance is in favour of the more collaborative model and support continues to move in that direction. This represents a fundamental element in the discussion of licensed retail franchising. It has informed a number of the issues that have been discussed so far in this chapter and it is central to most of the elements in this section.

Tied pubs of all kinds are provided with the equipment required to store and dispense the beer as appropriate, such as, cellar equipment, pumps, coolers and fonts, and there is often a contract, which provides maintenance for this equipment. The suppliers usually provide these free, which can be another powerful incentive not to change suppliers or to offer another company's products.

After the initial development of the leasehold approach in licensed retailing, immediately after the MMC Beer Orders, there was some underhand dealing from suppliers in this area. Some pubs wishing to stock guest beers from other suppliers, as legislated for by the Beer Orders, were threatened with having dispense equipment removed or not maintained if they went ahead. Though this practice appears to have almost died out, the use of a particular supplier's equipment for dispense is still a constraint on the retailing decision making of a large number of pubs.

Maintenance of product quality is a key issue, as opposed to the entire business format – i.e. ensuring that tenants/lessees are delivering the quality of product as specified by the brewer. This is a particular issue with cask conditioned ales. The 'Cask

Marque' scheme was originally set up by a small group of brewers to assure product quality in tied pubs selling the beer of the companies in the scheme. There are now over twenty companies in the scheme including Whitbread and Carlsberg Tetley. Also, the 1999 Guinness advertising campaign focused on educating customers as to what is required to produce a good pint, the aim being that they will insist on this quality delivery from the pubs they visit.

Area management support is available for all tenants and lessees. This is business management advice to assist tenants/ lessees in decision making about their pubs. However, it can also be surreptitiously about getting them to sell more beer! The level and availability of advice varies greatly. Some companies have one area manager per twenty pubs, another may have one per fifty to sixty pubs. The key issue is the extent that the retail organization is supporting franchisees as 'independent' businesses or attempting to control them in order to achieve exploitatively their own company goals. Where the role is more advisory and supporting the span of control will be narrower, so that the 'Business Development Manager' or 'Operations Consultant' can spend more time developing each individual tenant/lessee.

Staff training and development is provided in some enlightened companies; others provide support and advice for this, or require franchisees to undertake the British Institute of Innkeeping's qualifications. The *Publican* (1999) survey of 100 pub companies who promote some form of training shows a variety of requirements for managers, tenants and leaseholders. Most licensed retailers train managers of their directly managed properties. Inn Partnership (formally Greenall's) provided an impressive programme of courses for tenants and lessees, funded by a 2 per cent levy on turnover. This type of training and development offer reflects the movement of some companies away from the control model, to the business development focus mentioned earlier. There are other pub-owning companies moving in this direction, such as Punch Taverns, which has some interesting initiatives. Generally, however, support for tenanted leaseholder development is patchy. Worse still is the almost non-existent development offered to pub employees in these businesses. Such training that is provided is developed by the independent franchisee.

Specific promotional material is provided by brewers/drinks companies for particular brands of drink. This is becoming more targeted at the needs of particular outlets and their customers but is still largely generic. However, beyond this marketing support is limited. This represents a key difference with franchising in other sectors.

Empowerment

Operational decision making takes place at the tenant/lessee level, with the exception of the areas mentioned in the previous section. This is particularly the case if an independent managed licensed retailer, as opposed to a brewery-linked company owns the pub. There is also more independence in the smaller local and regional companies than in the larger nationals. The pub owners have a focus on beer sales as a key objective, and empowerment, if it exists at all, will be tied to this objective. Aspects like minimum barrelage and the wholesale pricing of beer are attempts to limit this empowerment. The franchisees in licensed retail businesses, whether tenants or leaseholders, have an immediate operational control over costs, and resource management. In some ways they have more freedom to operate in an empowered mode, but with less support from the centre, than in traditional hospitality retail operations.

The future

As licensed retailers develop their estates to maximum potential and improve their retailing skills they will look to diversify even more, and there will be increased opportunities to franchise in other sectors, such as hotels. Similarly, as brands develop it may be possible to franchise them out to other sectors. It could be speculated that the likes of the Rat & Parrot pub concept could be franchised to hotels, or All Bar One will be part of large-scale mixed retail and leisure developments. In addition, the growth of brands has not totally escaped the notice of the franchised sector, though as yet it has been slow to respond. It is a distinct possibility that within a short period of time there will be non-managed retailers offering brands to franchisees. These may be either brands they have developed themselves or ones which have in turn been franchised from the major retail players. It is our view that the benefits that franchising can bring to licensed retail organizations will cause rapid growth of franchising in the sector, for all the reasons outlined, for example, in Chapters 1, 2 and 4.

Internationalization through cross-border franchising will offer a tremendous opportunity, following on from the success of other franchise companies. Licensed retailers have long sought to expand abroad, both selling beer and in retailing. Indeed, there is evidence of franchising being used to lead a global distribution push for Guinness.

Pubs with business development potential may become available for 'franchise' as larger retailers develop new sites at the top end of their estate and are forced to release pubs at the bottom end. Further down the line it is possible that if the larger retailers do franchise out brands, it will be the smaller independently managed multiple licensed retailers, and not individuals, that take them on because of the capital needed and operational expertise required. It is proposed that the likelihood of early franchising of brands will come from single brand operators like Yates' Wine Lodge or Wetherspoons. Furthermore, it is anticipated that the high capital costs of branding will reduce as the requirements for brand development and implementation become better understood, and more standardized/structured.

Summary

The licensed retail sector is undergoing a period of rapid change. The effects of changes in the marketplace and in the legislative environment have resulted in important changes in the structure of the industry. Specifically, the Monopolies and Mergers Commission's recommendations limiting the links between breweries and the pub estate 'tied' to the brewer, and changes in the uses to which licensed premises are put in the UK, have resulted in some radical structural changes in the industry.

The larger brewers have held on to the high volume properties in a directly managed form. In other cases, licensed retail organizations have emerged with a variety of ownership and control arrangements for their properties. The licensed retailer will directly manage properties that have a high volume of sales and make good profits for the pub estate. Where properties are more marginal the licensed retailer has explored leasing properties as a way of encouraging entrepreneurship in the licensee. The longer term of the lease and the more substantial capital investment needed is felt to be an improvement on the tenancy agreement. In the latter case, the most marginal properties are still managed by tenants, and in some cases companies have emerged which are mostly concerned with property as an investment rather than the business use.

Franchising in the licensed retailing context has been chiefly concerned with securing outlets for brewery products. Traditionally the tenancy was a device that kept the licensed outlet in the brewery's control, and at the same time denied an outlet to competitors. Unlike many other service sector industries, franchising by the licensed retailer has not been viewed primarily as a means of funding expansion.

The change processes under way at the start of the twenty-first century have intensified the search for alternative organizational relationships, which create a more entrepreneurial climate for the licensee. That said, both the tenancy and lease are similar to, and different from, franchising systems based round business formats or highly defined hospitality service brands. In these circumstances, franchisees have restriction placed on them regarding the sources of supply and are supported, to varying degree, by the licensed retail organization. On the other hand, the less precise format allows the franchisee more scope to interpret service standards and resource usage than might be the case in more defined hospitality services. In the long, run it is possible to speculate that franchising will emerge as a strategy for expansion in licensed retail operations which has many similarities to other hospitality service operations.

Debate topics

- The 'tied' pub concept represents an original form of brand name franchising from which current franchising activity in hospitality services has evolved.

- A lessee of a licensed retail outlet can be defined as an intrapreneur.

- Franchisees in the licensed retail trade prioritize wealth maximization objectives over those of a more 'life-style' nature.

- Franchising in the licensed retail trade represents a product distribution, as opposed to a unit expansion, strategy.

Selected readings

Martin, P., Coulson, P. (1998) *M&C Report – June*. Benedict Books.
Price, S., Bleakely, M. and Pennington, J. (1999) *After the Precipice: Sector Update UK Breweries, Pubs & Restaurants*. Investment Report, Credit Suisse First Boston (Europe) Ltd.
Slade, M. (1998) Beer and the tie: did divestment of brewery owned public houses lead to higher beer prices? *The Economic Journal*, **108** (May), 565–602.

References

Ashness, D. and Lashley, C. (1995) Empowering service workers at Harvester Restaurants. *Personnel Review*, **19**(4), 17–32.
Guild, S., (1996) Lease is more. *Caterer and Hotelkeeper*, 31 October, pp. 76–7.

Key Note (1997a) *Breweries and the Beer Market*. Key Note Limited.

Key Note (1997b) *Public Houses*. Key Note Limited.

Lang, S. (1994) The Pub and Social Trends. In *Proceedings of 'The pub in 2000' Conference*. CAMRA, pp. 12–16.

Lincoln, G. (1996) The need for a new breed of licensee. *International Journal of Wine Marketing*, **6**(4).

Martin, P. and Coulson, P. (1998) *M&C Report—— June*. Benedict Books.

Mintel (1998a) *Pub Retailing March 1998*. Mintel.

Mintel (1998b) *Pub Visiting May 1998*. Mintel.

Price, S. (1999) The beer dilemma: higher prices and little profit. *The Hospitality Review*, **1** (2), 4–8.

Price, S., Bleakely, M. and Pennington, J. (1999) *After the Precipice: Sector Update UK Breweries, Pubs & Restaurants*. Investment Report, Credit Suisse First Boston (Europe) Ltd.

The Publican (1999) Industry trainers. No. 692, 26 April, pp. 24–33.

Sargeant, M. (1995) A bright forecast. *Caterer and Hotelkeeper*, 7 December, pp. 58–9.

Slade, M. (1998) Beer and the tie: did divestment of brewery owned public houses lead to higher beer prices? *The Economic Journal*, **108** (May), 565–602.

Whitbread Inns (1995) *The Changing Face of the British Pub*. Whitbread Plc.

Williams, C. (1996) The British pub: an industry in transition. *Cornell Hotel and Restaurant Administration Quarterly*, Winter, pp. 62–72.

Williams, C. and Lincoln, G. (1996) New directions for the licensed trade: a structural analysis. *International Journal of Wine Marketing*, **7** (1), 5–18.

Travel trade and transport

Lesley Pender

Key points

- Franchising is an emerging form of partnership for European travel trade and transport organizations.

- Airlines and retail travel agents are using franchising to meet various strategic objectives, including market growth, international market entry, and technology and distribution systems access.

- Travel trade and transport franchises display both standard and unique characteristics, management issues and critical success factors.

- The future of franchising as an organizational form, in the complex and dynamic travel trade and transport sectors, cannot be guaranteed.

Introduction

The travel trade and transport industries constitute a significant area of economic activity within the service sector. They are principally involved in the organization and sale of travel and tourism services and the movement of tourists to, from and within destinations. These represent two of the main components of travel and tourism distribution, particularly in the UK, which has a well-developed outbound tourism industry. Transport in this context relates to those transport forms for which a significant amount of business is derived from tourists.

In recent years, sectors of the travel and tourism industry have been experimenting with the concept of franchising. Holloway and Robinson (1995, p. 137), writing about tourism, define franchising as:

> an arrangement under which a business (whether principal or distributor) known as the franchisor grants an organization (the franchisee) the right to use the company's name and market its products in exchange for a financial consideration.

In this respect, tourism franchising is no different from franchising in other industry sectors. Furthermore, this definition applies equally to both the travel trade and transport sectors. There are none the less a number of ways in which the operation of franchising can vary between the different sectors and organizations, as will become evident as this chapter develops.

Essentially, airline franchising involves smaller operators adopting the brand image, uniforms and livery of the majors. As with more traditional areas of franchising, activities such as marketing may be undertaken on behalf of the franchisee. An important feature of the relationship is that the franchisee often acts as a feeder carrier for the franchisor. Acting as a franchisor appeals to airlines with high cost structures, especially in an environment of increasing price pressures. Travel agency franchising similarly involves smaller companies, known as 'independents'. They adopt the brand name and corporate image of a larger organization and gain access to some centralized business activities and resources.

Despite its short history, the development of franchising in certain areas of the travel trade and transport sectors has been rapid. In the US, airlines have used franchising as a method of extending their marketable networks since deregulation of their domestic airline industry in 1978. An early example from the US is that of Air Florida (1980), which used commuter flights provided by Air Miami (Davies and Quastler, 1995). US Air (now US Airways) is a further American example. The company's US Air Express division is purely composed of franchisees, although interestingly this division uses slightly different livery from the mainline company (Sloan, 1996). It is only more recently that European airlines have become involved in franchising, examples of which include British Airways, KLM and Lufthansa. Within the retail travel sector, franchising has also been applied with some success. A notable example is that of Uniglobe, a Canadian travel agency chain focusing on business travel which operated twenty-three franchises in Britain and over 1000 worldwide by 1999. Further chains to become involved in franchising more recently are Bonanza Travel and Advantage Travel Centres. Both these organizations are discussed in more detail throughout the remainder of this chapter.

However, other significant travel trade and transport sub-sectors have not, to date, shown evidence of franchise activity. In general, tour operators have displayed more interest in the consortia form of organization, and vertical integration, than they have in franchising. Some transport organizations, such as bus companies, operate franchises yet have less involvement in tourism as they exist mainly to service local communities. The focus of this chapter is therefore on two travel trade and transport sectors – retail travel agents and scheduled airlines. Together these sectors illustrate effectively the application of franchising within travel trade and transport whilst providing adequate scope to compare and contrast the organizational arrangements utilized within each sector.

The chapter content is divided into four main sections. The first two sections provide an overview of the structure, characteristics, dominant trends and franchisee benefits associated with the retail travel trade and scheduled airlines respectively. Section three integrates the two sectors in an analysis of the adoption of franchising as an appropriate strategy. Finally, the chapter concludes by making an assessment as to the future for travel trade and transport franchising.

Retail travel agencies

Retail travel agencies are located between principals and consumers in the chain of travel distribution. Their role is to sell travel products for the principals whilst acting as an information bureau and purchasing point for consumers. They provide an alternative to direct sales of leisure and business travel products. Currently, in the UK travel agents represent a significant force in terms of the distribution of particular travel services. A network of 7,276

Association of British Travel Agents (ABTA) travel agency offices, representing an average of 3.6 branches per member, are involved in the sale of around four-fifths of the overseas package holidays in the UK. Expenditure by UK residents at travel agencies reached an estimated £10.25 billion in 1997, the majority of which was on overseas travel (Key Note, 1998).

Retail travel trade: structure

Renshaw (1997) furthers our understanding as regards the structure of the retail travel trade sector in presenting a typology of different types of travel agent, which he divides in three ways, as presented in Table 10.1.

Defining factor	Explanation
Size of organization	Travel agents can be large firms referred to as multiples or smaller companies known as independents. Multiples can be further classed as *multinationals*, with a worldwide presence (e.g. Thomas Cook, American Express), as *national multiples*, with offices throughout the UK (e.g. Going Places, Lunn Poly, Advantage Travel Centres), or as *regional multiples* or *miniples* (e.g. Bakers Dolphin, Callers Pegasus). The latter are concentrated in particular areas of the country. Independents are often single shop agencies, although those companies with a small number of outlets are also classed as independents
Type of business conducted	Travel agents can be categorized as general or leisure agents, holiday agents and business agents. General (or leisure) agents sell most types of travel product and the majority of the multiples fall into this category. Holiday agents specialize in the sale of inclusive tours whilst business agents deal with commercial clients
Appointment	There are two main appointments sought by travel agents in the UK. These are Association of British Travel Agents (ABTA) licences and International Air Transport Association (IATA) licences. ABTA is a voluntary association of travel agents and tour operators. The role of ABTA is changing. IATA performs a crucial role in the industry as it is only once an IATA licence has been granted that an agency can sell scheduled airline tickets for international travel. These licences can be difficult to obtain due to conditions imposed by IATA. The organization has an investigation panel, which examines agencies applying for membership

Source: Adapted from Renshaw (1997 pp. 18–28)

Table 10.1 Travel agent types

According to Key Note (1999), between 1994 and 1998 the Association of British Travel Agents (ABTA) lost nearly a fifth of its members, yet the number of retail travel agency offices in the UK remained more or less the same. Most retail travel agents concentrate on the leisure sector of the outbound holiday market and are heavily reliant on the sales of All Inclusive Tours (AITs). With approximately 70 per cent of AITs sold through the retail travel trade, most of the major AIT tour operators have integrated forward to their own retail outlets. Between 1994 and 1997, concentration in the retail travel agency remained more or less stable, although there was scope for increased concentration. The principal reason for the marked stability was the investigation by the Monopolies and Mergers Commission (MMC) into vertical integration of the foreign holiday business. At the end of 1997, the MMC effectively ruled that vertical integration was not against the public interest. This paved the way for further consolidation, notably the tie up between World Choice Carlson and ARTAC (a buying group of independent travel agents) and the proposed merger between Carlson and Thomas Cook. The survey of travel agents conducted for the MMC's report on 'Foreign Package Holidays' (1997) found that 71 per cent of travel agencies had one outlet. The turnover of the average independent travel agency is far less than the turnover of the average branch outlet of a multiple chain. Consequently, the market share of the multiple retailers is much higher than their share of outlets. In 1997, the top four multiple retail owners accounted for 52.9 per cent, with only 31.7 per cent of outlets. Dominant retail travel agents are Lunn Poly owned by the Thomson Travel Group, Going Places owned by the Airtours group, and Thomas Cook.

Retail travel trade: characteristics

Four key characteristics associated with retail travel agents are: commission structure; concentration of ownership; entry barriers; and technology. These are now discussed.

- **Commission structure:** Traditionally principals have paid travel agents on a commission basis. The exact amount of commission paid varies in practice, but typically this might be between 7 and 11 per cent. Commission overrides (an increase upward in the amount paid which is not dependent on performance), and incentive payments (paid for reaching a certain level of sales) are also used. A move to fee-based payment systems for some companies has been implemented and further moves towards this may occur in the future.

- **Concentration:** The retail travel sector displays high levels of concentration. This is largely a result of horizontal integration, as discussed later in this chapter. Concentration in the travel agency sector grew rapidly in the late 1980s and early 1990s to plateau in the mid–1990s. According to Key Note (1998), since 1995 the number of travel agencies held by the top four companies has remained more or less constant at between 31 and 32 per cent. Renshaw (1997) examines this and other aspects of the retail travel sector in detail.

- **Entry barriers:** The travel agency sector traditionally had low barriers to entry but in recent years these have increased as more sophisticated technology is required and as price competition from the pervasive High Street marketplace has increased (Key Note, 1998).

- **Technology:** Technological developments have greatly affected the travel agency sector. As retail travel is concerned with the distribution of services the focus is on information provision and dissemination, which is ideally suited to technological methods of distribution. Computer reservations systems (CRS) have been particularly influential. The impact of CRS has been felt by independents that may not have sufficient financial backing to invest in the necessary technology. CRS are discussed fully by Inkpen (1998). More recent significant technological developments include CD-ROM technology, the Internet and multi-media kiosks. There is currently much debate as to whether these newer forms of distribution will eventually replace the traditional travel agents.

Retail travel agents: dominant trends

Given the structure and characteristics identified in the previous sections, established small independent retail travel agents are becoming increasingly vulnerable as their operating environment changes and becomes ever more aggressive. Many are looking for some form of interdependent umbrella support structure, as referred to in Chapter 4, as a strategy designed to sustain or grow market share. Where there is a strong desire to retain some degree of independence franchising can represent an attractive form of business relationship. Consequently, a major trend within the retail travel sector has been the creation of franchise organizations with strong power bases. This greatly improves the negotiating power of the travel agents with principals, and by

Description	Number of franchisees	Geographic locations	Start date
Specializes in dealing with independent travellers. It was established in 1995 and the first agreement with a franchisee was signed in 1997.	18 (2 pending)	Aberdeen	April 1998
		Bradford	February 1999
		Cornwall & Plymouth	January 1999
		Dundee	August 1997
		East Kilbride	December 1998
		Exmoor	November 1998
		Guildford	August 1998
		High Wycombe	September 1997
		Huddersfield	March 1998
		Isle of Man	Pending
		Lincoln	Pending
		London	May 1998
		Northampton	March 1999
		Norwich	March 1999
		Oldham	May 1998
		Reading	November 1998
		Stansted	June 1998
		West Lothian	March 1999

Source: Bonanza Travel (1999)

Table 10.2 Franchise system profile: Bonanza Travel

passing on any decrease in commission payments to consumers these travel agents can increase their market share considerably. Significantly, market share is often considered more important than profit by organizations in the travel trade. An example of one such retail travel agent, originating in the UK, is Bonanza Travel. Table 10.2 provides a profile of this organization.

Retail travel agents: franchisee benefits

Specific examples of benefits achieved through becoming a franchisee in a particular established franchise system can be identified in the form of: override commission; pooled marketing budget and expertise; brand image; and access to accounting systems. Advantage Travel Centres' franchisees obtain override commission. Commissions from the parent organization, the Airtours Group, range from a base of 13 per cent up to 17 per cent if targets are met (Harding and Noakes, 1999). Franchisees also

Hospitality, Leisure & Tourism Series

benefit from a £2 million annual marketing budget, and new brand image as reflected by new shop fascias (Harding and Noakes, 1998b). Access to accounting systems operated by franchisors can benefit franchisees, as was the case of the Exchange Travel Group. Although no longer operating, it was described by Holloway (1994) as having the attraction of accounting back-up provided by head office which freed up branch managers for other purposes, such as marketing. This has similarly been a feature of the more recent Advantage/Airtours franchise agreement, which is used as a mini-case study later in this chapter.

With respect to retail travel agent franchising in general, it is possible to identify some generic benefits for franchisees. The combination of these benefits may facilitate improvement to competitive position. In particular, franchising has the potential to:

- provide a means of **business start-up** for a relatively modest investment;

- serve to ease and speed **market entry** through the adoption of the established brand image of the franchise system;

- facilitate rapid movement up the **learning curve,** utilizing the knowledge and experience of the franchisor, particularly crucial to franchisees new to an industry sector and specifically one as specialized and complex as the travel industry;

- provide access to essential **technology** and **distribution systems** for smaller retail travel operators lacking in the resources and expertise to develop their own;

- enable franchisees to gain **negotiatory power** through consolidation within a franchise system where principals can influence commission rates, prices and levels of service;

- offer franchisees in the retail travel sector heavily **discounted personal travel**.

These benefits are illustrated within the context of Bonanza Travel (Illustration 10.1)

Scheduled airlines

According to Key Note (1999), since April 1997, non-UK airlines within the European Union (EU) have been allowed to operate domestic services within the UK, but almost all domestics services are served by UK airlines. In 1997, there were thirty-two

---

Illustration 10.1 Bonanza Travel

Initial investment in a Bonanza Travel franchise is relatively low, as **business start-up** can be from home and there is no stock to purchase. The company indicates that a typical initial investment including franchise fee would be £17,000 whilst the typical amount of working capital required is £5,000. Since its inception in 1996, Bonanza Travel has established brand awareness and recognition in the marketplace, which should assist in the ease and speed of **market entry** for new franchised retailers. The majority of Bonanza franchisees are new to the travel trade and draw on ongoing support from a team of both travel and franchise experts in order to fast track up the **learning curve**. The franchisor provides franchisees with modem connection to airlines, tour operators and private bulletin boards, along with computer software with more than 200,000 airfares and connecting franchisees to the computer reservation systems of every major airline. This enables access to essential **technology** and **distribution systems**. The franchisor **negotiates** relative to commission rates, prices and customer service levels on behalf of franchisees in the Bonanza system. The company's franchisee prospectus stresses that franchisees will work hard but can also enjoy playing hard through accessing a 'perk' of the system which is heavily **discounted personal travel.**

Source: Bonanza Travel (1999)

UK-registered airlines that carried more than 100,000 passengers and fifteen that registered more than one million passengers.

The airline industry is often described as consisting of two distinct types of carrier – scheduled and charter. Whilst a number of distinguishing features have been put forward, the fact that scheduled carriers predominantly sell seats directly to customers is important. Charter airlines are often either owned by tour operators or charter their services to them for particular periods of time. Scheduled carriers operate to a published timetable. The differences between the two airline forms are, however, lessening. Within the scheduled market a distinction can still be drawn on the basis of the size of different scheduled carriers with the largest airlines often referred to as the **majors.** In addition, there are smaller, regional carriers, which often service routes that feed into the majors' routes. A further category of scheduled carrier is that of low cost carrier. It is with scheduled carriers that this chapter is concerned.

Scheduled airlines: structure

In the scheduled sector, British Airways accounts for 60 per cent of scheduled passengers carried by UK airlines. The other major UK-registered scheduled airlines are British Midland, KLM UK

(Air UK until bought by the Dutch KLM in 1997), Virgin Atlantic Airways, British Regional Airlines, CityFlyer Express and Jersey European Airways, who all carried more than a million scheduled passengers in 1997 (Key Note, 1999).

In terms of international passengers, British Airways (BA) is the largest airline in the world and dominates all other UK airlines. This is primarily due to its history as the UK's national carrier following the merger of BEA and BOAC in 1974. Since its privatization in 1987, BA has been one of the world's most successful airlines in terms of profitability, recording profits during the recession of the early 1990s when most other major airlines produced losses. The company's mission is to be the undisputed leader in world travel, with a goal of being the first choice airline in key markets. In many respects, it can be said to have achieved its aims and is used as a blueprint for national airline privatization in an increasingly deregulated global industry.

Scheduled airlines: characteristics

The four key relevant characteristics associated with the scheduled airline sector are: competition, concentration, entry barriers and technology. These are now discussed.

- **Competition:** European liberalization occurred in three packages of measures, the last of which came into effect in April 1997. This rendered Europe's airline environment, like those in North America and other areas of the world, which have deregulated, far more exposed to competition. This process acted as a strong force of change within an increasingly slow-growing and competitive domestic market. Of significance has been the development of strategic location hub and spoke networks. This involves alliance relationships between smaller regional airlines, which feed into the hub, enabling major airlines to pick up on the longer-haul 'trunk' route. This complementarity of services helps both sets of carriers to become more competitive whilst also providing consumer benefits. Furthermore, the emergence of low-cost scheduled carriers is adding to the competitive environment. Offering extremely low fares, these carriers, including EasyJet and Ryanair, are meeting customer needs in Europe, as are the low cost airlines of North America. Airline competition extends to other transport forms and high-speed rail travel can be seen to be important in this respect. The London–Paris market is established and a service has been launched in Belgium. The

Channel Tunnel is also significant, with Eurostar rail services accounting for a 25 per cent fall in air passengers on the London–Paris route in 1996 compared to 1994.

- **Concentration:** The economies of scope that can be derived from operating a large, extensive network act as incentives towards mergers and alliances which in turn lead to a more highly concentrated industry. In common with the travel agency sector, the airline industry displays high levels of concentration. According to Hanlon (1996), there are approximately 1,200 scheduled airlines worldwide. Increasingly these carriers are involving themselves in some form of affiliation with other airlines in a bid to provide more extensive route networks. These relationships help to meet consumers' desires to have their needs satisfied on a global basis whilst also leading to a more highly concentrated airline industry. Indeed, some airlines rushed into partnerships as a form of damage limitation; they did not want their direct competitors to be linked to the most compatible carrier(s). These moves have led not merely to pairs of carriers with extended service offerings but significantly to groupings of airlines with a strong geographical presence. OneWorld and the Star Alliance are well-known examples, both of which involve major European members.

- **Entry barriers:** One characteristic of air transport markets is that they tend to exist at domestic or regional levels rather than there being one global air transport market. This is largely due to entry barriers, which result in competition on international routes being described as curtailed (Axelsson, 1993). Indeed, difficulties in this area are complicated further by the fact that air traffic rights are negotiated within the context of the 'freedoms of the air'. These freedoms, which provide a framework for governments and airlines to negotiate international airline movements, are discussed fully by Hanlon (1996). They can act as an incentive to airlines to form partnerships in order to achieve access to markets they otherwise would find barred to entry. Difficulties in obtaining take-off and landing 'slots' at busy airports can similarly act as an incentive to partnership. These slots are crucial to airlines wanting to operate new routes, yet access to them is according to a system of 'grandfather rights', whereby an airline has the right to a route in perpetuity unless it fails to make sufficient use of the slot. This acts as a significant barrier to entry even where other enabling factors exist, such as those resulting from deregulation. The impact of these restrictions can be seen on services from Heathrow to the USA. Currently only British Airways and Virgin from the UK, and American Airlines and United Airlines from the USA, can operate on the route.

- **Technology:** Airlines were instrumental in developing Computerized Reservation Systems (CRS) as a means to manage their inventory following deregulation and they still dominate their ownership today. Ownership of, or a share in, a CRS is regarded as highly important by airlines. Not only do they play a key role in seat distribution but they can also be highly profitable in their own right. In common with the airline industry itself the CRS market is highly concentrated, with the main players being Amadeus, Galileo, Worldspan and Sabre. It has been predicted that one system will eventually dominate the market. In addition, airlines, like travel agents, are adopting many new technologies to aid distribution. Once again the Internet, CD-ROMs and interactive kiosks can be seen to be important.

- **Scheduled airlines: dominant trends:** The factors identified relative to structure and characteristics reflect a sector that is moving to an ever-greater degree of consolidation, within which co-operative practices in their various forms, including franchising, are increasingly dominant. The concept of 'seamless services' has become an established feature of the airline sector, in the desire to more effectively meet customer needs. Complementary service providers joining forces to offer connecting flights can facilitate this. The adoption of a franchising strategy is one means of achieving this type of organizational arrangement. At the same time it facilitates market extension into tourism destinations, which were not previously easily accessible. Consequently, the airline industry has witnessed the formation of countless partnerships between major UK and foreign carriers, and smaller, regional niche players. For example, franchising has enabled smaller carriers to feed traffic into the British Airways network since July 1993, when CityFlyer Express became the first franchisee. At the time of writing a further nine franchise agreements had subsequently been signed. A profile of the British Airways franchise system is presented in Table 10.3.

Franchise	Date of agreement	Destinations served
City Flyer Express	July 1993	Amsterdam, Antwerp, Bremen, Cork, Cologne, Dublin, Dusseldorf, Guernsey, Jersey, Leeds/Bradford, London Gatwick, Luxembourg, Newcastle, Rotterdam
Maersk Air Ltd.	August 1993	Amsterdam, Belfast, Berlin, Birmingham, Copenhagen, Lyons, Milan, Newcastle, Stuttgart
Brymon Airways	August 1993	Aberdeen, Bristol, Cork, Edinburgh, Glasgow, Guernsey, Jersey, London Gatwick, Newcastle, Newquay, Paris CDG, Plymouth, Southampton
Logan Air Ltd.	July 1994	Barra, Campeltown, Fair Isle, Foula, Glasgow, Islay, Kirkwall, Lerwick, North Ronaldsay, Papa Stour, Papa Westray, Sanday, Stronsay, Tiree, Unst, Westray, Wick
British Regional Airlines (formerly known as Manx Airlines (Europe) Ltd.)	January 1995	Aberdeen, Belfast City, Belfast International, Benbecula, Bergen, Blackpool, Brussels, Cardiff, Cork, Edinburgh, Glasgow, Guernsey, Inverness, Jersey, Kirkwall, Knock, Leeds/Bradford, Liverpool, London Luton, London Stansted, Londonderry, Manchester, Newcastle, Paris CDG, Rotterdam, Shannon, Southampton, Stornoway, Sumburgh, Waterford, Wick
GB Airways	February 1995	Agadir, Casablanca, Faro, Funchal, Gibraltar, Jerez, London Gatwick, London Heathrow, Malaga, Malta, Manchester, Marrakech, Murcia, Oporto, Tangier, Tunis, Valencia
Sun Air	August 1996	Aarhus, Billund, Copenhagen, Digali, Gothenburg, Odense, Oslo, Manchester, Skive, Stockholm, Thisted
Comair	October 1996	Capetown, Durban, Gaborone, Harare, Hoedspruit, Johannesburg, Manzini, Port Elizabeth, Richard's Bay, Skukuza, Victoria Falls, Windhoek
British Mediterranean	February 1997	Amman, Damascus, Beirut

Source: Pender (1999, pp. 571)

Table 10.3 Franchise system profile: British Airways

Airline franchisee benefits

Within the scheduled airline sector, franchising can help smaller airlines to startup in business and to become established in the marketplace. Virgin Atlantic's franchise agreements with both South East European Airlines and CityJet eased and speeded market entry for the franchisees. Indeed, this was achieved to such an effective extent that CityJet subsequently severed the connection with Virgin once the airline had become established (Jones, 1996). However, not all airline franchisees have been start-up companies. Established carriers have also signed franchise agreements with majors. Furthermore, franchisees need not operate exclusively as franchisees. In addition, some service other routes in their own right. An example of this type of dual strategy, incorporating independent operation along with being part of a franchise system, is provided by Jersey European Airways (JEA).

With respect to scheduled airline franchising in general, it is possible to identify some generic benefits for franchisees. The combination of these benefits may facilitate improvement to competitive position. In particular, franchising has the potential to:

- provide access to the franchisor's **technology** and **distribution systems**, including the all important major airlines' CRSs;

- increase **market share** through participation in majors' frequent flyer programmes;

- defend a **niche position** in the marketplace, as many short domestic routes can only support one carrier, franchising can help a carrier to survive on such a route;

- enhance **customer added value** by allowing passengers to fly with a major on routes that these airlines could not otherwise afford to service, and providing access to the majors' executive clubs;

- achieve **quality assurance** through endorsement of the major's brand.

These benefits are illustrated within the context of British Airways (Illustration 10.2).

Franchising as a strategy

Structure, characteristics and strategy development

The environments in which both the retail travel agents and the scheduled airlines operate exhibit some common features. In

---

Illustration 10.2 British Airways

Franchisees of British Airways have access to the full range of **technology** and **distribution systems** operated by the company internationally. Franchisee Brymon's Airways experienced a rapid growth in **market share** relative to its business between Bristol and Aberdeen. It increased by 230 per cent in 1994 when compared to 1993 figures. The strength of being part of a franchise system assisted Brymon in successfully defending a **niche position** in the marketplace. Similarly, CityFlyer has seen a growth in passenger numbers averaging 20–30 per cent a year. Furthermore BA's agreement with SunAir allows the franchisee to compete more effectively in their domestic market through offering **added value** packages to their customers. The quality assurance achieved through **brand endorsement** and association with British Airways was a key factor in the increase in passenger numbers for each of these franchisees.

Source: Reed (1995); O'Toole (1998)

---

particular, there is increasing polarization between the numerous small, independent operations and the select few power broker corporations. Thus, for many of those in a weakened power position already in business, and for those smaller operators considering entering into business, the rationale for 'sheltering' under some form of umbrella support structure provided by stronger organizational formats is strong. This confirms propositions presented in Chapter 4, and is supported by analysis of the key characteristics associated with retail travel agents and scheduled airlines. It is possible to identify factors that have emerged from the structure of the sectors and their respective competitive environment. It is proposed that these require to be addressed at a strategic level if a competitive advantage is to be achieved and sustained. These required factors are summarized in Table 10.4.

These factors in combination lend themselves to the spectrum of forms of consolidation, partnership, affiliation and co-operation to a more intense level than has ever been experienced in the travel trade and transport business environment. Furthermore, there is no indication that this is going to lessen. Strategic options in this respect are presented by Hills and Jones (1995), and may be categorized as:

- **Horizontal merger**: is one means used to consolidate industries. Through the merging of a number of companies in the same industry sector, economies of scale or market security can be obtained. As a result, they are able to pursue a cost leadership or a differentiation strategy. This strategy had been evidenced in both the travel trade and transport sectors as a

Characteristics	Required factor
Commission structure	Critical mass and negotiatory power base
Competition	Complementarity of assets and services
Concentration	Economies of scale and scope
Entry barriers	Negotiated market entry and access through partnership
Technology	Access to information technology driven distribution systems

Table 10.4 Sector characteristics and strategic level factors

means to improve competitiveness, achieve growth and globalize.

- **Vertical integration**: means that a company is producing its own inputs or is disposing of its own outputs. A company pursuing vertical integration is normally motivated by a desire to strengthen the competitive position of its original, or core, business. It enables the company to build entry barriers to new competition, facilitates investments in efficiency-enhancing specialized assets, protects product quality, and results in improved scheduling. The UK's overseas package holiday industry is particularly characterized by high levels of vertical integration.

- **Joint venture:** makes sense for a company that has some of the skills and assets necessary to establish a successful new venture. Teaming up with another company that has complementary skills and assets may increase the probability of success. This could be in respect to embryonic industries or markets and involves an equity stake being taken in the new business entity by principals. Swissair, Austrian and Sabena airlines established a jointly held company in 1996 to operate a shared reservation centre in Frankfurt.

- **Consortium:** a growing importance of branding and the increase in competition has left independents and smaller chains little choice but to seek affiliation. As a consequence consortia membership has grown in the past decade. Such organizations offer affiliated members access to centralized resources and expertise which affords them the opportunity to remain independent whilst benefiting from the marketing, financial and education services provided. The mini-case study of Advantage Travel provides an example of this arrangement (Illustration 10.3).

- **Strategic alliance**: in certain circumstances companies can realize the gains linked with horizontal merger, vertical integration, joint venture and consortium without having to bear the bureaucratic costs, if they enter into long-term co-operative relationships with their trading partners. Such relationships are typically referred to as strategic alliances. They can facilitate the equivalent of horizontal merger and vertical integration. One example is that of code-sharing agreements with feeder airlines that achieve mutual objectives of extending market share and globalization. Code-sharing results when an airline attaches a designator code to a service provided by a different airline. This enables a single flight code to be used to show connecting flights as through services.

It is proposed that franchising represents a hybrid form of the above strategic options, and is a strategy employed chiefly by service companies. The franchisor does not have to bear the development costs and risks of opening up in a foreign market on its own, for the franchisee typically assumes those costs and risks. Using this strategy a service company can build up a global presence quickly and at a low price. Franchising is a particularly appealing strategy when the benefits of franchising for franchisees in the retail travel and scheduled airlines are analysed. It would appear that franchising presents one strategy that may be useful in addressing the factors identified in Table 10.4. A consolidation of the main benefits of franchising to franchisees is summarized in Table 10.5. Some are exclusive to each sector and some are common.

Currently, on the basis of the benefits that accrue through franchising, it would appear that the operating logic underpinning the adoption of franchising as a strategy in the travel trade and transport sectors appears to be sound. The rationale of franchising is founded on transaction cost economics

Retail travel agents	Scheduled airlines
Means of business start-up	Defence of a niche position
Gains from negotiary power	Enhance customer added value
Discounted personal travel	Achievement of quality assurance
Access to technology and distribution systems	
Increased market share	
Ease and speed of market entry	

Table 10.5 Main benefits of franchising for franchisees

(Williamson, 1975). Put very simply, in order that franchising is justifiable the costs must be outweighed by the profits. Linked to this is the uniqueness and quality of the product or service offering, effectiveness of added services, the regulatory environment in which the industry sector operates, and the strength of the brand. These combine to form a set of conditions that are either conducive to, or stifling of, the establishment and development of effective franchise systems.

However, early attempts at franchising in the travel trade did not possess a full set of these franchising conditions. As a consequence, it was beset with problems as exemplified by the UK chain, Exchange Travel. The company went into liquidation at the end of the 1980s. According to Holloway (1994), the Exchange agents (franchisees) had experienced low profit margins, and difficulties in achieving the required turnover to pay the 1 per cent management service fee. Exchange travel agent franchise offered neither price nor product advantages, the approval of principals was not guaranteed, and there was a lack of marketing support and territorial protection.

A further condition that was not conducive to franchising was that of the regulatory environment. Prior to the 1980s, the regulatory environment constrained the retail travel sector, and therein the possibilities for franchise system development. Commissions could not be split between an agent and another organization. It was only when travel agents were granted freedom in the 1980s both to discount and to split commission that franchising became a realistic opportunity for travel agents. Franchising has increased in popularity as travel agents are able to negotiate higher commission levels and so improve their profit margins (Holloway, 1994).

Finally, branding, often cited as a pre-requisite for successful franchising, has only been a feature of tourism marketing for a relatively short period of time. However, its adoption has been rapid, as Horner and Swarbrooke (1996, p. 150) describe: 'a flurry of service organizations in the tourism, leisure and hospitality industries that have been implementing branding strategies in the last decade.'

The establishment of clear brand identities is somewhat problematic in an industry as dynamic as travel, with a continuous round of changes in ownership and rebranding. Seaton and Bennett (1996), however, argue that the concept of branding is suited to airlines where differentiated brands can be developed based on differences in aspects such as service provision, carrier design and pricing. The basic product is none the less the same and so airlines can have difficulty differentiating their product from the competition. In addition, brand loyalty has become a feature of airline marketing, with frequent flyer programmes offered by most major scheduled carriers.

Times have changed, resulting in a strengthening of the justification of the operating logic and rationale on which franchising is built. The travel trade and transport sectors have gained experience of franchising as an organizational form. This has combined with supportive competitive and regulatory environments, and much more sophisticated application of branding practices.

Organizational arrangements

Organizational arrangements for franchising that typify those used in the travel trade and transport sectors are now discussed, and illustrated with mini-case studies, drawn from each sector. These highlight the manner in which a range of strategies are encompassed through franchising. Advantage Travel Centres provides the example from the travel agency sector (Illustration

Illustration 10.3 Advantage Travel Centres

The mass market tour operator Airtours provides an interesting example of the establishment of a franchised travel trade operation. The organization is a form of **joint venture**, holding a 15 per cent equity stake in a new franchise company within Advantage Travel following the announcement in 1998 of **vertical integration** between Advantage and Airtours. Advantage Travel was previously operated solely as a **consortium** of independent travel agents. Consortium members voted 66 per cent in favour of setting up a franchise-operating subsidiary in a secret ballot. Formal franchise offers were then sent out to all 950 branches. Members who chose to join up before Christmas 1998 paid £1, whereas the joining fee from the start of 1999 was set at £3,000. This was a clear incentive to agents to sign up early. The monthly royalty payment was set at £90. Over 350 shops, representing approximately 200 companies, had signed to the franchise deal by the end of February 1999. This equates to just less than half of the Advantage membership.

Operational aspects of the agreement include that franchisees are required to access Airtours' central accounting procedures whilst use of Airtours' Matchmaker reservations system is optional. Preferential Travel Insurance won an exclusive three-year contract to supply policies to Advantage Travel Centres' franchisees. Franchisees therefore have more **commercial freedom** in some areas than others. An interesting aspect of this particular franchise agreement is that it involves vertical integration between a tour operator and the franchised travel agency company. This reflects the extent of integration within the industry. The tour operator, a well-known middle-market mass tour operator, involves a number of other brands including Bridge Travel, Cresta and Panorama. Each of these brands aims to attract different market segments.

Source: Compiled from *Travel Trade Gazette*

10.3). This has been selected because it proved to be the most public franchising arrangement in the travel trade in the UK during the 1990s. The well-known example of British Airways is used to illustrate the operation of franchising in the airline sector. British Airways (Illustration 10.4) has been selected as it has led the field in terms of European airline franchising.

Illustrations 10.3 and 10.4 serve to highlight some key strategic issues. First, the Advantage Travel Centres' franchise system provides examples of:

- a strategy of vertical integration between a tour operator, seeking to extend its brand portfolio, and a franchised travel agency company;

Illustration 10.4 British Airways (BA)

In just a few years the BA franchised fleet has grown to consist of 115 aircraft. BA franchisees carry more than 6 million passengers and together the **franchise partners** have over 3,600 employees. The franchisees fly to destinations in the UK, Ireland, Europe, the Middle East, Africa and the USA, as shown in Table 10.3. In 1997–98 franchisees' carriers flew 5.9 million passengers, the franchise partners had a net revenue of £542 million and provided 392,000 connecting passengers. BA's mainline operations serve 165 destinations in 82 countries. This **horizontal merging** of franchise partners adds 74 more destinations and nine countries to the network. Franchises provide 15 per cent of BA destinations. This highlights the strategic importance of franchising for BA. Airlines generally experience problems controlling franchisees and this creates costs for British Airways, who are always mindful of the fact that the reputation of their brand is at stake. Audit and ongoing training of franchisees plays a part in the control process. BA also has the ultimate say regarding route development.

BA continually searches for franchise partners and the development of agreements is the responsibility of the franchisee concerned, BA's general manager franchising and **alliances** and BA's legal department. The franchisees consist of both UK and overseas carriers. The Danish regional airline SunAir is an example of the latter, which operates under the BA Express brand. Franchising has had an added advantage in the Levant where BA's flight frequencies were restricted. The political situation in the Middle East has prevented BA operating routes to Beirut, Amman and Damascus profitably. A franchise agreement was therefore signed with British Mediterranean to service these destinations.

BA's agreements with franchisees vary in nature. Brymon Airways was acquired in August 1993 as a wholly owned subsidiary company, yet it operates as a franchised carrier under the British Airways Express brand. Similarly, BA acquired CityFlyer Express as a wholly owned subsidiary in November 1998. BA also entered into a form of **joint venture**, taking a 49 per cent stake in franchisee GB Airways in February 1995. Not all aircraft in the franchised fleet display BA livery, as evidenced by two Dash 7 aircraft used by Brymon.

Sources: Reed (1995); Jones (1996); British Airways (1999)

- a form of joint venture with the tour operator taking an equity stake in the franchise retail travel trade operation, thus gaining control within the value chain;

- a franchised organizational form that is a result of a conversion from a voluntary consortium, representing a more formalized partnership relationship;

- a franchise contract that can be termed as 'soft', in that it provides latitude for a certain degree of commercial freedom and franchisees are not legally bound to subscribe to all systems and services provided.

Second, the British Airways illustration provides examples of:

- consolidation and market coverage achieved through horizontally merging smaller airlines into a global network;

- strategic alliances of franchisees formed as a means of route extension, foreign market entry, and achieving globalization;

- a joint venture which is established through an equity stake and may provide a means of control within the value chain;

- a franchise contract that can be termed as 'hard' to satisfy the need to protect brand equity through control, audit and on-going training of franchisees.

Thus, from these two sector mini-case studies it can be summarized that a range of outcomes from adopting franchising as a strategy may include:

- brand portfolio extension;

- a degree of value chain control;

- formalized partnership relationships;

- franchise agreements that can be termed either 'soft' allowing a large degree of commercial freedom, or 'hard' protecting brand equity;

- increased market scope and reach;

- foreign market entry and globalization.

Summary

Operating in a highly regulated environment, the franchise relationship in the travel trade and transport sectors is by no means easy to implement. Furthermore, the layers of complexity that characterize the airline industry highlight the necessity for flexibility, yet franchising generally relies upon a level of standardization to be successful. The retail travel sector is similarly complex. For franchising to be selected and implemented as an appropriate strategy, its basic rationale must be present and defendable, and pivotal in the establishment of a strong brand in the marketplace is the quality of the franchisees selected, recruited and trained.

If franchising is to have a future in the travel trade and transport sectors, various authors (for example, Holloway, 1994; Davies and Quastler, 1995) caution that it is necessary to guard against the following features that are associated with the franchise relationship:

- franchisees may become over-reliant on the major for business and there is a danger that their position can become vulnerable;
- negative effects experienced by the major can cascade out to the franchisees;
- franchisees' commercial freedom and independence of management may be compromised;
- environment factors, such as economic recession and political unrest, may impact on different parts of the franchise system to lesser or greater degree;
- revision of original franchise agreement terms and conditions may affect franchise benefits and, consequently, the degree of support accorded to the franchisor.

Clearly there are areas of travel trade and transport where franchising has had little if any impact to date. Some of these could offer potential for future development, motivated by drivers that have been identified (Jones, 1996; Rogers, 1999) as:

- perpetual growth in the size and value of the travel market;
- increased globalization of companies;
- enhanced confidence in, and experience of, franchising within the sectors;
- continued practice of horizontal and vertical integration, and general consolidation;
- the implementation of sophisticated branding strategies.

At a sub-sector level, Holloway (1994, p. 195) expressed scepticism about the future of franchising in the retail travel sector describing this as uncertain:

> Arguably, a franchise, if it is to succeed, must offer a unique product of some kind which is not available through other distributive outlets; this a travel franchise signally fails to deliver.

This is particularly pertinent given the increased use of technologies, such as the Internet, by consumers which may impact upon the *raison d'être* of travel agents in general, never mind whether they are franchised or not!

Relative to the airlines, demand for air travel is increasing and franchising appears to be one effective way for airlines to meet this demand, especially with newer airport developments, which are occurring away from the more traditional destinations. However, Axelsson (1993) identified a number of pre-requisites for carriers to benefit from franchising. These included well-known brands, a willingness to enter foreign domestic markets, a supportive corporate culture and a growth strategy, which is both clear and aggressive. Not all airlines display these characteristics. In addition, the emergence of low cost carriers in Europe poses a threat to airline franchising as they create new markets and displace existing ones. However, the long-term prospects of these low cost carriers is not certain. Also, the development of high speed rail networks may also prove to be a significant threat.

In conclusion, it is still extremely early to comment on the success or otherwise of franchising in the travel trade and transport sectors which is emerging in these sectors. Although we have the North American example to look to regarding airline franchising, the operating environment is very different to that in Europe and so no universal conclusions can be drawn from this. Ultimately much will depend on the competitive environment of the future.

Debate topics

- Characteristics of the travel trade inhibit the applicability of franchising within the sector.

- Franchising in the European airline sector could be viewed as a short-term defensive strategy by majors facing increasing threats from low cost carriers, high speed rail travel and integrated travel companies.

Hospitality, Leisure & Tourism Series

- Franchising offers an ideal method for travel trade and transport organizations to expand internationally.

Selected readings

Hanlon, P. (1996) *Global Airlines: Competition in a Transnational Industry.* Butterworth-Heinemann.

Inkpen, G. (1998) *Information Technology for Travel and Tourism.* Longman.

Renshaw, M. (1997) *The Travel Agent.* Business Education Publishers.

References

Anon (1997) Brussels comes closer. *Sunday Times*, 14 December, p. 6.

Anon (1999) CARTA blasted for dropping franchisees. *Travel Trade Gazette*, 26 April, p. 88.

Axelsson, R. (1993) Cloning a winner. *Airline Business*, September, pp. 70–3.

Barrow, C. and Golzen, G. (1996) *Taking up a Franchise.* Kogan Page.

Bonanza Travel (1999) http://www.bonanzatravel.co.uk

British Airways (1999) http://www.british.airways.com

Burns, P. and Holden, A. (1995) *Tourism – a New Perspective.* Prentice Hall.

Davies, P., Macefield, S. and Baneree, T. (1999) Airtours chiefs stand firm over franchise. *Travel Trade Gazette*, 26 April, p. 6.

Davies, R. and Quastler, I. (1995) *Commuter Airlines of the United States.* The Smithsonian Institute, pp. 135–77.

French, T. (1997) Global trends in airline alliances. *Travel and Tourism Analyst*, **4**, 81–101.

Hanlon, P. (1996) *Global Airlines: Competition in a Transnational Industry.* Butterworth-Heinemann.

Harding, L. and Noakes, G. (1998a) Members see deal as their best Advantage. *Travel Trade Gazette*, 2 December, p. 4.

Harding, L. and Noakes, G. (1998b) Yes vote victory for Airtours' retail plans. *Travel Trade Gazette*, 2 December, p. 1.

Hills, C. and Jones, G. (1995) *Strategic Management: an Integrated Approach.* Houghton Mifflin.

Holloway, J. (1994) *The Business of Tourism.* Pitman.

Holloway, S. (1997) *Straight and Level: Practical Airline Economics.* Ashgate.

Holloway, J. and Robinson, R. (1995) *Marketing for Tourism.* Pitman.

Horner, S. and Swarbrooke, J. (1996) *Marketing Tourism, Hospitality and Leisure in Europe*. International Thomsons Business Press.

Inkpen, G. (1998) *Information Technology for Travel and Tourism*. Longman.

Jones, L. (1996) Keeping up appearances. *Airline Business*, October, pp. 38–42.

Key Note (1998) *Travel Agents and Overseas Tour Operators*. Key Note Publications.

Key Note (1999) *Transportation*. Key Note Pubications.

Mayling, S. and Richardson, D. (1999) BA franchises to follow suit on commission cut. *Travel Trade Gazette*. 22 March, p. 88.

Mendelsohn, M. (1996) *The Guide to Franchising*. Pergamon Press.

O'Toole, K. (1998) Widening the franchise. *Flight International*, 25–31 March, pp. 34–5.

Oliver, C. (1990) Determinants of interorganizational relationships: integration and future directions. *Academy of Management Review*, **15**, 241–65.

Pender, L.J. (1999) European Aviation: the emergence of franchised airline operations. *Tourism Management*, **20** (5), 565–74.

Reed, A. (1995) Buying into the game. *Air Transport World*, February, pp. 96–7.

Renshaw, M.B. (1997) *The Travel Agent*. Business Education Publishers.

Richardson, D. (1998) Franchising could reduce subs income. *Travel Trade Gazette*, 2 December, p. 11.

Rogers, D. (1999) TTG Travel Marketing Column. *Travel Trade Gazette*, 12 April, p. 13.

Seaton, A. and Bennett, M. (1996) *Marketing Tourism Products – Concepts, Issues, Cases*. International Thomson Business Press.

Sloan, G. (1996) USAir Express – a scale apart. *All in the Family*, Issue 6, June, p. 2.

Turpin, A. (1997) Airlines seek strength in partnership. *The Scotsman*, 4 February, p. 22.

Uniglobe (1999) http://www.uniglobe.com

Westbrooke, J. (1996) Fast track into Europe. *Financial Times*, 7 October, p. 5.

Williamson, O. (1975) *Markets and Hierarchies*. Free Press.

The case of McDonald's Restaurants Limited

Conrad Lashley

Key points

- McDonald's Restaurants Limited adopts a range of new market entry strategies. The company combines new construction and conversion of properties, varied size of production/service capacity, location in prime and secondary sites, and a mix of franchised and directly managed units.

- As a franchise organization it represents a 'hard' brand, which imposes 'tight' systems within which franchisees' freedom of operation and innovation are restricted.

- The company typifies an approach to managing service encounters that includes four dimensions: efficiency; calculation; predictability; and control.

- McDonald's makes a substantial investment in the selection and training of franchisees, a key component of which is their immersion in the company's culture prior to being eligible for a franchise.

Introduction

McDonald's Restaurants Limited is the world's largest restaurant chain, with units on every continent and in almost every country. In the UK, McDonald's had approximately 1000 restaurants by the end 1999, having opened the first restaurant in the UK in 1974. After just twenty-five years trading, UK sales revenue is estimated to exceed £1.4 billion, and profits will be in the region of £90 million. The company is in a dominant position within its marketplace. It currently controls 74 per cent of the hamburger restaurant business, and accounts for 18 per cent of the quick service restaurant market. Table 11.1 provides a summarized overview of the company's growth in total numbers of restaurants in the United Kingdom from 1979.

One of the most influential factors in shaping the growth of the company's restaurants during the past ten years has been the change in the construction of the basic restaurant unit. In the early days, the company tended to locate units in major city centres using existing premises on prime sites, involving large capital investment and high running costs. In the late 1980s the company developed a pre-fabricated construction for new units that could be assembled on site in a matter of hours, and operational within weeks. The Doncaster unit, for example, was open for business within 18 days of commencing construction. New site development costs have fallen from average of £1.5 million per unit to just under £700,000 per unit. Apart from the lower break-even point that flows from reduced capital investment, and the opening up of business opportunities that might have been marginal in the past, these new units are located in positions that open up new markets. No longer restricted to city centres, recent openings are located in suburban sites, on arterial roads and in retail parks.

The number of franchised restaurants is an unusual feature of the British company compared to the rest of the McDonald's Corporation internationally. The company directly manages over

Year	1979	1984	1989	1994	1999
Number of restaurants in UK	38	165	338	579	927

Source: Company records

Table 11.1 Total McDonald's restaurants in the UK, 1979–1999

Hospitality, Leisure & Tourism Series

70 per cent of the UK company's restaurants and the remainder are franchised. In most other countries, the proportions would be roughly reversed, with approximately 70 per cent of the international stock of restaurants franchised. Recently, the parent company has put pressure on the British company to increase the number of franchised units to around 30 per cent. This unusual aspect of the UK operation makes the study of the franchises in the British McDonald's company interesting because franchised restaurants are in the minority. Table 11.2 shows that the UK company's involvement in franchising restaurants dates from the mid-1980s, with a more rapid growth over the 1990s. At the time of the research (August 1999) there were 277 of the company's restaurants franchised to 152 franchisees. This represents 28 per cent of the company's UK restaurant stock. Recent years have seen the growth of multi-unit franchising.

Interviews with senior British management suggest that the reason for the low level of franchised restaurants is due to a combination of history and culture in the British context. When McDonald's starts to trade in a new country it looks for a person who understands the company and the country concerned. In the UK it chose an American called Bob Wray, who had been in the UK as a serviceman. He developed the first chain of restaurants

	Restaurants franchised		Franchisees appointed	
	That year	Total	That year	Total
1986	2	2	2	2
1987	3	5	3	5
1988	7	12	7	12
1989	1	13	1	13
1990	16	29	12	25
1991	8	37	7	32
1992	14	51	11	43
1993	29	80	21	64
1994	38	118	25	89
1995	31	149	21	110
1996	40	189	15	125
1997	27	216	9	134
1998	48	264	13	147
1999*	13	277	5	152

*Figures up to August 1999

Source: Company records

Table 11.2 Total franchised McDonald's restaurants in the UK, 1986–1998

as a licensee and brought several key executives with him from the USA. When Bob Wray retired in the mid-1980s, the 150 units formed the basis of the new managed business, and the company continued to develop new units within the now directly owned business. One manager described this situation thus:

> We had developed pretty good systems for managing a chain of restaurants and it seemed to make sense that we would keep on running the business that way. I suppose it's a cultural thing. A bit like when you throw a ball at an American boy he picks it, whereas you throw a ball at a British boy and he kicks it.

It is also interesting to explore McDonald's as a case study because it is proposed that the company is a representative type in franchising hospitality services. McDonald's is a firmly established brand, based round a tightly defined operating system that the franchisee buys into. In Price *et al.*'s (1999) terms, it is a 'hard' brand with strong franchise potential, but the system presents franchisees with a tension to manage. The McDonald's system provides franchisees with a successful formula that limits entrepreneurial risk, but that also restricts entrepreneurial freedom and constrains innovation. Franchisees have to be prepared to work within the operating system, and innovate, in a way that does not challenge brand values. Consequently, McDonald's franchisees are carefully selected and there are considerable barriers to entry to becoming a McDonald's franchisee.

Operating system

McDonald's operate quick service restaurants in a manner which has been described as a 'production line' or 'service factory' approach to service delivery (Levitt, 1972; Schmenner, 1995). That is, the production and delivery of the company's services are informed by Weberian 'formal rationality' and have much in common with Taylor's (1947) approach to factory production. The extreme division of labour of production and service, and routine tasks require minimal discretion by operational crew. Operating manuals and procedures specify not just product standards but also a detailed breakdown of service times and targets.

McDonald's Restaurants is the eponymous object of Ritzer's *McDonaldization of Society* (1993; see also Ritzer, 1998). The company typifies an approach to managing service encounters that includes four dimensions in managing the service process.

Hospitality, Leisure & Tourism Series

We don't have to agree with Ritzer's somewhat ill-informed analysis to agree that these dimensions are important sources of customer satisfaction – what people are buying into.

The first dimension is that McDonald's offers **efficiency**, in that 'it offers the best way of getting from the state of being hungry to the state of being full'. Work is designed to maximize the use of labour most efficiently through technology and simplified job design. The second dimension is that McDonald's offers services, which can be easily quantified and **calculated**. Customers can specify what they are going to get and the time it will take. Tight job design and productivity levels allow managers to be more certain as to the level of outputs from a given level of labour inputs. Customers are able to **predict** products, services and prices; they know what they will be offered in different McDonald's Restaurants, and even the prices to be charged. From an employment perspective, employee performance and the need for labour hour by hour can be predicted with reasonable accuracy. Finally, customers, through the impact of these other dimensions, can experience a sense of personal **control**. From an employment perspective the design of jobs and management hierarchy aim to ensure maximum control of employee performance.

Standardization and the accompanying psychological benefits are therefore an important feature of the offer made by the company to its customers, and this shapes much of its management of human and other resources. Its brand values are tightly drawn and closely managed. In these circumstances performing tasks in 'the one best way' is an essential feature of delivering the company's highly standardized and uniformity-dominant offer to customers. Production and service operations are tightly defined and the subject of detailed training and quality auditing programmes. Within each restaurant crew are trained against these standards and a management development programme supports manager training for each stage of the management hierarchy up to unit management level.

The delivery of the standardized customer service does not just relate to standard operation procedures, crew training and management development. Each restaurant offers the same range of services to its customers. Though there have been some experiments with salads and pizzas in some restaurants, all units offer the same menus, special offer programmes, money taking systems, and are usually covered by the same nationally devised promotional and advertising campaigns. Managers are very concerned to ensure that there is no confusion about the offer to customers, and there are no additional games or vending machines allowed in restaurants.

In addition to the training and tight specifications mentioned above, the quality of service delivery is monitored through an elaborate system of management. Area supervisors and operations consultants conduct regular service audits of each restaurant. A 'full field' audit involves managers auditing each restaurant in all aspects of service and production. Until recently, monthly visits by Mystery Customers to each restaurant evaluated the restaurant against the company's measures. Three themes – **Quality, Service** and **Cleanliness** (QSC) drive through **all** quality audit systems.

Customer comments are also sought through a restaurant feedback system based on a simple questionnaire, which is a more elaborate version of a customer comment card that provides customers with an incentive to complete the questionnaire. In addition, information from customer comment cards and letters to 'head office' also form part of the company's quality monitoring process. Again, a monthly quality audit grade is awarded to each restaurant on the basis of this array of measures. Current service targets expect restaurants to achieve 80 per cent or above against the cumulative scores gathered from the sources mentioned above. Any restaurant achieving a score of below 70 per cent would give cause for concern.

As well as these quality audits, the company also conducts monthly audits of training activities in each restaurant. Each restaurant has to achieve the correct level of fully trained crew, and progress crew through the Observation Checklists that monitor individual performance both during and after training. The monthly monitoring of staff turnover and an annual employee attitude survey, together with the requirement to hold regular 'RAP' sessions with crew. These sessions facilitate open communication and mean that crew satisfaction is also monitored in each restaurant.

Finally, and perhaps unsurprisingly, each restaurant is subject to monthly monitoring of revenue and profit. Restaurants have to be seen to be 'progressing and developing' through a combination of sales growth, profit growth and cost reduction. These measures and objectives are common across many hospitality retail businesses. What is interesting in the McDonald's case is that they cannot be achieved at the expense of other measures such as training, customer satisfaction and employee turnover. Unit managers, for example, are paid bonuses on profit performance only if the other quality, training and employee turnover audits achieve the target requirements.

The management structure, inside each restaurant and externally, further supports the processes of monitoring and controlling overall performance. Within individual restaurants the management structure tends to represent a fairly tight span of control. Typically each restaurant will have one restaurant manager, one or more first assistants, and two or more second assistants, who are all salaried full-time employees of the company in the managed estate. Below these, four or more floor managers are hourly-paid, working supervisors. Though restaurants vary in size, on average the span of control is one manager to six crew. Outside of the restaurants the span of control, though growing, is still quite small in comparison to many hospitality retail businesses. Each area supervisor used to be responsible for just two restaurants, though the growing number of experienced unit managers now means the company is moving to an average of six franchised units, and eight in the managed units. In addition, franchised restaurants work with field consultants who are responsible for about eight franchised restaurants.

It is expected that the company's systems and standards will be applied in all restaurants, whether managed or franchised, and the contract ties the franchisee into a requirement to manage the business in line with the company's systems and controls. Indeed, it is possible that any franchisee that consistently failed to meet quality audit measures would be judged in breach of their contract.

Franchise arrangements

McDonald's Restaurants is the classic example of a 'hard' and 'tight' customer franchise (Price *et al.*, 1999). It has a tightly defined standardized offer to customers in both the tangible product and service elements of the offer. Customers know what to expect, how much it will cost, and how long it will take. The operating systems and approach to quality management are focused at ensuring that these expectations are met. As a consequence the brand has powerful market recognition and value that makes it a strong franchise brand that is able to generate high value.

Company promotional material for potential franchisees states up front that:

> Fundamental to our success, both here and internationally, is the way the McDonald's brand stands for uncompromising quality, unbeatable value for money, friendly and efficient service, impeccable hygiene and unerring consistency.

The nature of the brand and the need for consistency across all outlets, whether they be franchised or managed, represents a strong message from the company and its literature to potential franchisees.

National advertising and sales promotional campaigns are chiefly co-ordinated and organized by the company. The franchisee interprets these and works within the McDonald's system and, 'benefits from over 40 years' food service experience' (McDonald's, 1999, p. 12). Therefore, apart from quality and business performance constraints on franchisees, much of the marketing and sales promotional strategy relating to the conduct of the brand are dealt with at national level, and largely outside of the control of the franchisee. Thus major promotions like the famous 'two for one' promotion in January 1999, and the successful 'teeny beanie babies' promotion in May the same year, were national campaigns in which franchisees 'had' to participate. Similarly, key elements of the menu offer are not up for negotiation with franchisees. For example, no franchisee would be allowed to drop the 'Big Mac' from the menu.

The franchise agreement is normally set up to cover a twenty-year period and the links between the company and franchisees are ongoing during the period of the contract. Field consultants are appointed by the company to work with franchisees and provide advice and support, as well as links with the company's specialist and technical departments. The franchisee pays an initial 'one-off' franchise fee of £30,000 and an ongoing service fee of 5 per cent of monthly sales.

The company retains the real estate interest in the site and the building, and the franchisee leases the buildings and land from the company. Current rental arrangements work on a stepped payment system based on monthly sales. These vary between 5.75 and 18.5 per cent. The higher the sales the higher the rental, until the maximum figure. The franchisee purchases the fixtures and fittings, equipment and the right to operate the restaurant during the period of the agreement.

McDonald's franchisees are required to join the McDonald's Marketing Co-operative Limited and have to pay a monthly contribution equivalent to 5 per cent on net sales. They have to gain approval for all local promotional materials and are only allowed to use the company's name and trademarks for genuine promotional circumstances and after written approval.

There are two ways of becoming a McDonald's franchisee. The **Conventional Franchise** is the usual long-term arrangement based round a twenty years' lease. For those who have less capital available, the **Business Facilities Lease** allows the franchisee to trade and purchase the franchise within the first three years. Table 11.3 provides an indication of the typical investment needed for existing and new restaurants.

	Existing restaurants	New restaurant
Purchase price	300,000	270,000
Security deposit	10,000	10,000
Franchise fee	30,000	30,000
Total cost	340,000	315,000
Maximum borrowings	255,000 (75%)	189,000 (60%)
Unencumbered cash required	85,000 (25%)	125,000 (40%)

Source: Franchising: McDonald's Restaurants Ltd (1999)

Table 11.3 Typical investment needed (£) for existing and new restaurants

The Conventional Franchise

There are slight variations depending on whether the unit is a new or existing restaurant, and in the case of an existing unit depending on the size of the current sales. In the main, franchisees take on existing restaurants, though there are, potentially, higher earnings to be made from a new business built up by the franchisee. The purchase price for an existing restaurant is based on current sales and cash flow, and is from £150,000 upwards. Typically this would be about £300,000–£275,000 for a new restaurant. In addition the franchisee needs to put up the £30,000 franchise fee plus a further £10,000 'non-interest bearing security deposit'. Typically an existing restaurant will cost the franchisee £340,000 and the company requires a minimum 'capital commitment of 25 per cent of the total purchase price', which is typically £85,000. In the case of a typical new restaurant the 'unencumbered cash required is £125,000' because the company requires 40 per cent of the total purchase price to meet the 'greater start-up costs', albeit on a lower purchase price. Where a franchisee needs to raise loans to meet the purchase price the company advises the use of banks, and makes no loans to franchisees itself.

The Business Facilities Lease

The Business Facilities Lease (BFL) arrangement is for those franchisee who are 'right for McDonald's but don't have enough capital to meet the requirements above' (McDonald's, 1999, p. 13). It allows franchisees to use the restaurant's cash flow to buy the lease within the first three years. There is, however, a need for franchisees to fund themselves through the initial training period and this will typically cost £30,000. Using the figure given above, this would mean raising £85,000 within the three-year period, once installed as a franchisee on the BFL arrangement.

In addition to the funds needed for the purchase of the franchise and restaurant contents, all franchisees are advised that they require £10,000 for inventory items such as food, paper, cleaning equipment and cash floats.

Ongoing fees are summarized in Table 11.4 and comprise the three elements mentioned earlier: rental, service fee and marketing fee. All are computed retrospectively based on the previous month's total restaurant sales.

Ongoing fee	Monthly fee as % of restaurant sales
Monthly rent	5.7–16.75
Marketing spend	5
Service fee	5

Source: Franchising: McDonald's Restaurants Ltd (1999)

Table 11.4 Ongoing fees payable by the franchisee

The franchisee's rights largely operate within a framework that is prescribed by the company. Most strategic decisions relating to the development of the brand and its promotion are undertaken at company level. There is involvement by representatives of the franchisees 'on virtually all our decision making committees and vote on the direction of our substantial marketing programme' (McDonald's, 1999, p. 12). As we have seen, the operating systems together with administrative and management systems are devised by the company. Freedom of action is further restricted because the company monitors franchisee perform-ance; in particular the service quality and general conduct of the business have to be assessed as being to the required standard.

It is not surprising therefore that the selection of franchisees, and the franchise contract are much concerned with recruiting franchisees who are prepared to be bound by the hard brand definition and tight operational specifications. The company's draft contract requires that franchisees 'operate the Restaurant in a wholesome manner in compliance with the prescribed standards of Quality, Service and Cleanliness' (McDonald's, 1999, p. 2). The contract also requires the franchisee to keep to planned opening hours, to use only McDonald's supplies, standard uniforms and packaging, and to work within the company's procedures for food handling and safety practices. The contract restricts the franchisee from introducing credit card payment, or to operate in the restaurant: 'any coin, or token operated equipment, machine, device or apparatus for the supply of any service or goods or for amusement or gaming purposes including but not limited to pay telephones, pay toilets, scales, amusement devices and machines for the sale of confectionery, cigarettes, foods and beverages and other commodities . . .' (McDonald's, 1999, p. 4).

When selecting franchisees the company insists that it will not deal with partnerships or businesses owned by absentee investors, and franchisees are required to 'divest themselves of other business interests' (McDonald's, 1999, p. 12). Franchisees are required to live in the area in which the restaurant is located. The franchisee is expected to have a 'hands on' approach to the business, and the company limits franchise ownership to four, or in exceptional circumstances five, restaurants. Table 11.5 highlights the current profile of franchisee control of restaurants. This confirms that most franchisees control just one or two restaurants. Interviews with company executives confirm a view that franchisees benefit the business by bringing an entrepreneurial focus to immediate business operation and service delivery. Senior executives state that several of the company's lead products – including the Big Mac – have been suggested by franchisees. There is also a frequently expressed cultural reference to the early days of the company when the McDonald brothers allowed a franchisee too much freedom and the whole business suffered as a result. These two concerns are important to understanding both the franchise system and the relationship with franchisees. In Chapter 4, Morrison focuses specifically on this issue.

	Number of restaurants controlled					Total
	1	2	3	4	5	
Number franchisees	68	59	13	10	3	153
Number restaurants	68	118	39	40	15	280

Source: Company records

Table 11.5 Franchisee control of restaurants in the UK (October, 1999)

Franchisees have to be prepared to work within a tightly defined and constrained operating environment in which details of their business control and quality management are subject to scrutiny by the company. Key strategic decisions relating to the brand and marketing are also shaped in a way that franchisees have to acquiesce to decisions made at corporate level. Franchisee decision making authority therefore, is mostly tactical in nature, such as, staffing levels, local sales promotions, some choice over the food offer, say in stocking salads or other products which the company allows on the margin of the brand. They have more control over capital investment in equipment and building maintenance, though the franchise agreement sets limits on the minimum standards. Hence franchisees may be allowed to spend more than is required but would not be allowed to under-invest in these things.

Franchisees are also, however, encouraged to show initiative and to make suggestions that will develop the business. Although all variations to the premises, or product and service offer, have to be approved by the company, the company is keen to support franchisees and learn from innovative suggestions. One senior manager said:

> We are keen to support all reasonable requests, though sometimes we have to protect some franchisees from themselves. Being so large we can usually find someone who has tried different suggestions and the franchisee can benefit from their experiences.

When asked for an example of a recent suggestion that had been approved he mentioned one franchisee who had constructed a security grille sealing off part of the unit. This enabled him to open for late night business without having the whole unit in operation. On other occasions the use of express tills might be permitted if the business demanded it owing to a high number of individual sales.

Selecting franchisees

Currently franchisees are drawn from both company personnel, who have achieved the level of area supervisor (one level above unit manager) and above, and from people external to the company. As indicated earlier, the process of selection and recruitment of external applicants involves considerable barriers to entry and is a long way from the 'have you got the money?'

approach that is common to many franchisors in the hospitality retail sector.

All applications are subject to an initial sifting process that sorts out those who are serious applicants. After an initial interview, all external applicants are required to work in a restaurant for an initial test period of five days. During this time, the unit manager evaluates the applicant, and a senior executive will also check on progress. Following this first 'pilot' experience applicants who continue to express interest are required to attend a second interview with three senior managers including the chief operations director.

Every external franchisee (registered applicant) is required to complete the company's training programme. During this time they work, without pay, in one of the company's restaurants and undertake the various courses and management development activities delivered in the unit and at regional and national training centres. Typically a franchisee would take nine months to complete the programme on a full-time basis and it might take a couple of years part-time. Apart from detailed training in the various operational activities working as a crew member, i.e. griddle, fries etc., the training programme includes a period in junior management prior to taking on full restaurant management. The registered applicant will only be eligible to take on a franchise when he or she has been 'signed off' after successfully completing all training, and when the restaurant in which he or she has been 'shifting running manager' has been audited three times. The aim of the detailed training is to both equip franchisees with skills needed for success and ensure that they operate their restaurant in a manner consistent with the brand.

Step 1	Initial enquiries received and subject to initial review
Step 2	Selected applicants' first interview with franchise team
Step 3	Performance review over one week in restaurant
Step 4	Second formal interview with three senior managers
Step 5	Unpaid work in a restaurant – training and performance review
Step 6	'Signed off' after three audits of the restaurant under the applicant's control
Step 7	Allocation of franchise restaurant

Source: Company records

Table 11.6 Selecting franchisees for McDonald's Restaurants

Table 11.6 provides a simple overview of the stages in the selection process for franchisees. On the surface, figures show a low conversion rate of appointed franchisees from initial expression of interest. The problem is that many applications are from people who for one reason or another merely see the McDonald's franchise as one of many possibilities, and after the first contact can be ruled out of consideration. All applications are scrutinized at this point by senior company managers, and approximately 12.5 per cent are invited to attend the exploratory first interview. From this approximately one in three become registered applicants. Ultimately most of these go on to become franchisees and the conversion rate is approximately one in four of the people sifted out as potentially suitable. Senior management's aim in the process is to ensure that people who are selected as registered applicants are all potentially successful franchisees.

Internal applicants require a different process of selection, though depending on what jobs they have occupied and their recent experience they may need some additional operational experience. Typically, however, support for existing employees is aimed at providing advice and assistance on small business management. In fact, all registered applicants attend a quarterly programme of two-day courses designed to enhance their skills as independent business managers. Inputs from banks and lawyers supplement those from the company's functional and support departments (marketing, human resource management, purchasing, etc.). In addition, these courses help to develop networks and support mechanisms for franchisees through the social contacts developed through the programme of meetings.

In many ways the company is looking for individuals who are more consistent with Morrison's **intrapreneurs** mentioned in Chapter 4. As one executive said:

> Traditional entrepreneurs wouldn't give us a look, because our systems do not correspond to the way they work. We have spent a lot of time talking about the sorts of people we are looking for – it's difficult. At one time we thought that the Services [Armed] were a good source of recruits for us, but that one's been disproved. We have all sorts of people – even from farming, but I suppose we generally prefer to see some experience of the retail sector. There are a lot of people out there running small retail businesses who feel under pressure from the big retailers like Tesco's and they come to us for protection.

Hospitality, Leisure & Tourism Series

The current profile of franchisees suggests that the average franchisee is male and in his late thirties when appointed to the franchise. In fact, 93 per cent of franchisees are between the ages of 30 and 49 when they take on their first franchise with the company. Over 50 per cent have a higher education. Despite stringent efforts by the company, and positive profiles in the company's promotional literature and case studies in franchise material, just fifteen of the franchisees are female and sixteen come from ethnic minorities, though this is above the national average.

Former occupations reveal that just under 40 per cent of franchisees are former McDonald's managers. Typically, these employees would have been area supervisors and above within the operational structure, or at equivalent grade in the organizations. The remaining franchisees have all been appointed from outside the organization. Most have come from occupations such as managers, self-employment or the professions. Of the franchisees appointed from outside, almost half declared their former status as manager or director, and about 20 per cent said they had been self-employed. Few had previously worked in the hospitality industry, though former experience in service industries does seem to be a common theme.

The match between the franchisee and the unit starts almost from the time the potential franchisee is accepted as a 'registered applicant'. Through the interview stages and various contacts with the applicant the company discusses the likely geographical location and type of restaurant that the person has in mind. These issues sometimes change as the applicant works through the training programme. There is no formal negotiation over the selection of the units. The Head of Franchising states that:

> We hope that our knowledge of the candidate's wishes; our assessment of their skills and interests; and knowledge of the restaurants available, will come up with a suggested restaurant that is acceptable to the applicant.

There is no formal policy of franchising out only the more marginal properties, as is the case in the licensed retail sector, discussed in Chapter 9. The company clearly has some interest in getting a franchisee to turn round properties that have not been successful under direct management. Often the extra motivation and direct personal interest can produce the innovation and enthusiasm needed. In other cases, there are properties on the geographical margins of a region that present difficulties for direct management, and they can be conveniently hived off from the formal operational structure. From the franchisee's point of view there are financial benefits in taking on a property with potential, rather than one that is already producing booming sales and profits. While successful restaurants are more expensive to buy and have less potential growth, the banks view such properties favourably relative to lending funds (see Chapter 6).

There are short-term benefits in separating a not so successful restaurant from the directly managed operational statistics because these units represent a drag on average growth, profit levels and regional performance audit ratios. However, the long-run success of the company is seen as dependent on all units performing effectively. Consequently, the company's field consultants support and advise franchise operators so that they can develop the business to its full potential.

The franchise experience

The success of the company and the formula is clearly an important attraction to franchisees. Apart from the obvious success of the business as in hospitality retailing terms, there is perceived benefit from the way that the company responds to the various crises and difficulties that the sector has experienced. The BSE scare for example was a general threat to all businesses that relied heavily on beef and the company acted quickly to change suppliers, which many saw as a positive action. More specifically, the effects of the 'McDonald's Two' libel case was put to one side and the company has bounced back with some aggressive marketing campaigns that have lifted sales dramatically.

Profiles of franchisees provided by the company stress issues raised by franchisees in their relationships with the company. Whilst these have to be seen as key selling points selected by the company, they do quote comments made by individual franchisees in their views about the experience of working with the company. Several of the franchisees' comments emphasize the appeal of the business to individuals who are extrovert and people-orientated. For example, Gill Eastwood is quoted as saying: 'One of the biggest pleasures I get is watching people develop; seeing them move from crew to training squad to floor manager.' Keli Watts brings in customer relationships: 'I love going out into the dining area, the regular customers always expect a chat with their coffee.' Finally, Martin Cuthbert said: 'I love dealing with my customers face to face.' Flowing from this extroverted theme, several comments relate to the activity and hands-on practical appeal of the business. Phil Parkin is quoted as saying: 'McDonald's is a very much a hands-on business. It's a case of rolling your sleeves up, and getting in there!' Sean Quirke makes a similar point: 'I don't like being behind a desk too much, and I prefer being on the floor; it's where the atmosphere is.'

Apart from these appeals to people who are essential activists and have clear extrovert tendencies – characteristics frequently found in hospitality operators – the comments reveal other interesting elements of the appeal to franchisees. The business format, strength of the brand, training and support given by the company are all elements that are featured in other comments from franchisees in this case study. Gary Mealing is quoted as saying: 'McDonald's stood out with the amount of training I was required to do. McDonald's showed they were as committed as I was prepared to be, and I was very impressed with the brand.' Ron Mounsey reflects on the nature of the franchise system: 'The more I found out about it the more I realized what a great opportunity it was. The back-up you get is tremendous.'

Pru Naik makes several comments about the business opportunity: 'It was simply a great business opportunity'; and 'working with McDonald's is great fun, and it's a business that's definitely growing'. Jasmine Johnson also picks up the entrepreneurial opportunity linked in with the support from the company in comments: 'I had the drive and ambition to make my business a success'; and later she says: 'if I have any problems I can just pick up the phone'.

Finally, several of the comments relate to the appeal of people working closely with their communities and families. Several franchisees commented on the fact that their partner helped with some aspect of the business administration. In Jasmine's case her son, who is a shift running floor manager, joins her husband: 'It's a real team effort!' Siobhan Fitzpatrick is said to feel a local business woman: 'The local kids really believe it's their McDonald's and later she says, 'It's nice to see the regular customers; it's a small town and I recognize faces.' Jimmy Patrick is also quoted as feeling the links with the community are important: 'We're built into the bricks of Kirkcaldy.' Another franchisee enforces this point, 'McDonald's is a well-known brand' and 'there is potential to build strong links with the community'.

In summary, the company's selection of comments from franchisees stress benefits that will appeal to people who want to work with people, and who are most likely to have extrovert personalities. That said, they are people who probably have a strong desire to limit risk. The success of the company, the security of the operating system, initial training and on-going support, all appeal to risk-aversion, or at least risk-minimizing. Finally, these comments also emphasize two messages that may well have appeal to two different groups with slightly different motives. Both groups clearly want business and financial success, but one set of messages emphasize the business opportunity and potential for growth, whilst the other set of messages emphasize lifestyle, family and community links. These two sets of messages reflect issues that have been highlighted in other research on small firms (Beaver and Lashley, 1998). It is unlikely, therefore, that all McDonald's franchisees have ambitions to have several restaurants. Like their counterparts in other small firms, many will be interested in keeping a balance between financial success and links to family and local community.

A franchisee on franchising

This impression of the dual motives of business success and social involvement is supported by the case study of Mike Mathews, a former senior executive with the company and who now runs two franchised restaurants in the Midlands. Mike started working for the company as a management trainee after a successful career in both the British and Danish merchant navy. Given his background and experience, Mike was soon promoted to manage a restaurant, and subsequently moved on through area supervisor to operations manager within the Midlands Region. After just over ten years with the company Mike had a national role advising and negotiating with local and national government on behalf of the company. His final role with the company involved managing the Total Quality Management project across the company. In 1996 Mike took on two franchises in his home town. This is somewhat unusual, because most new franchisees would initially be allowed to franchise a single restaurant, but given his former experience and resources he was able to take on the two units.

Mike agreed that the role of franchisee was different to the classic entrepreneur because the relationship with the company involved a number of tensions. In part the company wanted the ideas and local enthusiasm that franchisees bring to running their restaurants. He said: 'Most franchisees out-perform the managed units. The franchisee can bring a lot of enthusiasm to the role of running restaurants, but without the right support franchisees can be isolated.' At the same time the company wants to standardize much of the customer experience and encourage franchisees to conform to management polices and initiatives. On some occasions, relationships with field consultants can be difficult because they have limited direct controls over franchisees and have to negotiate or persuade franchisees to act in the desired way. He said: 'It's a fine line between giving instructions and negotiation, not all field consultants can do it. To be successful it has to be a partnership with give and take and sensitivity to the needs of the other party.'

Mike expressed the view that the company was getting better at listening to and learning from the experiences of franchisees. Andrew Taylor, the Chief Executive Officer, meets regularly with franchisees in different regions of the company. Mike valued this approach because it enabled the senior management to learn from the experiences at local level. The company was also supportive of some initiatives that were being taken by the franchises themselves: 'Locally we have formed an informal group of franchises. We meet every few months and visit each other's restaurants. We even share detailed information, because this helps us learn from each other.'

Generally the relationship with the company was supportive and encouraging. The company would give additional resources where either future development was of mutual benefit or where company promotions had an impact on costs. Mike quoted the 'two for the price of one offer' which achieved national fame early in 1999. The company paid compensation to franchisees for the added costs of the promotional offer. Similarly, the company is encouraging franchisees to refurbish older city centre restaurants by sharing the refurbishment costs with the franchisee: 'It's in everyone's interests, because there are always dramatic sales increases when the older units are given new shop fronts and interiors. The company is helping the franchisees develop the business, but also helping itself grow sales', Mike explained.

The freedom to develop the sales and profile of the business was clearly an important source of satisfaction for the franchisee. Although operational aspects of the McDonald's business are a given, each franchisee has discretion over investment decisions, such as when to replace or buy new equipment . The franchisees could also make decisions about pay rates and when to arrange for pay increases, and over the management and development of employees. Mike was very proud of the fact that he had reduced staff turnover to around 24 per cent per year. The rate had been over 208 per cent when he became the franchisee. He had managed this by paying rates above local averages, and by developing the employees with the business. He also had very good contacts with local schools, colleges, and community organizations. One interesting practice that he had initiated was inviting family members of employees to a series of open evenings so that all 'are singing from the same song sheet'. He also produces a restaurant newsletter that is sent to the homes of all employees. He notes with pride that he had a waiting list of people wanting to come to work in his restaurant, where many of the local managed restaurants were constantly advertising for staff.

Similarly, sales growth and initiating local promotions were a source of satisfaction. He had introduced several promotions that had an impact on bringing customers back to the unit. Customers at his restaurant who arrived with a dog in the car were given a dog biscuit: 'When we started we used a couple of pounds a month, now we give away a five pounds every fortnight, People like it. We have generated a lot of repeat business with this approach.'

Summary

McDonald's Restaurants Limited represents an ideal type of hospitality operation. The 'uniformity dominant' nature of the product and services means that much of the management tactics are concerned with ensuring that quality, service, cleanliness and value are consistent through all units. As one franchisees said, 'the customer should not be aware that they are in a managed or a franchised unit'. The management structure and control systems are concerned with doing things in the 'one best way'. In these circumstances, entrepreneurial flair and creativity could be positively harmful if franchisees started introducing a range of different products and services to customers. Yet the company wants to encourage franchisees to be flexible within the confines of the brand.

Franchisees are clearly attracted to McDonald's because it is successful and has well worked-out systems for managing the business in all its dimensions. It represents an ideal opportunity for people to be 'intrapreneurial'. That is, it is attractive to people who want to have personal control over their lives and want the freedom of running their own business but who are, if not risk-averse, are risk-minimizing. The company has undergone a number of phases in recruiting franchisees. At different times, franchisees drawn from the company's management structure have been encouraged and subsequently discouraged. Currently approximately 40 per cent of McDonald's franchisees are former company managers. Those recruited from outside the organization tend to be people with a small business background, ideally from within retailing or services contexts. Clearly, these two groups represent different sets of benefits to the company as a whole. Former employees know the systems and have contacts in the organization that can resolve difficulties quickly, whilst new franchisees bring new vision and ideas to the operation.

The company's approach to working with franchisees is not without tensions, though interviews with the parties concerned created an impression that the company values its franchisees and wants to 'play the long game' with them. There is limited sense of franchisees being used to operate more marginal units, as is the case in licensed retailing. The fact that the franchisees get a 21-year lease allows for business planning processes that encourage commitment and investment in the future. That said, the relationship can experience difficulties, particularly where the company opens a new restaurant that impacts on the franchisee's business. On another level, there are bound to be problems that arise from a big firm dealing with a small firm, different operating systems and resources are bound to influence the expectations and mind sets of both parties. By using a number of techniques, the company is attempting to resolve tensions through discussion and consultation.

Debate topics

- Investment in a McDonald's franchise guarantees financial success for a franchisee.

- Despite being part of an international company, individual franchised units have the capability and freedom to integrate into the local community.

- In relation to the conversion rate of applicants to franchisees, the McDonald's selection process appears to be inefficient.

Selected readings

Alfino, M., Caputo, J. and Wynyard, R. (1998) *McDonaldization Revisited: Critical Essays in consumer culture.* Praeger.
Love, J. (1986) *McDonald's Behind the Arches.* Bantam.
Ritzer, G. (1998) *The McDonaldization Thesis.* Sage.

References

Alfino, M., Caputo, J. and Wynyard, R. (1998) *McDonaldization Revisited: Critical Essays in Consumer Culture.* Praeger.
Beaver, G. and Lashley, C. (1998) Barriers to management development in small hospitality firms. *Journal of Strategic Change,* **4** (4), 223–35.
Levitt, T. (1972) Production line approach to service. *Harvard Business Review,* September/October, pp. 41–52.
Love, J. (1986) *McDonald's: Behind the Arches.* Bantam.

McDonald's (1999) Franchising. McDonald's Restaurants Ltd, company document.

Price, S., Bleakley, M. and Pennington, J. (1999) *After the Precipice: UK Brewers, Pubs and Restaurants.* Credit Suisse First Boston de Zoete and Bevan Limited.

Ritzer, G. (1993) *The McDonaldization of Society.* Pine Forge.

Ritzer, G. (1998) *The McDonaldization Thesis.* Sage.

Schmenner, R.W. (1995) *Service Operations Management.* Prentice-Hall.

Taylor, F. (1947) *Scientific Management.* Harper & Row.

Index

Hospitality, Leisure & Tourism Series

Hospitality, Leisure & Tourism Series